Contents

Notes on contributors

Yana Beigulenko is currently in the process of completing her PhD on the topic of *Homelessness in Russia: a women's perspective* at the School for Policy Studies at the University of Bristol.

Paul Cloke is Professor of Geography in the School of Geographical Sciences at the University of Bristol. He has longstanding research interests in the society, economy and culture of rural areas, and has published 15 books on these topics, the latest of which are *Contested countryside cultures* (with Jo Little) and *Rural Wales: Community and marginalisation* (with Mark Goodwin and Paul Milbourne). He is also editor of *Journal of Rural Studies*. Most recently he has been involved with ESRC-sponsored research on rural middle classes, rural life-styles and poverty, and rural homelessness.

David Cowan is a lecturer in the Law Department at the University of Bristol. He is the author of *Homelessness: The (in)appropriate applicant* (Dartmouth, 1997), editor of *Housing: Participation and exclusion* (Dartmouth, 1998) and *Housing law and policy* (Macmillan, forthcoming). At present, David is part of a team researching 'Allocation of social housing to sex offenders: an examination of good practice', funded by the Joseph Rowntree Foundation.

Gary Fooks is a lecturer in Criminal Justice at Thames Valley University. His principal research interests lie in the area of white-collar crime, particularly serious fraud.

Ray Forrest is Professor of Urban Studies at the School for Policy Studies, University of Bristol. He has published widely on housing and related topics including *Selling the welfare state: The privatisation of public housing* (Routledge, 1990) and *Housing and family wealth: International comparative perspectives* (Routledge, 1995) (both with Alan Murie). He is currently carrying out research with Patricia Kennett on 'Social change on council estates' (Economic and Social Research Council), with Ade Kearns (University of Glasgow) on 'Social cohesion and neighbourhood change' (Joseph Rowntree Foundation), and with Patricia Kennett and Alex Marsh on 'Harassment and unlawful eviction' (DETR).

Rose Gilroy is Senior Lecturer in the Department of Town and Country Planning, University of Newcastle. Prior to joining academia in 1988 she was a housing officer in local government. Rose retains her practice links through her membership of the Chartered Institute of Housing and of a housing association's management committee. Her research interests focus on anti-oppressive practice in planning and housing. Recent publications include 'Barriers, boxes and catapults: social exclusion and everyday life' (with Suzanne Speak) in A. Madanipour, G. Cars and J. Allan (eds) *Social exclusion in European cities* (Jessica Kingsley, 1998) and 'Planning to grow old', in Clara Greed (ed) *Social town planning* (Routledge, 1999).

Malcolm Harrison is a Senior Lecturer in the Department of Sociology and Social Policy at Leeds University. He has taught in the fields of housing, 'race', and welfare state theory since the 1970s, and has published in a wide variety of books and journals.

Brian Harvey is a social research consultant based in Dublin, Ireland. He specialises in the issues of poverty, social exclusion, homelessness and the work of non-governmental organisations, with a particular interest in the European dimension to these issues. He was President of FEANTSA, the European Federation of National Organisations Working with the Homeless, for 1991-95. His recent publications include 'The problem of homelessness: a European perspective', in S. Hutson and D. Clapham (eds) *Homelessness: Public policies and private troubles* (Cassell, 1999).

Derek Hawes is visiting fellow at the School for Policy Studies, University of Bristol. He was a director of housing in local government for over 20 years prior to becoming lecturer in housing policy and practice at the School in 1992. His most recent research includes *Older people and homelessness: A story of greed, violence, conflict and ruin* (The Policy Press, 1997) and he is currently undertaking a long-term study for the DETR on housing and community care.

Patricia Kennett is a lecturer in Comparative Policy Studies in the School for Policy Studies at the University of Bristol. She has published material on the comparative dimensions of homelessness, citizenship and social exclusion, as well as the coping strategies of householders with negative equity. She is currently working on a book entitled *International comparison in social policy: Theory and research* and research on the future of home ownership, and housing and welfare in the Asia Pacific.

Alex Marsh is a lecturer in the Centre for Urban Studies, School for Policy Studies, University of Bristol. His research centres on housing policy and housing economics. He has published work on housing-related topics in a variety of academic and professional journals. He is editor (with David Mullins) of *Housing and public policy* (Open University Press, 1998).

Paul Milbourne is Senior Research Fellow in the Countryside and Community Research Unit at the Cheltenham and Gloucester College of Higher Education. His research interests include issues of housing and homelessness, poverty and social exclusion, and cultural change and conflict in rural Britain. He is editor of *Revealing rural 'others': Representation, power and identity in the British countryside* (Pinter, 1997) and co-author of *Rural Wales: Community and marginalisation* (University of Wales Press, 1997). He is currently writing a book on poverty in rural Britain to be published by Routledge.

Jenny Pannell is Visiting Research Fellow at the Faculty of Health and Social Care, University of the West of England, Bristol. She has been a senior manager and board/committee member with a wide range of social housing and voluntary organisations, including specialist associations working with homeless people.

Christina Pantazis is a researcher in the Centre for the Study of Social Exclusion and Social Justice, School for Policy Studies, University of Bristol. She has edited (with David Gordon) *Breadline Britain in the 1990s* (Ashgate, 1997).

Siân Parry has been a Senior Consultant at Bristol City Council since 1998. She undertakes a range of consultancy and research-related projects on behalf of council directorates and other agencies. Previously she has held a number of research posts in universities and local authorities, the most recent of which was as Senior Research Fellow at the University of the West of England, Bristol.

Sophie Watson is Professor of Cultural Studies at the University of East London. She has published extensively on gender, housing, and homelessness and has a longstanding interest in culture and difference in the city. Her recent and forthcoming publications include editing (with Lesley Doyal) *Gender and social policy* (Open University Press, 1999) and (with Gary Bridge) *The Blackwell companion to the city* (Blackwell, forthcoming).

Rebekah Widdowfield has spent the last two years as a research associate at the University of Bristol working on an ESRC-funded project looking at rural homelessness (directed by Paul Cloke and Paul Milbourne). Following the completion of this project, Rebekah has a three-year fellowship funded by the British Academy to examine representations of, and attitudes towards, homelessness and homeless people.

Acknowledgements

The initial impetus for this collection was a seminar held at the School for Policy Studies in September 1997. The contributors to the seminar examined homelessness from a number of different angles and disciplinary perspectives. We would like to thank all those whose participation contributed to making the day an enjoyable and fruitful occasion. A number of the contributions to this volume have their origins in presentations made at the seminar. Thanks to all those who agreed to turn their presentations into written pieces.

Some of the contributions to this book were commissioned by the editors to address particular topics or issues which it was felt should be reflected in a book seeking to survey the 'new terrain'. Considerable thanks goes to those who agreed to come 'on board' at this later stage in the venture.

Thanks to all contributors for responding both thoughtfully and patiently to editorial comments on their chapters and, typically, doing so promptly.

ONE

Exploring the new terrain

Alex Marsh and Patricia Kennett

Introduction

Homelessness has been a feature of the social landscape for centuries, but over the last 25 years in the industrialised countries of the West there has been a growing concern with the 'new homelessness'. Rapid social and political change has seen the post-war settlement undermined through the end of full employment, the erosion of the welfare safety net, and the marketisation and residualisation of the welfare state. These changes have been accompanied by a dramatic rise in the number of households without adequate secure accommodation. More recently the countries of the former communist bloc have undergone fundamental political and economic transformations which have been accompanied by substantial levels of poverty and social deprivation. So it is in the context of widespread impoverishment that the phenomenon of homelessness has become a component of housing debates in Central and Eastern Europe (Esping-Andersen, 1996). Furthermore, the emergence of the new homelessness in Europe and the other industrialised countries needs to be seen in the context of the global shelter crisis discussed by Ray Forrest in Chapter Two.

It is against this backdrop that the new homelessness has often been connected with debates about other emerging social phenomena such as the 'new urban poor' (Room et al, 1989; Minigione, 1993; Silver, 1993), the 'underclass' (Morris, 1994) and 'social exclusion' (Lee et al, 1995; Lee, 1998; Pleace, 1998; Somerville, 1998). In popular discourse, homeless households are classified as members of an 'underclass' or as the archetypal 'socially excluded group'. The complexity of the problems and the trajectory and coalescence of the social processes which result in households finding themselves homeless requires explanations with a clear focus on process. It is essential to move beyond broad labels such as 'socially excluded' and, indeed, 'homeless' to understand both the varied processes involved and the differentiated impact which these processes have on particular social groups.

The new homeless are a heterogeneous group. The increasing visibility of the young, those in retirement, and women among the homeless population is evidence of the inappropriateness of the stereotypical perception of the homeless as comprising mainly single white middle-aged males. An increasingly hostile and complex social and economic environment means that it is more difficult for households to secure adequate accommodation and to retain it, resulting in extended periods of homelessness for those who find themselves dispossessed. Some may be more at risk than others, but in the current environment relatively few can be viewed as entirely secure.

The uncertain dimensions of the problem

While it is widely accepted that the number of households experiencing homelessness has increased in many industrialised countries (see, for example, FEANTSA, 1995), there is little if any way of arriving at a precise and widely accepted measure of the size and nature of the phenomenon, even when attention is restricted to a single society at a single point in time (see, for example, Bramley, 1988). The difficulties in exploring changes in the extent of homelessness over time within a society, or across a number of societies, are formidable. This is for two broad reasons.

First, homelessness is a high profile, politically sensitive issue with a strong normative dimension. Where housing is seen as a basic right of citizenship of a particular society, the presence of homeless households could be taken as an indication that the social system is functioning inadequately and/or the government is failing in one of its key tasks. As a consequence, the meaning of the term 'homeless' is fundamentally unstable (see Jacobs et al, 1999, for a recent discussion). Contests over the precise definition of homelessness and the appropriate means of measuring the extent of homelessness have been a prominent feature of debates around housing policy, in Britain at least (Somerville, 1994, 1999; Hutson and Liddiard, 1994; Lowe, 1997; Mullins and Niner, 1998). All state assistance is rationed and governments are typically keen to exert strong pressure towards tightly circumscribing the 'official' definition of homelessness. In this respect Britain is unusual in having a definition of statutory homelessness, which in principle requires state intervention to provide accommodation for those finding themselves in particular circumstances.

All statistical measures are socially negotiated, but in the case of homelessness – along with other key political issues like crime and unemployment – the fragility of official definitions and measures is particularly stark. Societies with different socio-political traditions are likely to come to very different understandings of the term. The British approach to defining statutory homelessness highlights the arbitrariness of the issue clearly. While it is recognised that single homeless households have a range of housing and other social needs at least as great as other homeless households (Anderson et al, 1993; Kemp, 1997), many single households are excluded from consideration as being statutorily homeless by the very fact of being single. Yet one consequence of the operation of a statutory definition of homelessness in Britain is that the incidence of homelessness may appear higher than elsewhere (see, for example, the figures presented in Table 12.1 on p 269). The apparent difference between countries in the incidence of the problem is at least in part a result of a greater willingness on the part of the state to recognise the problem, rather than because a larger proportion of British households find themselves in extremely precarious housing circumstances.

Second, research in policy implementation (Hill, 1993a, 1993b; Smith and Mallinson, 1997) has demonstrated the existence of a considerable degree of local discretion regarding the interpretation of legal frameworks. Examinations of the English system of homelessness legislation (Niner, 1989; Lidstone, 1994; Mullins et al, 1996; Evans, 1999), for example, highlight the fact that beyond a core of households whose circumstances would mean that they would be treated as homeless by the vast majority of local administrations, there is a range of households whose status as officially 'homeless' depends critically upon which locality they find themselves in. Whether a household is considered by a local housing authority to be statutorily homeless and eligible for assistance is likely to depend on a number of contingent factors such as the political complexion of an authority or the demand for social housing locally. Aspects of this issue are explored in greater detail in Chapter Eight.

Explaining the new homelessness

Arriving at an understanding of the dimensions of the homelessness problem is undoubtedly problematic: arriving at an adequate understanding of the processes giving rise to homelessness is even more complex. Much research effort over the last decade has been expended in an attempt to further our understanding of the emergence of the new homelessness. While studies of considerable depth and insight exist (for example, Wolch and Dear, 1993), in many respects our picture of homelessness remains relatively broad brush.

There are two basic questions around which popular, political and theoretical explanations of homelessness have revolved. First, is homelessness a product of individual choice, and therefore best treated as an individual responsibility, or are the causes structural and consequently individuals should not be held responsible for their circumstances? Second, do the roots of homelessness lie primarily in the operation of the housing market or should we look elsewhere for the origins of the phenomenon?

Dominant approaches to these issues have changed over time (Neale, 1997). The terms of the political debate in Britain moved from a sympathy with the structural view to something more akin to the individual 'pathology' view over the period from the mid-1970s to the mid-1990s (Jacobs et al, 1999). At a theoretical level during this period the move was, broadly speaking, further towards an emphasis on structural causes. The establishment of social exclusion at the centre of contemporary policy debate might be thought to herald a move back towards a focus on structural causes, although the extent to which the government's conception of social exclusion departs from explanations based on pathology can be questioned (Marsh and Mullins, 1998).

Whether homelessness is best seen as primarily a question of housing market functioning and failure is somewhat less clear cut: a range of opinions can be sustained. Perhaps more importantly for current purposes is a recognition that attempting to fashion an explanation that gives primacy to one factor – such as inadequate housing market functioning or a lack of affordable housing – is misconceived. Homelessness is the product of the convergence of factors operating at the local, national and global scales. Moreover, the combination of processes operating in different localities at different points in time is unique. That is not to argue that broader theoretical understandings are either unobtainable or inappropriate, but that such work needs to be sensitive both to the particularities of specific empirical application and the extent of the domain to which they can usefully be applied.

Homelessness can be approached theoretically at a number of different levels. Much of the debate has, in Britain at least, started from issues of policy, definition and public administration (see, most recently, Hutson and Clapham, 1999). The concern with policy and policy impacts is not restricted to housing or homelessness policy per se. Change in a range of other policy arenas including community care, social security, mental health, and penal policy have all been examined as a vehicle for understanding the growth of homelessness. Mapping the changes in policy provides an insight into key proximate causes for some of the increase in homelessness. It does not, however, provide a framework within which to comprehend the impetus behind policy change itself.

The search for such a framework can take us in at least two different, but not necessarily mutually exclusive, directions. On the one hand, policy and policy change around homelessness can be theorised with reference to the influence of political ideology and normative issues as a means of comprehending how particular societies understand the rights or responsibilities of citizens and the consequent responsibilities of government. The focus of debate here is individual choice and responsibility, with much of the political rhetoric around homelessness being directed at (re)negotiating the boundaries between the 'deserving' and 'undeserving' poor (Lowe, 1997; Neale, 1997; Mullins and Niner, 1998).

A second avenue for theoretical development is to seek to account for policy directions with reference to broader structural factors. The notion of a fiscal crisis afflicting many states in Western industrialised, and more recently Central and Eastern European, countries has particular currency here. The fiscal crisis can, however, be read at two levels. First, it can be taken as an external pressure upon governments of all political complexions which required them to manage expenditure levels downwards (Foster and Plowden, 1996). From this perspective fiscal crisis has played a role in governments' attempts to reduce welfare spending and to externalise expenditure through, for example, deinstitutionalisation, care in the community and the return of the locus of caring responsibilities to the informal sector. Equally it has played a role in government attempts to restrain social security expenditures and to minimise government responsibilities for dealing with the housing market effects of change in other policy areas.

A second, more critical, reading of the notion of fiscal crisis is as an element in a discourse surrounding the rise of a new right anti-state and pro-market ideology in Western industrial countries. From this perspective governments did not face unavoidable external pressure to reduce spending, but rather propagated the rhetoric of crisis as a means of justifying an ideological programme which the electorate may otherwise have found unpalatable.

Regardless of whether the link is viewed as primarily discursive or in some sense 'real', the fiscal crisis of the state is linked to key structural changes which have been affecting local, national and global economies since the mid-1970s and government perceptions of appropriate policy responses. Government attempts to restrain welfare spending are here not interpreted simply as a means of easing the burden upon the private sector by lowering social overheads. They are also seen as part of a drive to increase incentives and enhance the competitiveness of national economies by attempting to foster a culture of entrepreneurialism and individual responsibility. Such entrepreneurial economies are portrayed as the only realistic basis for survival in the contemporary global economy.

Again it is possible to read these changes in different ways. They can be treated as the continuing evolution and elaboration of a world economy in which the demands of the capitalist system of production are both inevitable and unavoidable. Alternatively, they can be located within more explicit theoretical frameworks for analysing macro-social change such as regulation theory (Aglietta, 1979; Amin, 1994; Kennett, 1994). From within the regulation theoretic perspective the events since the 1970s are taken to signify a clear disjunction in socio-economic development as the world economy moves out of the Fordist regime of accumulation. Whether rampant neo-liberalism represents the basis of a new post-Fordist era or is a period of turbulence before stabilising around a new regime of accumulation is a question which remains to be resolved (Peck and Tickell, 1994a, 1994b).

However change at the macro-level is interpreted, the contemporary context is one in which it is perceived that there has been a marked increase in risk, precariousness and individualisation for the mass of the population and not just for a particular social group labelled the 'new poor' or the 'new homeless' (Beck, 1992; Douglas, 1992; Adams, 1995). From this starting point we can develop an understanding which recognises that households and individuals have differential social resources upon which to draw. Despite the pressures towards minimal intervention which national governments perceive they face, it is important to recognise that convergence to a minimal welfare state is by no means complete and thus that the impact of economic change at the global level is mediated through different regimes of welfare (Esping-Andersen, 1990). Thus the social resources upon which households can draw in the face of risk and insecurity are likely to vary in both extent and type between households and between nations. It is the progressive exposure to risk and an accumulation of problems which eventually exhausts these resources and shifts some households into the sphere of homelessness (Paugam, 1995). This perspective sensitises us to the likelihood that different social groups will experience very different routes into homelessness.

We are coming to a greater recognition that individuals and households both experience, and place meaning upon, housing in different ways (Munro and Madigan, 1993; Harrison, 1998). We must therefore be equally willing to explore the way in which households experience and ascribe meaning to homelessness (Somerville, 1992). The meaning and experience of homelessness differ across key social dimensions such as race, gender, impairment and age and as yet we have relatively limited understanding of the nature of these differences. Edwards' (1995) exploration of the social impact upon homeless households of the different ways in which the use of temporary accommodation is managed in different localities gives one clear illustration of the need to recognise the experiential diversity that is subsumed within the category 'homeless'.

Responding to homelessness

While policy implemented at both local and national level can be implicated in the emergence of the new homelessness, it is equally the case that the state, along with the voluntary sector, is simultaneously acting directly to cope with the resulting problem. Depending on one's analysis of the root causes of homelessness, it is possible to take the view that much of this activity is focusing on symptoms rather than causes. Nonetheless, there is a whole range of innovative activities currently being explored in practice. In line with broader thinking on combating social exclusion (Taylor, 1998), contemporary approaches to homelessness are likely to take an holistic view and attempt to address a number of facets of the problems facing particular households, rather than focusing on housing alone (see for example, Quilgars and Anderson, 1997). Such an holistic view is typically accompanied by an argument in support of multi- or interagency working. The problems and practices of interagency working are therefore of paramount importance in policy towards homelessness (Oldman, 1997).

At the broader, theoretical level Perri 6 (6, 1998) has called for the notion of risk and risk management to be located more centrally in debates around the appropriate form for housing policy. He suggests that the language of risk provides a fruitful vocabulary for strategic thinking and enhances our understanding of the way in which politics influences policy. He argues that policy approaches need to move away from the 'curative' and towards 'anticipatory and holistic government', which is very much in tune with rhetoric of contemporary policy. Furthermore, Perri 6 argues that when we consider policy in terms of risk we are not simply concerned with individual risks – such as the risk of homelessness or of illegal eviction – but we are also concerned with policy seeking to manage risks affecting particular social groups: either at the community or systemic level. This theme is picked up in the discussion in Chapter Eight.

The scope of the book

The contributions to this volume approach homelessness from different disciplinary perspectives and with variations in focus, but key concerns include consideration of the relevance of theory, the policy process and implementation, and the recognition of the diversity of experience among those who are themselves homeless.

Ray Forrest provides a context for the rest of the contributions by surveying the new landscape of precariousness. He ranges from the global to the local in a bid to illuminate the social and economic changes which are increasing the housing and non-housing risks to which households are exposed and which mean that both risk and homelessness should be seen as central to contemporary policy. He is particularly concerned to highlight the way in which the reconfiguration of the socio-economic landscape results in previously secure households finding themselves drawn into precarious positions. In Chapter Three Patricia Kennett seeks to link homelessness with the concepts of citizenship and social exclusion. She argues that the new homelessness has been accompanied by a renegotiation of citizenship rights: the discourse of the Keynesian era has broken down and a new narrative has been forged. Kennett argues that it is important to situate current initiatives aimed at rough sleepers and other homeless households in the context of an increasingly productivist approach to urban policy and local economic development: the emergence of the rhetoric around the entrepreneurial city seeking to compete on an international stage is an important factor in understanding the motivations behind policy.

Issues of narrative and social construction are central to Chapter Four in which Paul Cloke, Paul Milbourne and Rebekah Widdowfield examine why homelessness is typically seen as an urban issue. Is it that homelessness is not a problem in rural areas or is it that the problem is ignored, unrecognised or denied in rural areas? Drawing on their recent empirical research, the authors find that homelessness is clearly a problem in rural areas and seek an explanation for the neglect of this problem in the way in which notions of the rural are constructed and idealised in Britain. During the course of their discussion the authors highlight the mobility of many homeless people and suggest that to draw the distinction between an 'urban' and a 'rural' homeless population would be misconceived.

The principal concern of the next two chapters is to move beyond treating 'the homeless' as an undifferentiated whole. They explore the particular social processes which result in certain social groups finding themselves homeless and consider how the experience of homelessness differs between social groups. In Chapter Five Sophie Watson returns to a theme of her earlier research and examines how issues of gender are central to our understanding of homelessness. She starts to develop the argument that visible homelessness among women presents a particular challenge to our social order because the gender role of women is tied up with notions of domesticity, caring, nurturing and cleanliness. Drawing on Foucault, Watson considers that in a society where, despite major increases in labour market participation, many women are still dependent on others for support, the very presence of homeless women in society acts as a disciplining device for those housed women who might be tempted to step out of line.

In Chapter Six Malcolm Harrison develops a model of exclusion for thinking about the way in which minority ethnic groups experience processes leading to homelessness. He considers the complex interaction between structural factors and experiential diversity to explore the range of potential outcomes for black minority ethnic households. The argument is that an adequate explanation of housing exclusion processes requires reference to both labour and housing market factors, to the relative socio-economic status and resources of groups, to change occurring at both household and community level, to racialised practices, and to the impact of choices and constraints facing individuals and groups. While the focus of the chapter is homelessness among black minority ethnic groups, the framework is of wider applicability.

Chapters Seven and Eight bring the sensibilities of socio-legal studies to the examination of policy toward homeless people. An underlying theme of both chapters is the tension embedded in policy between care for those experiencing homelessness and control of the activities of homeless households. In Chapter Seven Gary Fooks and Christina Pantazis examine the way in which begging and street homelessness are policed, focusing on a particularly high-profile example from central London. The discussion raises important questions about the thrust of current policy towards rough sleepers. While at a rhetorical level front-line police officers distance themselves from intensive policing of the 'zero tolerance' variety, the authors argue that the activities of rough sleepers none the less appear to be exposed to considerably greater police scrutiny and intrusion than other groups in society.

This concern with the law is broadened in Chapter Eight when David Cowan and Rose Gilroy revisit some of the debates about the nature of the homelessness legislation and its application. They take the example of a contemporary 'folk devil' – the paedophile – and examine how homelessness legislation has been applied. They argue that notions of risk and risk management need to be central to our understanding of policy in this area. The case of the paedophile highlights particularly starkly the importance of understanding the incompleteness of the legislation and the opportunities thereby opened up for local bureaucratic discretion in determining who should be considered as needing, and meriting, assistance. The authors demonstrate the way in which housing allocation and management decisions shade into questions of risk management and social control. They argue that housing managers now find themselves mediators of the new criminal justice. The chapter provides much food for thought regarding the current and future role of housing organisations.

In Chapter Nine Derek Hawes considers the way in which older people became an increasingly significant sub-group among the homeless during the 1990s. It is wrong to see older households as insulated from the increased risk of homelessness. Hawes argues that a range of social pressures and policy changes have placed many older people in a more precarious position. He concludes by suggesting that a creative policy response to this issue could be combined with an attempt to tackle the issue of less popular sheltered housing.

The importance of social and economic change and the deficiencies of policy in giving rise to homelessness is thrown into sharp relief by Yana Beigulenko's contribution which outlines the growth of homelessness in Russia (Chapter Ten). The collapse of the old order, deficiencies in housing supply and an uncoordinated policy response have meant that homelessness has increased and has impacted differentially upon households. Beigulenko sees the position of women and children as a particular concern.

Responding to homelessness is the concern of Chapters Eleven and Twelve. In Chapter Eleven Jenny Pannell and Siân Parry reflect upon The HUB and other multiagency initiatives in Bristol. The initiatives examined are held up as an example of relatively successful multiagency working to address the problems of single homeless people. The HUB has involved partners from a range of statutory and voluntary organisations and has attracted considerable attention both nationally and internationally. The HUB has experienced many of the well-known tensions associated with working across boundaries and Pannell and Parry reflect upon the reasons why the initiative seems to have overcome the obstacles and delivered. However, the authors recognise the difficulty of seeking to disentangle precisely what it is that has made the initiative successful. It exhibits an unusually high degree of interagency working, which could be seen as the key, but separating that out from other changes to service delivery – such as increased targeting and improved accessibility – which were also introduced under the initiative is by no means straightforward.

In Chapter Twelve the level of analysis switches from the individual innovative case to the range of resettlement activities occurring across the European Union. Brian Harvey argues that it is possible to identify three different models of resettlement in operation in different countries: the normalisation, tiered, and staircase of transition models. The different models carry with them different resource implications and different rates of successful resettlement. By broadening the horizon from the detail of the British case the chapter invites reflection upon the particularities of the British approach to addressing homelessness and offers the chance to draw some lessons regarding the appropriate shape for future policy.

Conclusion

A comprehensive understanding of homelessness will require theoretical approaches that bridge the gap between macro- and micro-social change. It will need to encompass explicitly an understanding of the way in which such changes are mediated by the institutions and processes specific to particular welfare regimes. It will need to be fully cognisant of the heterogeneity of both the people and processes involved and the way in which they make sense of their circumstances. It will recognise that policy is not only concerned with the response to homelessness, but is inextricably linked to the construction and perpetuation of the phenomenon. Such an understanding is likely to draw on the full range of theoretical resources offered by the social and human sciences. In bringing together authors from a range of disciplines to explore the new terrain of homelessness from a variety of perspectives we hope that this book makes a contribution towards attaining the goal of a comprehensive understanding.

References

6, Perri (1998) 'Housing policy in the risk archipelago: towards anticipatory and holistic government', *Housing Studies*, vol 13, no 3, pp 347-76.

Adams, J. (1995) *Risk*, London: UCL Press.

Aglietta, M. (1979) *A theory of capitalist regulation*, London: New Left Books.

Amin, A. (ed) (1994) *Post-Fordism: A reader*, Oxford: Blackwell.

Anderson, I., Kemp, P. and Quilgars, D. (1993) *Single homeless people*, London: HMSO.

Beck, U. (1992) *Risk society: Towards a new modernity*, London: Sage Publications.

Bramley, G. (1988) 'The definition and measurement of homelessness', in G. Bramley, K. Doogan, P. Leather, A. Murie and E. Watson (eds) *Homelessness and the London housing market*, Occasional Paper 32, Bristol: SAUS Publications, pp 24-43.

Douglas, M. (1992) *Risk and blame: Essays in cultural theory*, London: Routledge.

Edwards, R. (1995) 'Making temporary accommodation permanent: the cost for homeless families', *Critical Social Policy*, vol 43, no 2, pp 60-75.

Esping-Andersen, G. (1990) *The three worlds of welfare capitalism*, Cambridge: Polity Press.

Esping-Andersen, G. (1996) *Welfare states in transition*, London: Sage Publications.

Evans, A. (1999) 'Rationing device or passport to social housing? The operation of the homelessness legislation in Britain in the 1990s', in S. Hutson and D. Clapham (eds) *Homelessness: Public policies and private troubles*, London: Cassell, pp 134-54.

FEANTSA (European Federation of National Organisations Working with the Homeless) (1995) *Homelessness: The rising tide*, Brussels: FEANTSA.

Foster, C. and Plowden, F. (1996) *The state under stress*, Buckingham: Open University Press.

Harrison, M. (1998) 'Theorising exclusion and difference: specificity, structure and minority ethnic housing issues', *Housing Studies*, vol 13, no 6, pp 793-806.

Hill, M. (ed) (1993a) *New agendas in the study of the policy process*, Hemel Hempstead: Harvester Wheatsheaf.

Hill, M. (ed) (1993b) *The policy process: A reader*, Hemel Hempstead: Harvester Wheatsheaf.

Hutson, S. and Clapham, D. (eds) (1999) *Homelessness: Public policies and private troubles*, London: Cassell.

Hutson, S. and Liddiard, M. (1994) *Youth homelessness*, Basingstoke: Macmillan.

Jacobs, K., Kemeny, J. and Manzi, T. (1999) 'The struggle to define homelessness: a constructivist approach', in S. Hutson and D. Clapham (eds) *Homelessness: Public policies and private troubles*, London: Cassell, pp 11-28.

Kemp, P. (1997) 'The characteristics of single homeless households in England', in R. Burrows, N. Pleace and D. Quilgars (eds) *Homelessness and social policy*, London: Routledge, pp 69-87.

Kennett, P. (1994) 'Modes of regulation and the urban poor', *Urban Studies*, vol 31, no 7, pp 1017-31.

Lee, P. (1998) 'Housing policy, citizenship and social exclusion', in A. Marsh and D. Mullins (eds) *Housing and public policy*, Buckingham: Open University Press, pp 57-78.

Lee, P., Murie, A., Marsh, A. and Riseborough, M. (1995) *The price of social exclusion*, London: NFHA.

Lidstone, P. (1994) 'Rationing housing to the homeless applicant', *Housing Studies*, vol 9, no 4, pp 459-72.

Lowe, S. (1997) 'Homelessness and the law', in R. Burrows, N. Pleace and D. Quilgars (eds) *Homelessness and social policy*, London: Routledge, pp 19-34.

Marsh, A. and Mullins, D. (1998) 'The social exclusion perspective and housing studies: origins, applications and limitations', *Housing Studies*, vol 13, no 6, pp 749-60.

Minigione, E. (1993) 'The new urban poverty and the underclass', *International Journal of Urban and Regional Studies*, vol 17, no 3, pp 324-6.

Morris, L. (1994) *Dangerous classes: The underclass and social citizenship*, London: Routledge.

Mullins, D. and Niner, P. (1998) 'A prize of citizenship? Changing access to social housing', in A. Marsh and D. Mullins (eds) *Housing and public policy*, Buckingham: Open University Press, pp 175-98.

Mullins, D. and Niner, P. with Marsh, A. and Walker, B. (1996) *Evaluation of the 1991 Homelessness Code of Guidance*, London: HMSO.

Munro, M. and Madigan, R. (1993) 'Privacy in the private sphere', *Housing Studies*, vol 8, no 1, pp 29-48.

Neale, J. (1997) 'Homelessness and theory reconsidered', *Housing Studies*, vol 12, no 1, pp 47-61.

Niner, P. (1989) *Homelessness in nine local authorities: Case studies of policy and practice*, London: HMSO.

Oldman, C. (1997) 'Working together to help homeless people: an examination of inter-agency themes', in R. Burrows, N. Pleace and D. Quilgars (eds) *Homelessness and social policy*, London: Routledge, pp 229-42.

Paugam, S. (1995) 'The spiral of precariousness: a multi-dimensional approach to the process of social disqualification in France', in G. Room (ed) *Beyond the threshold: The measurement and analysis of social exclusion*, Bristol: The Policy Press, pp 49-79.

Peck, J. and Tickell, A. (1994a) 'Jungle law breaks out: neoliberalism and global-local disorder', *Area*, vol 26, no 4, pp 317-26.

Peck, J. and Tickell, A. (1994b) 'Searching for a new institutional fix: the after-Fordism crisis and the global–local disorder', in A. Amin (ed) *Post-Fordism: A reader*, Oxford: Blackwell, pp 280-315.

Pleace, N. (1998) 'Single homelessness as social exclusion: the unique and the extreme', *Social Policy and Administration*, vol 32, no 1, pp 46-59.

Quilgars, D. and Anderson, I. (1997) 'Addressing the problem of youth homelessness and unemployment: the contribution of foyers', in R. Burrows, N. Pleace and D. Quilgars (eds) *Homelessness and social policy*, London: Routledge, pp 216-18.

Room, G., Lawson, R. and Laczko, F. (1989) 'New poverty in the European Community', *Policy & Politics*, vol 17, no 2, pp 165-76.

Silver, H. (1993) 'National conceptions of the new urban poverty: social structural change in Britain, France and the US', *International Journal of Urban and Regional Research*, vol 17, no 2, pp 336-54.

Smith, S.J. and Mallinson, S. (1997) 'The problem with social housing: discretion, accountability and the welfare ideal', *Policy & Politics*, vol 24, no 4, pp 339-57.

Somerville, P. (1992) 'Homelessness and the meaning of home: rooflessness or rootlessness', *International Journal of Urban and Regional Research*, vol 16, no 4, pp 529-39.

Somerville, P. (1994) 'Homelessness policy in Britain', *Policy & Politics*, vol 22, no 3, pp 163-78.

Somerville, P. (1998) 'Explanations of social exclusion: where does housing fit in?', *Housing Studies*, vol 13, no 6, pp 761-80.

Somerville, P. (1999) 'The making and unmaking of homelessness legislation', in S. Hutson and D. Clapham (eds) *Homelessness: Public policies and private troubles*, London: Cassell, pp 29-57.

Taylor, M. (1998) 'Combating the social exclusion of housing estates', *Housing Studies*, vol 13, no 6, pp 819-32.

Wolch, J. and Dear, M. (1993) *Malign neglect: Homelessness in an American city*, San Francisco, CA: Jossey-Bass.

TWO

The new landscape of precariousness

Ray Forrest

So, what's new? There is certainly nothing new about homelessness. What may be new is the scale of the problem, its visibility, duration and the context in which it is occurring. Part of this changing context is the policy and academic discourse in which references to homelessness are now embedded. Well-worn debates about pathological and structural causes of homelessness have given way to references to social exclusion and social polarisation. The underlying narrative is one of division, fragmentation and of a widening gap between the majority which participates in social and economic life and the minority of the multiply excluded. Just as majorities are, however, differentially included, so minorities are differentially excluded. In other words, there is a continuum of security and insecurity in terms of factors such as employment, income, family life and social networks. This view recognises that homelessness can have both different causes and consequences and that while for some the experience of homelessness may be a temporary episode set within a portfolio of more secure formal and informal resources, for others it is a manifestation of a more general poverty of resources. Equally, for some the foothold on housing and employment, on participation in relatively resource rich social networks of friends and neighbours, may prove to be highly insecure.

The idea that society is now more polarised and that there are widening social fissures does not necessarily imply impermeable boundaries. The implication is that there are well entrenched minorities of privilege and underprivilege at either end of the social spectrum. Between those minorities lies a middle mass in varying degrees of comfort and security. Flexible labour markets, greater job insecurity, the erosion of the Keynesian welfare state and a greater fragility in relationships may, however, mean that it is possible to fall further and faster and that risk and insecurity are now more pervasive. Homelessness in this chapter is used therefore as a general metaphor for severe and typically multifaceted experiences of marginality and exclusion from mainstream society. The experience may be short and sharp or progressively corrosive, longstanding and debilitating.

Before pursuing these and other related issues it is as well to remind ourselves that marginality and subsistence living is the common experience in the everyday life of millions of people when viewed on a global scale. While the last century has seen enormous changes in housing standards and conditions in the developed 'north,' the reality for vast numbers of households in developing countries remains one of absolute housing deprivation.

As we approach the end of this century we are it seems finally entering the urban age, when the majority of people will be living in cities of varying scale. In the developing and newly industrialising countries, many of these cities will be on a mega scale with mega problems of environmental pollution, transport congestion, poverty and shantyism. The accelerated pace of urbanization and the commercialization of land markets in the cities of the south are creating new pressures of eviction and displacement. Rural–urban migration and the related housing pressures remain dominant forces in the world (see United Nations Centre for Human Settlements, 1996).

It is a sobering fact that, on whatever estimates, the scale of homelessness remains significant in Europe and North America. It has been suggested, for example, that in the early 1990s there were around 18 million citizens of the European Union in some state of homelessness (FEANTSA, 1995). However, if we then include even more heroic estimates of those living in various states of housing precariousness in other parts of the world, the scale of the global housing problem appears truly unmanageable:

> ... worldwide, the number of homeless people can be estimated at anywhere from 100 million to 1 billion or more, depending on how homelessness is defined. The estimate of 100 million would apply to those who have no shelter at all, including those who sleep outside (on pavements, in shop doorways, in parks or under bridges) or in public buildings (in railway, bus or metro stations) or in night shelters set up to provide homeless people with a bed. The estimate of 1 billion homeless people would also include those in accommodation that is very insecure or temporary, often of poor quality – for instance squatters who have found accommodation by illegally occupying someone else's home or land and are under constant threat of eviction, those living in refugee camps whose home has been destroyed and

those living in temporary shelters (like the 250,000 pavement dwellers in Bombay. (United Nations Centre for Human Settlements, 1996, p 229)

So one answer to the question of what's new is that the scale of urban homelessness is on the increase worldwide. Urban poverty and deprivation accelerate as cities fail to provide the opportunities for an adequate income for many of those displaced from the rural hinterland. But there is also a new perspective on the connections between the urban poor in the traditional 'Third World' and the displaced and disadvantaged within the old capitalist core countries. The assumption of progressive inclusion is now questioned. It is no longer assumed that the poor of today will be members of tomorrow's middle class. The big picture is no longer one in which there are localised pockets of poverty within the industrialised or post-industrialised world which are merely waiting their turn at the end of the queue to receive their share of burgeoning affluence. Reich (1993), for example, refers to the increasing dominance of the symbolic analysts, the manipulators of signs and symbols, whose incomes and related rewards are progressively diverging from those in other occupational categories – what he refers to as routine production workers and those involved in in-person-servicing.

Controlling for family size, geography, and other changes, the best estimate ... is that between 1977 and 1990 the average income of the poorest fifth of Americans declined by about 5 percent, while the richest fifth became about 9 percent wealthier. During these years, the average incomes of the poorest fifth of American families declined by about 7 percent, while the average income of the richest fifth of American families increased by about 15 percent. (Reich, 1993, p 197)

Similar statistics can be found for other nation states associated both with transformation in the labour market and in welfare regimes which have become increasingly shaped by the perceived competitive demands of the global economy. Lipietz (1998), drawing on data taken from taxable income declarations by households, gives this process of social transformation a particular French flavour when he refers to the transition from a *montgolfier* to an *hour glass* society. He characterises the income distribution in post-war France which resulted from a virtuous combination of rapid and durable productivity gains systematically redistributed via "a network of collective agreements, social legislation and the welfare state" as a "hot air balloon, ascending harmoniously". He continues:

> **There were a few poor people, a few rich people and a huge waged middle class, all of them growing richer together. The income hierarchy was rigidly constrained by collective agreements. Higher classes, middle classes, popular classes, each successively reached similar consumption patterns, which rose along similar trajectories but were lagging after each other in time. The lifestyle of the engineer preceded that of the technician by a few years, which showed the way for the highly skilled factory worker, which, in turn pointed to the path for the unskilled worker. (Lipietz, 1998, p 178)**

In the evolving hour glass society, shaped by factors such as flexibilisation, stricter eligibility criteria for state benefits and higher returns for wealth holders, incomes become increasingly polarised. Lipietz evocatively captures these social changes as an hour glass "where grains of sand represent households desperately falling to the bottom and money is like air accumulating in the upper part". According to Lipietz this metaphor not only describes the shape of the evolving income distribution in France but refers to a change in the essential economic mechanism. Under Fordism he argues the "rich lived off the expenditure of the poor" whereas in the post-Fordist hour glass society "the poor live off what trickles down from the expenditure of the rich" (p 182). There is, of course, considerable debate about the extent to which wage polarisation between those appropriately skilled for the contemporary labour market and the unskilled is generating a trapped and chronically impoverished minority. What *is* evident is a pervasive downward pressure on the wages of the least well qualified. The consequences of this trend for social mobility are mediated by the nature of welfare systems, the structure of national labour markets and social investment strategies (Esping-Andersen, 1996).

Nor is the gap closing between the developed and developing world. Most notably, in Africa poverty and unemployment levels have been increasing and the income gap between Sub-Saharan Africa and, for example, Europe, has widened rather than diminished. Castells (1998) refers to the increasing 'structural' irrelevance of people and places in what he has termed the global, informational age. These people and places are concentrated in Africa, Latin America and parts of Asia but the old core-periphery distinctions are breaking down. Instead, according to Castells, a new fourth world is emerging which comprises the 'black holes' of this new informational capitalism.

> **The fourth world comprises large areas of the globe, such as much of Sub-Saharan Africa, and impoverished rural areas of Latin America and Asia. But it is also present in literally every country, and every city, in this new geography of social exclusion. It is formed of American inner city ghettos, Spanish enclaves of mass youth unemployment, French banlieus warehousing North Africans, Japanese Yoseba quarters and Asian mega-cities' shanty towns. And it is populated by millions of homeless, incarcerated, prostituted, criminalized, brutalized, stigmatized, sick and illiterate persons. (Castells, 1998, pp 164-5)**

This is a powerful and apocalyptic view of the new world order. But Castells stresses that these divisions are neither immutable nor inevitable. The forces of the new informational age can be harnessed in different ways and are subject to political will and action. Nevertheless, the implication is that the demands of this new age are such that those lacking the necessary social and educational qualifications – those with least bargaining power in an increasingly competitive labour market – are likely to fall further behind in terms of life chances and living standards. The general point is that there are new forces at work which are marginalising sections of the population. These places, without the necessary infrastructure to tap into informational networks, will see themselves progressively disconnected from those embedded in the global flows. These forces are most apparent in the poorest nation states where minority elites dominate an otherwise subsistence existence for majorities. Their precarious existence is nothing new but it is apparently more deeply entrenched by the forces at work in this new global order. Within richer societies, however, these forces bear down on a diversity of poorer minorities and vulnerable groups in novel ways to create new dimensions of social exclusion from the social and consumption norms of the majority. At the extremes, perhaps, and most visibly, they produce increasing levels of street homelessness and rough sleeping. It is in this context that Marcuse, echoing Castells' reference to "structural irrelevance", refers to "structural homelessness, that is a core level of homelessness which seems to be independent of fluctuations in the business cycle" (Marcuse, 1993, p 359). In other words, there is a level of homelessness which seems to be with us whatever the general state of the economy. And the composition of the homeless population is also changing. There may be a variety of routes into homelessness but once there, the dangers of social exclusion multiply. Again, Castells provides an evocative summary of US research evidence on this issue:

> **The homeless population of the 1990s is composed of a mixture of 'old homeless', classic skid-row types, or de-institutionalized mentally ill persons, and of newer characters, such as 'welfare moms', young families left behind by deindustrialization and restructuring, tenants evicted by gentrification, runaway teenagers, migrants without a home, and battered women, escaping from men.** (Castells, 1998, p 162)

New homelessness then is the product of a combination of processes. The reshaping of labour market opportunities, the changing geography of employment, the erosion of welfare safety nets for the most vulnerable and changing social norms produce new groups at risk of being without shelter either temporarily or for longer periods. The particular configuration of circumstances will vary in relation to welfare regimes, cultural norms, employment structures and policy shifts. Homelessness is, of course, a particularly severe example of marginality and exclusion and may be the product of a combination of adverse factors. One general and central question is how far the risk of falling into or towards the abyss of homelessness has spread beyond those groups traditionally most vulnerable. In other words, are new groups being drawn into this new landscape of precariousness or is it simply that the incline is steeper and the penalties harsher for the poor and the least educated? Are there processes at work drawing more people into these risk scenarios which may culminate in the experience or real threat of homelessness?

Commentators on the transformations affecting our everyday lives most commonly refer to changes in the labour market as the key factor creating greater instability and risk for households. References to casualisation, part-time work, zero-hour contracts and core-periphery models of firms' employment structures in the contemporary era are contrasted with a post-war Fordist Keynesianism of relative security and permanence in job opportunities and experiences. For example, a recent review of available evidence on the changing nature of work concluded, inter alia, that:

> ... in the past, risk was shared between employers and employee,
> with employers implicitly accepting responsibility for smoothing
> out the bad with the good. That responsibility is no longer as
> widespread. The increase in risk has been most marked for those
> working in manufacturing, for the less skilled and the less healthy.
> However, there are indications that these risks are increasingly
> shared by well-educated middle-class men, which is part of the
> reason we have come to hear more about them. (Joseph Rowntree
> Foundation, 1996)

To what extent these risks are real or imagined among different groups is
a matter of some debate among labour market analysts. Wadsworth (1995)
observes that while there has been growing job insecurity "the average
job tenure and turnover is little different now than twenty years earlier"
(p 4). He goes on, however, to argue that inactivity and detachment from
the labour market has grown dramatically and that men "in the lowest
quartile of the skills distribution are now more than twice as likely to
leave/lose their jobs than the top quartile" (pp 4-5). He concludes: "Whilst
full-time permanent posts as an employee have almost certainly not
become more unstable, there has been a switch towards ... more unstable
forms of employment". And he continues:

> For those at the margins, employment in the nineties has become
> far more unstable and the penalties attached to job loss in terms
> of durations out of work and the wage penalty on return have
> risen. Hence their labour market has become far riskier.
> (Wadsworth, 1995, pp 10-11)

For Wadsworth, then, there is a strong sense of polarisation of opportunity
and experience in the labour market with the risks concentrated on a
minority, albeit a growing one. Doogan (1998), addressing some of the
same issues, draws on OECD data to argue that contrary to some of the
more dystopic post-Fordist accounts of economic restructuring, job tenure
and long-term employment "have borne up remarkably during three
recessions" (p 7). For Doogan, feelings of anxiety and insecurity are not
consistent with OECD data on employment stability which show, for
example, that in Germany, Canada and the USA average job tenure has
actually increased over the last decade or so.

> These statistics are global figures for each country and they
> conceal differences by industry and gender, particularly with male
> job tenure declining and female job tenure increasing. But the
> phenomenon of long term employment enduring and increasing
> throughout periods of boom and recession is remarkable, and
> present a serious challenge to advocates of labour market
> restructuring and the decline of stable employment. (Doogan,
> 1998, p 10)

Some caution is therefore required when attributing growing risk and
instability in everyday life to transformation in the labour market. There
has been an increase in temporary employment but it still represents only
around 5% of all employees in employment. The substantial increase in
part-time work is associated to a great extent with the higher participation
rates of women in the labour force, the majority of whom are not seeking
full-time work. The flexibilisation of the labour market has increased
levels of self-employment and subcontracting and thus the numbers on
fixed-term contracts. However, fixed-term contracts can be of varying
durations and will include highly paid professionals as well as those with
low incomes and lower skills. Contract work does not necessarily equate
with precariousness and casualisation and is as likely to indicate choice as
constraint in work regimes. Moreover, employees flow in and out of
different employment situations. For example, the British Household Panel
Survey (BHPS) shows that among males with seasonal or casual
employment status in 1991, a third had permanent jobs a year later. And
45% of males on fixed-term contracts in 1991 had permanent jobs in
1992. This could suggest an increased use of temporary or fixed-term
contracts by employers as a filter prior to either firing or hiring on a more
permanent basis. However, the flows between more stable and less stable
employment circumstances are heavily biased in one direction. The same
data from the BHPS show that 39% of male employees in seasonal or
casual employment and a fifth of those with fixed-term contracts in 1991
were not working in 1992. Conversely, 90% of those in permanent
employment in 1991 had the same status a year later – 7% were not working
and 3% had either seasonal or fixed-term contracts (CSO, 1996, p 88).

This suggests that much of the risk in the labour market is associated
with churning and turnover on the fringes and that there is an increasing
differentiation between a secure primary core and a less stable periphery
of workers moving in and out of various employment circumstances.
Moreover, there are strong ethnic differences in overall employment

patterns. Whereas in 1995, 72% of white males of working age were employed full time, only 49% of black males were in this category. And while a third of Pakistani/Bangladeshi males of working age were officially classified as inactive, only 15% of white males were in this category (CSO, 1996, p 83). Ethnicity, class, gender and educational levels combine to produce an uneven pattern of opportunity and risk in employment. A number of studies internationally have shown a progressive growth in knowledge intensive jobs requiring high education levels and a decline in lower level jobs where only basic qualifications are needed (see, for example, Castells, 1989, Chapter 4). The implication is that those without the necessary educational and social skills for the informational age are likely to fall progressively further behind in terms of income and job opportunities. In this context a commentary on the BHPS by Gershuny et al (1996) observes that:

> ... as unemployment has tended, on average, to increase slowly since the 1950s with a more dramatic rise in the late 1980s and early 1990s, successive generations of this less well qualified group of men have experienced increasing levels of unemployment. To a lesser extent, generations of highly qualified men have also experienced rising levels of unemployment. (CSO, 1996, p 35)

Hunter (1995) sums up general trends in the British labour market as follows:

> Employers have responded to the new market and technological environment by varying the *form* of employment. High unemployment and a plentiful supply of low-skill, low wage labour have enabled employers to develop their shrinking internal labour markets (where they seek commitment and flexibility) while drawing supplementary labour from the highly competitive external market – labour that can be hired to meet specific time-related needs or occasional functional specialisms. (Hunter, 1995, p 9)

Changes in the labour process, with greater intensification and scrutiny, have affected those in relatively secure positions contributing perhaps to a stronger general sense of insecurity. Real insecurity, in the sense of risk of job loss, is however, spread unevenly and is more likely to affect those in lower skill, lower paid jobs. There is a strong sense of polarisation in the labour market captured in the conception of primary and secondary circuits of employment.

Precariousness and stability as multidimensional phenomena

Precariousness is not, however, solely or even perhaps always centrally about jobs. The consequences which may flow from job loss, loss of income or some other change in circumstances such as marital breakdown will depend on the overall portfolio of formal and informal resources of an individual or family. Paugam (1995), writing with particular reference to France and drawing on a major empirical study of the living conditions of households in the late 1980s, refers to a "spiral of precariousness" and the need for a multidimensional approach to social disqualification. His multidimensional approach is operationalised via correlation and regression techniques to link employment situations to income, the degree of stability of relationships and the strength or otherwise of social networks. Paugam classifies job situations in a hierarchy of stability and "the extent of social and economic advantage acquired through the occupation". In the survey material he is analysing, "stable jobs not under threat" accounted for 52% of employees. At the other end of his hierarchy are those who have been unemployed for more than two years which accounted for just over 5% of the sample. Linking this hierarchy to other demographic and social characteristics he observes that:

> **People with jobs not under threat are generally in good health, live in comfortable housing and have many professional advantages (higher educational qualifications). People who say their job is under threat are all, by their age, occupation and status, in the less dynamic and protected sectors of the labour market, which makes them more vulnerable to economic fluctuations. People with jobs that are unstable do not all have difficulty in getting another job – this is only a case with a fraction of them. On the other hand the others can be regarded as overall employed but working in sectors of the labour market which rely on considerable mobility between firms, in the building industry or public works, for example. (Paugam, 1995, p 51)**

Paugam goes on to illustrate the various interactions between employment insecurity, income loss and conjugal instability to produce what he refers to as a general "decline in social life". With this latter term he is referring to a reduction in the intensity of social relationships, a progressive emptying out of kinship and friendship networks which finds particularly concentrated expression in chronically disadvantaged neighbourhoods where the socially excluded become increasingly concentrated. This spatial exclusion is a further dimension of 'social disqualification' through the external negative labelling of such neighbourhoods and the pervasive weakness of the social networks of the people who live there (see, for example, Forrest and Kearns, 1999).

It is inappropriate to report the full details of Paugam's complex analysis here. Two further issues are, however, particularly relevant to this discussion. First, what does it tell us about the spread of risk and vulnerability across the population? For example, recent research on youth homelessness in Britain suggested that the middle classes are increasingly represented among the young homeless – that new groups are now at risk (CHAR, 1996). Paugam suggests that while even those with secure employment may be vulnerable to social exclusion, the risk is undoubtedly less than for those furthest removed from the labour market. But he is more concerned to emphasise that precariousness can come in different forms with different relational contingencies.

> **It is certain that the case of the civil servant who is made redundant, and at the same time suffers a marital breakdown, loses his home, breaks contact with his family and goes down the rungs of the social ladder one by one until he finds himself on the street, is no longer exceptional. Charitable organisations are dealing more and more with people who have suffered a serious social displacement. It must not be deduced from this that the risk of exclusion strikes all individuals in an identical fashion independent of their social situation. There are various forms of precariousness spread across French society, and it is not true that in all cases they are the result of accumulated problems. It would be false to say that no one is protected from the risk of social exclusion. (Paugam, 1995, p 69)**

So Paugam's answer is that risks have spread beyond the traditionally vulnerable groups but longstanding and deep-seated inequalities continue to structure propensities to vulnerability and the depth of the abyss into which people may fall.

The second and equally pertinent question concerns cross-national comparisons. Would a similar study of Britain produce similar results given differences in welfare regimes, labour market structures and institutions and cultural differences in relation to, for example, the role of the family? Paugam reports preliminary results of a comparative study which offers some tentative conclusions. While there are close correlations in Western European countries between employment precariousness, low income, bad housing and conjugal breakdown there are apparently significant areas of divergence in relation to family ties and social networks. In the UK and France, unstable employment and unemployment are more likely to lead to a weakening of social networks and family ties than in, for example, Spain or the Netherlands (Pauham, 1995, pp 73-7). Whatever the underlying reasons for these apparent differences the important point is that we need to look beyond traditional measures of vulnerability to understand fully the risks and the nature of social exclusion faced by different groups in particular cultural settings. The significance of informal networks, and specifically of friends, has been emphasised in recent work by Pahl (1997). In a world where the role of the family, formal voluntary association and other formal institutional supports may be weakening, friendship networks may be playing an increasingly important role. To be friendless or to have few friends in times of difficulty may be a significant element of the divide between the haves and have nots and a major factor in social isolation. Pahl, drawing on data from the BHPS shows that, for example, "unemployed men enjoy potentially less social support than those in employment. One in ten of the unemployed had no-one to turn to, to provide help in a crisis or to offer comfort" (p 9).

Precariousness and the British housing market

Changes in housing opportunities, subsidy regimes in housing and the specific risk of losing one's home sit then within the broad context outlined above. And particular features of British housing policy and the British housing tenure structure have undoubtedly and observably spread vulnerability into middle-class domains. A number of commentators have observed that home ownership, a form of housing provision best suited to circumstances in which households have relatively stable earnings, secure employment and predictable life paths, has been promoted and expanded in an era in which social and economic changes are creating greater risk and uncertainty (for a general discussion see Forrest and Murie, 1994).

Homeowners through the 1980s and 1990s have experienced periods of rapidly rising unemployment, rapidly rising house prices, rapidly falling house prices and escalating interest rates. The general statistics relevant to this scenario are well known. For example, mortgage repossessions, which had been a marginal problem in 1980 with around 3,500 households affected, stood at 75,600 in 1991. Similarly, serious arrears of more than 12 months, around 5,000 in 1982, peaked at over 151,000 in 1993 (CML, 1995). Negative equity, an unknown phenomenon a decade earlier, affected an estimated 1.8 million households in 1992 (Thomas, 1996). In 1993, 8% of households accepted as homeless by local authorities in England were attributed to mortgage arrears. In parts of the country such as the South East (outside London) and East Anglia the percentage of mortgage arrears cases were 13% and 15% respectively (CSO, 1995).

Until the mid-1980s homelessness was a phenomenon associated mainly with either outright vagrancy or the rental tenures. Home ownership was the secure tenure of the middle classes. Beyond a few unlucky or particularly profligate souls, entry into home ownership was a one-way ticket indicating and consolidating relative security of income and employment. As the growth of home ownership has accelerated over the last two decades a number of things have happened. Most obviously, a mass tenure takes on different characteristics from one which is a minority tenure accommodating mainly households in middle to higher income categories. Home ownership now includes more lower income households and households in less secure employment. Wilcox and Ford observe that:

> ... home buyers now make up two-fifths of all households in the lower half of the bottom income decile. In 1979 they made up just 14 per cent of the households in the lowest income band.... More generally one in six home-buying households do not now have household heads in full-time employment, twice as many as there were at the beginning of the 1980s. (Wilcox and Ford, 1998, p 25)

At the same time the subsidies to homeowners through mortgage interest tax relief have been substantially reduced and more restrictive and less generous provision has been introduced for homeowning households which get into difficulties. Income support for homeowners with a mortgage has been restricted in scope and with no entitlement for nine months. Homeowners are now expected to take out private insurance to cover themselves against such risks. Moreover, the prospect of an era of low or zero inflation is a mixed blessing for homeowners with mortgages. High inflation rapidly erodes the value of the mortgage debt and builds up a cushion of positive equity. Low inflation leaves borrowers more exposed to the prospects of negative equity and generally increases debt exposure. Bootle (1996), among others, has offered a particularly cautionary analysis of this new world of low inflation in which both lenders and borrowers need to adapt to a higher risk environment.

> **Because property prices will go up and down and, in general, pay will rise only slowly, it also means that people need to adopt a more cautious and conservative attitude towards borrowing money for house purchase. The 80, 90 or even 100% mortgages which were prevalent in the heyday of the housing market at the end of the 1980s could now be downright dangerous. (Bootle, 1996, p 86)**

In a similar vein Wilcox and Ford comment that:

> **... the medium-term prospects are for far slower equity growth than in earlier decades, and with lower inflation the ratios of mortgage payments to earnings will only slowly ease over the lifetime of a mortgage. In this context, home-buying households will typically be more at risk in the event of any short-term economic or domestic events that disrupt their incomes than they would have been during earlier more inflationary decades. (Wilcox and Ford, 1998, p 26)**

These changed economic circumstances have affected not only those on lower incomes but reached well into the middle classes, directly in the sense of arrears difficulties or even repossessions associated with high interest rates and negative equity and less directly through job losses in housing market related professions. For example, one building society reported in August 1990 that almost half its repossession cases were professional borrowers such as doctors or solicitors (reported in Forrest and Murie, 1994). Negative equity, which was concentrated in the South East of England, inevitably encompassed significant numbers of higher income professional and managerial households (Forrest et al, 1999). It was higher income households which had the highest mortgage debts and thus the highest amounts of negative equity. But it was mainly lower income homeowners which experienced the worst consequences of rising costs or negative equity. To return to our earlier discussion of Paugam's work, the arrears, repossession and negative equity statistics undoubtedly include examples of 'serious displacement', of professional households ending up in very changed housing circumstances through a combination of negative factors. In the main, however, it was households with the most limited portfolio of assets in terms of property values and conditions, incomes, savings, relationship stability and job security which were most likely to get into serious difficulties.

The Survey of English Housing (ONS, 1998) provides an analysis of the main characteristics of those households having difficulties with mortgage repayments and the main reasons. Loss of income through reduced hours, redundancy, unemployment, sickness or injury was mentioned by over two thirds of respondents with mortgage arrears. Those groups most likely to be in arrears or having payments difficulties were households with unemployed persons, households headed by an economically inactive person of working age, households with gross incomes of under £100 per week and lone parents. Arrears were also associated with that cohort of homeowners which had bought at the peak of the housing boom in 1989/90. Unemployed heads were seven times more likely to be in arrears as those in full employment. Being self-employed more than doubled the likelihood of being in arrears (ONS, pp 37-8).

The same survey found that in 430,000 households, "at some time in the past, someone in the household had had to give up their home because of difficulties paying their mortgage" (p 38). Of those 430,000 people who had all been in home ownership, 147,000 were now renting from the council, 55,000 were in housing association tenancies, 92,000 were in the privately rented sector and 14,000 were no longer householders. Only 29% were homeowners. A quarter had given up their homes as a result of a court order rather than left of their own accord. It is evident, therefore, that for many households entry into home ownership has not been a one-way ticket.

This section has focused on the new risks associated with an expanded home ownership in a changed set of social and economic circumstances. In emphasising the problems of homeowners and home ownership it is important, however, not to lose sight of the fact that the poorest and most vulnerable households are concentrated in the rental sectors or are on the street. Private renting in particular remains strongly associated with problems of insecurity and homelessness. Harassment and illegal evictions are still experienced by private tenants who are often already seriously disadvantaged. Security of tenure has been eroded and rents are more freely set and negotiated. But there is nothing new in this. Private renting has traditionally served a shifting mass of households adjusting to short or longer-term difficulties. Social renting has increasingly become the tenure of last resort coping with the casualities of recessions, marital breakdown and other adverse events in people's lives. Concentrated poverty, areas saturated with disadvantage, is a particular feature of the 1990s landscape. But the fall out from home ownership and the growing instability around the tenure is the dominant new element.

The new landscape of oppression

Changes in the structure of housing opportunities and housing-related risks have impacted on a wide variety of households. For those on the extreme margins, however, there is another, and perhaps starker and more novel dimension to the way the world is experienced. This is the literal change in the architecture of cities and the greater scrutiny of those living on or near the streets. As metropolitan cores become increasingly marketed as chic, vibrant, glamorous residential niches for young professional cityphiles they become simultaneously more oppressive and exclusionary for the poor and homeless. New technology permits 24–hour surveillance of the public spaces which are in turn increasingly private spaces. The steel gates close on the shopping malls and arcades at the end of the day and the libraries and museums, the traditional shelters for those with nowhere else to go, require entrance fees in a progressively privatised environment. And the more affluent city dwellers retreat behind gates and walls to protect themselves from the hostile world outside. These developments, often in the form of gated communities with security guards, are increasingly popular, particularly in the USA. Lang and Danielson (1997) draw on various studies to show that some 19,000 such communities currently exist in the United States containing more than 8.5 million residents. They remark that "Gated communities represent a major reordering in the physical, social, legal and civic arrangements by which Americans live" (p 868). They are themselves a reaction to "general societal angst": a reaction to often unspecified fears about a world outside which has become more unstable, threatening and insecure. In the same context Judd (1995) refers to shopping mall "fortresses" as symptoms of new and more extreme forms of spatial and social segregation. The fortress metaphor is taken up by Christopherson (1994) who argues that "as social disintegration and increasing economic inequality have made the city more dangerous, designs in response to danger, particularly those to secure property, have altered the spatial relationship between public and private, a relationship built around a sense of common ownership and control of the street" (p 410).

The control of the street and the 'hardening' of the city surface has been most provocatively captured in Davis' account of contemporary Los Angeles where he refers to "a merciless struggle to make public facilities and spaces as 'unliveable' as possible for the homeless and poor" (Davis, 1992). He goes on to describe "the new barrel-shaped bus bench that offers minimal surface for uncomfortable sitting, while making sleeping utterly impossible. Such 'bum-proof' benches are being widely introduced on the periphery of Skid Row. Another invention, worthy of the Grand Guignol, is "the aggressive deployment of outdoor sprinklers ... an elaborate overhead sprinkler system programmed to drench unsuspecting sleepers at random during the night" (pp 232-3). The experience of being on the outside looking in has, it seems, become sharper than ever.

Concluding comments

This chapter set out in search of novel processes at work in the creation of insecurity and precariousness in our everyday lives. In particular, it has been concerned to provide a broad context within which to situate contemporary debates about homelessness and situations which may precipitate homelessness. It has not attempted to explore the various debates around forms of homelessness nor to provide any substantial data on homelessness in the UK or elsewhere. These issues are examined in greater depth elsewhere.

There are three points which have been emphasised. First, in exploring issues around homelessness in the UK we should acknowledge that from an international perspective there is little doubt that problems of lack of shelter, poverty and subsistence living are increasing rather than diminishing. Castells' 'fourth world' may well encompass people and places in London, Manchester, Bristol and other parts of Britain, but rampant urbanisation combined with economic vulnerability is producing misery on a breathtaking scale in parts of Asia, Latin America and Africa.

Second, the chapter has stressed the need to look beyond the labour market to appreciate new forms of vulnerability. Unemployment and underemployment remain a central factor but it is job instability combined with instability or lack of resources elsewhere which will combine to produce major problems of social exclusion. And it is more complex than simply the combined effects of relationship breakdown and job loss. In a world where the associational institutions of the workplace and kinship networks are under stress and where state safety nets are being generally reduced in scope and scale, the experience of adversity is an increasingly individuated one. In those circumstances it is the informal networks of neighbours and friends and the level of market-based insurance against risk which increasingly separates the survivors from the serious casualties. Risk is spread wider but does not strike in some random manner. Traditional and systematic inequalities remain which affect the degree to which certain groups are in danger of falling over the precipice. But these inequalities are not simply economic but refer to a broader portfolio of formal and informal resources.

Third, there are particular new risks associated with the housing market. Essentially there are more vulnerable households in less stable markets. These circumstances include the particular features of households such as low income, job insecurity and the tenuous nature of contemporary personal relationships *and* structural changes in the nature of housing markets in which price stability and asset appreciation are no longer assured. Home ownership is no longer such a secure domain of the middle classes or middle classness. The particular features of the British housing market and tenure structure combine then with factors such as the specific ways in which state support has been reduced and reoriented, the nature of labour market change and practices and the strength of social networks to produce a particular landscape of precariousness. In this landscape what is new is not so much the characteristics of those groups which are most vulnerable. It is the familiar list of the poor, lone parents, ethnic minorities and the sick. What are novel are the combination of processes contributing to vulnerability. These include the pressures of a more competitive labour market, the reshaping of welfare benefits and entitlements and the stresses and strains on family networks and conjugal relationships. While those processes have impacted primarily on minorities, the consequences have become more visible not only in relation to street homelessness but in relation to neighbours, friends or colleagues who may have been downsized, casualised or repossessed. Some may be further from the precipice than others but there is a common perception, rooted in everyday experience, that it is no longer quite so far away.

References

Bootle, R. (1996) *The death of inflation*, London: Nicholas Brealey.

Castells, M. (1989) *The informational city*, Oxford: Blackwell.

Castells, M. (1998) *End of millennium*, Oxford: Blackwell.

CHAR (1996) *The inquiry into preventing youth homelessness*, London: CHAR.

Christopherson, S. (1994) 'The fortress city: privatized spaces, consumer citizenship' in A. Amin (ed) *Post-Fordism: A reader*, Oxford: Blackwell, pp 409-27.

CML (Council for Mortgage Lenders) (1995) *CML market briefing*, February, London: CML.

CSO (Central Statistical Office) (1995) *Regional trends 30*, London: HMSO.

CSO (1996) *Social trends*, London: HMSO.

Davis, M. (1992) *City of quartz*, New York, NY: Vintage.

Doogan, K. (1998) 'Labour market forces versus labour market structures', Paper presented to the 14th World Congress of Sociology, Montreal, Canada, July.

Esping-Andersen, G. (ed) (1996) *Welfare states in transition: National adaptations to global economies*, London: Sage Publications.

FEANTSA (European Federation of National Organisations Working with the Homeless) (1995) *Homelessness in the European Union: Social and legal context for housing exclusion in the 1990s*, Brussels: FEANTSA.

Forrest, R. and Kearns, A. (1999) *Joined-up places? Social cohesion and neighbourhood regeneration*, York: York Publishing Services for the Joseph Rowntree Foundation.

Forrest, R. and Murie, A. (1994) 'Home ownership in recession', *Housing Studies*, vol 9, no 1, pp 55-74.

Forrest, R., Kennett, P. and Leather, P. (1999) *Home ownership in crisis? The experience of negative equity in Britain*, Aldershot: Avebury.

Gershuny, J. et al (1996) 'The British Household Panel Study', in Central Statistical Office, *Social trends*, London: HMSO, pp 16-26.

Hunter, L. (1995) 'What price labour market flexibility?', Draft paper presented at seminar on Economic Flexibility and Housing, Glasgow, 5-7 September.

Joseph Rowntree Foundation (1996) *The future of work: A contribution to the debate*, Social Policy Summary 7, York: Joseph Rowntree Foundation.

Judd, D. (1995) 'The rise of the new walled cities', in H. Liggett and D. Perry (eds) *Spatial practices*, London: Sage Publications.

Lang, R.E. and Danielson, K.A. (1997) 'Gated communities in America: walling out the world', *Housing Policy Debate*, vol 8, no 4, pp 867-77.

Lipietz, A. (1998) 'Rethinking social housing in the hour-glass society', in A. Madanipour, G. Cars and J. Allen (eds) *Social exclusion in European cities*, London: Jessica Kingsley, pp 177-88.

Marcuse, P. (1993) 'What's so new about divided cities?', *International Journal of Urban and Regional Research*, vol 17, no 3, pp 355-65.

Meadows, P. (1996) *Work out-or work in? Contributions to the debate on the future of work*, York: Joseph Rowntree Foundation.

ONS (Office for National Statistics) (1998) *Housing in England 1996/97*, London: HMSO.

Pahl, R. (1997) 'The ties that bind: creating communities', Paper presented to ESRC Social Science Conference, QE2 Centre, 25 June.

Paugam, S. (1995) 'The spiral of precariousness: a multidimensional approach to the process of social disqualification in France', in G. Room (ed) *Beyond the threshold: The measurement and analysis of social exclusion*, Bristol: The Policy Press, pp 49-79.

Reich, R. (1993) *The work of nations*, London: Simon and Schuster.

Thomas, R. (1996) *Negative equity: Outlook and effects*, London: CML.

United Nations Centre for Human Settlements (1996) *An urbanizing world: Global report on human settlements, 1996*, Oxford: Oxford University Press.

Wadsworth, J. (1995) 'Mind the gaps? An overview of the changing structure of the UK labour market', Paper presented at seminar on Economic Flexibility and Housing, Glasgow, 5-7 September.

Wilcox, S. and Ford, J. (1998) 'At your own risk', in J. Wilcox, *Housing finance review*, York: Joseph Rowntree Foundation, pp 23-9.

THREE

Homelessness, citizenship and social exclusion

Patricia Kennett

This chapter considers the relationship between homelessness and the concepts of citizenship and social exclusion. The connections are complex and numerous while at the same time nebulous and changing. The meanings of the concepts themselves represent 'contested terrain'. This chapter will argue, however, that this conceptual framework contributes to an understanding of the multiple connections between the ensembles of social rights, institutional and policy arrangements within and through which homelessness has been understood and through which the boundaries of citizenship and social exclusion have been drawn. The discussion will be located in the context of the contemporary 'entrepreneurial' city.

This chapter will begin with a brief discussion of the concepts of citizenship and social exclusion (for fuller discussions see Turner, 1993; Room, 1995; Bulmer and Rees, 1996; Jordan, 1996; Levitas, 1998; Lister, 1998). Developments in the post-war period will then be explored to establish the institutional, ideological and discursive context through which homelessness was constructed and the boundaries of citizenship and inclusionary and exclusionary criteria were established. The chapter will then consider the emergence of the new homelessness within an alternative policy discourse. Particularly from the early 1980s, this discourse was accompanied by the renegotiation of the content and meaning of citizenship rights. The chapter will argue that the current model of social integration and citizenship seems to be one in which there has been a re-evaluation of the notion of civil rights and an increasing emphasis on the 'privatised' citizen (Lister, 1990), active in the workfare state of the stakeholder society.

Citizenship and social exclusion

The concept of citizenship has a long history but is most commonly associated with the work of T.H. Marshall (1950) for whom citizenship is based upon rights and entitlements. His central theme was that the rights of citizenship involve national constitutional rights such as civil and political rights, as well as embracing social rights, each of which is closely associated with social and political institutions. The hallmark of advanced industrial democracies is the eventual institutionalisation of all three types of rights and, in particular, social citizenship. For Marshall, the citizenship rights that accrue to members of a political community integrate previously unintegrated segments of the population and serve to mitigate some of the inequalities of class, thus altering the pattern of social inequality. Marshall discusses 'class fusion' which he refers to as the "general enrichment of the concrete substance of civilised life, a general reduction of risk and insecurity, and equalisation between the more or less fortunate at all levels" (Marshall, 1950, p 6). This leads "... towards a fuller measure of equality, an enrichment of the stuff of which the status is made and an increase in the number of those on whom the status is bestowed" (p 29). Marshall's thesis has been criticised for its evolutionary and Anglocentric nature (Giddens, 1982; Mann, 1987), as well as its emphasis on class. As Marsh (1998) points out, general accounts of citizenship often render other social divisions in society, such as gender and ethnicity, invisible. Marshall (1950) also fails to recognise the contingency, flexibility and fragility of the social contract between the state and the individual and that the attainment of citizenship rights and the opportunity to exercise such rights is a process of constant struggle and negotiation. The progression from civil to political and social rights is not the smooth, inevitable process Marshall suggests, but has always been dependent on political struggles between social movements, groups and classes. Retrogression and the erosion of the rights of particular groups are an ever-present possibility.

Byrne (1997) describes the term social exclusion as "currently the most fashionable term" (p 28) for describing social divisions in European capitalist societies. It has been the catalyst for extensive debate regarding the nature of social differentiation (for example, Rodgers, et al, 1995; Room, 1995; Jordan, 1996) and is now widely utilised both in national and international policy arenas (for example, European Commission, 1994; Social Exclusion Unit, 1998). Saraceno (1997) argues that the reconstruction of debates from poverty to social exclusion has involved "an actual conceptual shift, and a change in perspective; from a static to a dynamic approach, as well as from a distributional to a relational focus" (p 177). Lee and Murie (1997) point out that the term social exclusion is more explicitly concerned with the social rights of citizenship and the ability to exercise such rights, particularly in relation to accessing services such as housing, employment and healthcare. And, according to Abrahamson (1997) "the element that distinguishes social exclusion from poverty and makes it, perhaps, more potent, is ... the affiliation with the issue of citizenship rights" (p 148). So while Room (1991) had defined social exclusion in relation to social rights and the inability of 'citizens' to secure these social rights, for Tricard social exclusion refers to:

> **... processes and situations by which persons or groups tend to be separated or held at a distance from ordinary social exchange or positions which promote or allow integration or 'insertion' – that is, from participation in institutions or from access to rights, services or resources which imply full membership of society. (Tricard, 1991, p 2)**

The relational dynamics between housing and social exclusion have recently been explored by Lee and Murie (1997) who seek to show "the way in which the housing system forms part of the process through which poverty and deprivation arises and is experienced" (p 4). Somerville (1998), in applying the theory of social exclusion to housing processes, explores the themes of housing production, housing tenure, residential segregation, mobility and processes associated with homelessness and leaving home. He seeks to show "how housing processes cut across the different social levels (labour process, social reproduction and ideology), how they reflect prevailing patterns of social exclusion, and how they can mitigate or reinforce those patterns" (p 761). Anderson (1999), however, argues that debates linking housing and social exclusion have tended to "neglect a significant group of people who have *no* accommodation, or have shelter which is much less secure than council housing – single homeless people" (p 157). Yet, Pleace (1998) argues that the concept of social exclusion offers the opportunity to reconceptualise single homelessness and rough sleeping. He states that "'homelessness' does not actually exist as a discrete social problem" (p 50). Single homelessness is best seen as an outcome of processes of social exclusion, particularly "the inability of a section of the socially excluded population to get access to welfare services and social housing" (p 50). He sees the recent policy initiatives around resettlement and inclusion for single homeless people (for example, the Rough Sleepers Initiative) as a "development of the relationship between the understanding of single homelessness and the concept of 'social exclusion'" (p 51).

This chapter will argue, however, that while recent policy initiatives have indeed brought the issues of rough sleeping and single homelessness back onto the agenda it has been in the context of the promotion of a 'productivist' rather than a redistributive social policy agenda, emphasising the active rather than the passive citizen, with labour market insertion the key to inclusion (Levitas, 1998). These themes are encapsulated in the 1994 White Paper of the European Union, *European social policy – A way forward for the Union*:

> ... it is clear that there needs to be a move away from more passive income maintenance measures towards active labour market measures designed to ensure the economic and social integration of all people. This means giving a top priority to employment, securing new links between employment and social policies by developing a 'trampoline' safety net, and recognising that those who are not in the labour market also have a useful role to play in society.... (European Commission, 1994, p 34-5)

As Esping-Andersen (1996) argues, "the idea is to redirect social policy from its current bias in favour of passive income maintenance towards active labour market programmes that 'put people back to work', help households harmonise work and family obligations, and train the population in the kinds of skills that post-industrial society demands" (p 3). The promotion of the active citizen is now said to be an essential element of the enterprise culture and the entrepreneurial, competitive city. It signifies the emergence of an alternative mode of integration to that maintained and supported through the post-war era of Keynesian welfare capitalism. The dimensions of citizenship, social exclusion and homelessness during this period will now be explored to highlight the contingent and temporally specific nature of citizenship, social rights and integration.

Homelessness: a thing of the past

A mode of integration in any phase of capitalist development emerges through the relationship between the state, the family, the individual and the institutional framework. Its sustainability depends on its resonance with broader public and ontological narratives, that is, narratives which are attached to cultural and institutional formations larger than the single individual, and "personal narratives rooted in experience" (Sommers, 1994, p 619). The narratives encapsulated within the institutions of the post-war welfare state provide an insight into the nature of the webs of relationality within a mode of inclusion and their cultural and temporal specificity. The economic and political context was the promotion of Keynesian welfare capitalism organised around mass production and mass consumption of capital goods, within a largely national context. The welfare consensus emphasised an explicit commitment to state intervention through universal access to direct public provision of welfare benefits. It accepted an extended role for the state in economic and social policy and implicitly guaranteed social rights of citizenship for the whole population as a right. The discourse was that the state would ensure all citizens enjoyed a certain minimum standard of life and economic security as a matter of right. The mass consuming, mass producing, wage-earning society of the Fordist era was supported by a mode of integration encompassing a commitment to Keynesian capitalism, universal citizenship and collectively minimised individual risk, in that the state was seen as the primary guarantor against the vagaries and uncertainties of everyday life. Radical class struggle faded from political discourse and, according to Bowles and Gintis, "the language of liberal democracy, the lexicon of rights, was ... installed as the nearly universal means of political discourse" (Bowles and Gintis, 1982, p 64). The boundaries of social rights, however, were constructed within a specific narrative and that narrative reflected the privileged status of the white, male working class and the "partial citizenship" of women and black men (Kennett, 1998). While the Fordist welfare state linked the interests of capital and labour in a programme of full employment and social welfare it also involved the interplay of forms of social power other than class, such as racism and patriarchy (Williams, 1994). Thus the welfare settlement of the post-war period was a product of the "interrelation between capitalism, patriarchy and imperialism" (Williams, 1994, p 61).

In Britain the ethos of egalitarianism prevailed and the trends were towards decreasing social inequality and the gradual inclusion of previously excluded or marginal populations. On the new housing estates the move was to a more fragmented, home-centred culture as rising working-class living standards started to establish themselves. This was a period in which growing middle-class affluence enabled the further development of home-owning suburbia, while the 'estate' provided mass housing for the 'respectable' working class. The Fordist regime could be characterised in terms of housing as a social right, universalism of subsidies and tax breaks and as an era of mass suburbanisation and direct state housing provision (Florida and Feldman, 1988). Personal disposable incomes rose, the rate of inflation was modest, the scale of unemployment was low and the majority of the population were well-housed. However, for the poor to be incorporated into the home ideal they had to meet certain criteria relating to personal decency and the acceptance of established behavioural norms. Issues relating to class, race, gender and sexuality were major considerations in how home was defined and who was able to gain access. Women and people from ethnic minorities were unlikely to have equal access to the capital through which the suburban home ideal could be achieved, and were likely to be denied access to local authority waiting lists (Rex and Moore, 1967; Castles and Kosack, 1973; Rex and Tomlinson, 1979; Henderson and Karn, 1987; Smith, 1989).

Nevertheless, the provision of state housing served to justify the institutions of the Keynesian welfare state and support the hegemony of the post-war settlement at the micro level. In Britain in 1960 7.5 million people were living in poverty (Coates and Silburn, 1970) and there were 2,558 households (10,270 by 1976) in temporary accommodation (Burke, 1981). Yet for the majority of individuals the ideological commitment to equality and welfarism was compatible with the 'lived' experience at the micro level. As Byrne points out:

> **... in the Fordist era, good council housing was the locale in space of an employed working class and movement into it from poor council housing and out of it to the cheaper end of the owner-occupied system was simply an incremental matter. (Byrne, 1997, p 33)**

The prevailing ideology was one in which income and housing need had been met and poverty and homelessness involved a small number of people on the margins of society. The homeless population, under the 1948 National Assistance Act, was to be the object of welfare services rather than housing departments. This served to construct and maintain the undeserving status of the homeless and reinforce the individual, pathological model of homelessness. The way in which the homelessness problem was constructed, "which stressed the deviant characteristics of homeless individuals rather than issues such as housing shortage" (Neale, 1997, p 37), contributed to a policy agenda which served to render the homeless population 'invisible' and perpetuate the logic of the public narrative that this was an era in which poverty and homelessness were a thing of the past.

Redrawing the boundaries of citizenship: risk, insecurity and the active citizen

The last 25 years have been a period of substantial flux and change during which the landscape of capitalism has been reshaped: economic, political, social and cultural activities are said to have created a new set of conditions from the past. According to Jessop selective narratives of past events generate distinctive accounts of current economic, social and political problems, from which emerge "a limited but widely accepted set of diagnoses and prescriptions for the economic and political difficulties now confronting nations, regions, and cities and their populations" (Jessop, 1996, p 3). The redrawing of the boundaries of citizenship can be seen in this context. Allen argues that "discourses of citizenship are shaped not only by the material and political realities which they (selectively) reflect, but also by the way they seek to provide justificatory explanations for, and principles to guide, the social activities which organise that reality" (1998).

As economic conditions deteriorated during the mid-1970s, the post-war consensus began to crumble. The institutional arrangements of the post-war period which had supported specific configurations of citizenship were increasingly perceived as barriers and impediments to the deploying of new methods of production and consumption. In Britain, the erosion of the post-war consensus occurred in the context of rampant inflation in the wake of the oil crisis, and involved the acceptance by the 1976 Labour government of the International Monetary Fund's prescription of income restraint, cuts in social expenditure and, ultimately, the abandonment of Keynesian policy. By the 1980s a major structural reform of the welfare state was underway linked to an alternative economic doctrine, philosophical tradition and an anti-collectivist orthodoxy. Economic individualism and supply-side economics, as advocated by Hayek and Friedman, provided the framework for the policy formulations of monetarism, and the rhetoric for the devaluation of the welfare state portraying it as a barrier to economic recovery and the road to 'serfdom' and economic ruin. Writers such as Nozick (1974) influenced the notions of the minimal state and the atomistic individualism. The critique and devaluation of state intervention incorporated all three elements as governments sought to reintroduce market processes into the welfare state and public sector. Connotations of a bloated, self-interested and inefficient bureaucracy were introduced and supported by 'public choice' theorists (Niskanen, 1971, 1973) with recommendations for the reduction in the size and power of government agencies and the introduction of competition and market forces into welfare provision. By the end of the 1980s there was an explicit policy emphasis on market-based approaches to the delivery of services, the role of local authorities became more focused on that of enabler rather than provider, and the 'desirability' and increased role for voluntary and private agencies in social policy was enhanced. As Dean argues, "the burden of welfare provision was shifted from the state to the informal, voluntary and commercial sectors and the character of welfare transactions became, if not literally private, more akin to contractual relations in the marketplace" (Dean, 1999, p 218).

These developments were accompanied by the erosion of the relative predictability and certainty of the mass producing, mass consuming Fordist era of welfare capitalism, and a change in the balance of class relations reflecting the changing relative status of different groups and their relationship with the state. The Fordist industrial order of stability in which the life cycle of the "working-class [male] masses was predictable and, mobility wise, generally flat" (Esping-Andersen, 1993, p 227) has come to an end. The decline of Fordism has been accompanied by the rise in both professional and lower-end service occupations, changes in class composition and a recrystallisation of class forces, resulting in a declining overall standard of living for large sections of the population and a reduction in the number and quality of employment opportunities. As discussed in the last chapter, the stable, predictable patterns of the conventional Fordist life cycle, underpinned by the institutions of the welfare state, have given way to greater variety and less predictability. Thus, in contrast to the post-war period, there seems to be increasing insecurity not only in the labour market but in many aspects of day-to-day life. Changes in the structure of employment combined with the reorientation of the welfare state are said to have created an arena of risk, insecurity and uncertainty for the majority of the population, not just the poor (Forrest and Kennett, 1997), in contrast to the previous mode of inclusion.

According to Beck (1992) insecurity has emerged in the context of the increasing individualisation and autonomisation of contemporary society, and Giddens (1991, 1992, 1994) argues that in this era of reflexive modernity "the concept of risk becomes fundamental to the way both lay actors and technical specialists organise the social world" (Giddens,

1991, p 3). Within this risk culture individuals are constantly required to assess their risk status and make decisions regarding potential risk "through contact with expert knowledge ..." (Giddens, 1991, p 5). Life-style choice, life-planning and the reflexivity of the self are central to the construction of an individual's identity in this risk environment and, in turn, are linked to the notion of ontological (or emotional) security (Giddens, 1991). Increasingly, the social relations of everyday life have come to be associated with complexity and uncertainty, independence and individualism. The 'collective management' of uncertainty during the post-war period has given way to what Marris refers to as "the competitive management of uncertainty" (Marris, 1996, p 14) where strategies for containing uncertainty and risks must be developed individually. Thus, there has been a transfer of risk from the state and the employer to the family and the individual and a redrawing of the boundaries of citizenship (Kennett, 1998). This reorientation is an indication that the nature and significance of the social relations of welfare change over time as does the relationship between the individual and the state. This relationship is encapsulated in the institutions and ideology of the welfare state through which the inclusionary/exclusionary boundaries of citizenship are articulated and perpetuated.

This restructuring of relations between state and civil society and the establishment of new forms of intervention were most evident during the Conservative era in Britain when there was the most profound shift towards 'welfare pluralism' (Dean, 1999). However, following their election in May 1997, the Blair government has pursued similar strategies indicating according to Marquand (1998) that New Labour "has turned its back on Keynes and Beveridge" (quoted in Dean, 1999, p 221). According to Dean (1999) "New Labour has combined the economic liberalism of the Thatcher/Reagan orthodoxy, with something approaching socially conservative Christian democracy" (p 221). Key policies of New Labour have been Welfare-to-Work and the New Deal. Initially introduced to overcome the problem of unemployment among young people the scope of the New Deal has been extended to include, for example, lone parents and those over 25. According to King and Wickham-Jones:

The policy recast in fundamental fashion Labour's strategy to tackle poverty: previously, Labour administrations and social democratic thinkers had placed much weight on amelioration of general destitution through State-directed public spending programmes. New Labour, by contrast, emphasised paid work,

seemingly to the exclusion of other approaches. (King and Wickham-Jones, 1999, p 271)

They go on to point out that in contrast to the commitment to universal and unconditional social rights which was central to Marshall's conception of citizenship and to the Labour Party's welfare agenda between 1945 and 1992, conditionality, compulsion and coercion appear to be the hallmarks of the policies of the Blair administration. Sanctions and penalties, such as loss of benefit, will fall on those who either refuse to participate or who are unable to finish the New Deal programmes. The implications of this move towards conditional citizenship are as yet unclear. King and Wickham-Jones (1999) point out the uncertainty in calculating the numbers denied benefit because of Welfare-to-Work. The most recent figure they cite is that of "1,352 individuals who had lost benefit because of their failure to participate" (p 279). Dean (1999) argues that in the context of conditional citizenship one outcome might be that "more citizens will defect from their contract with the State, in the sense that they will 'disappear' into the shadowy world of the informal economy. If welfare reform does not work with the grain of everyday survival strategies the result may be more not less social exclusion" (p 232). And similarly, the emphasis on labour market insertion as the means to social inclusion fails to take account of the nature and content of employment and the fact that low pay and casualisation characterise large sectors of the labour market today.

Drawing on the work of Jessop (1994) Dean argues that "the space between the individual and the State is itself 'hollowed out' as it is subordinated to economic forces and made increasingly conditional on the citizen's individual 'stake' in the economy as a paid worker" (p 225). While recognising the importance of the political and cultural dimensions to inclusion and exclusion Madanipour argues that:

> ... the main form of inclusion is access to resources, which is normally secured through employment.... Marginalization and long-term exclusion from the labour market lead to an absence of opportunity for production and consumption, which can in turn lead to acute forms of social exclusion. (Madanipour, 1998, p 77)

However, participation in the labour market does not necessarily guarantee inclusion, particularly because of inadequate access to resources and the nature of employment available. For example, a recent study on the distribution of poor households within the countries of the European Union indicated that 35% of poor households were classified as working poor (EAPN, 1997). As Levitas (1998) argues, labour market insertion as the key to inclusion serves only to obscure the differential access to resources which exists *within* the working population not just between those within the labour market and those outside. This approach obscures the complex interplay of processes which structure opportunities particularly in relation to gender and ethnicity (issues discussed further in Chapters Five and Six of this volume) and which enable people to access and maintain a reasonable standard of life. Evidence suggests that the restructuring of capitalism combined with a renegotiation of the context of citizenship rights has been accompanied by a shift towards increasing inequality, social exclusion and homelessness, particularly among young people, women and people from ethnic minorities who are increasingly likely to enter into the sphere of the state and be reliant on more basic and coercive forms of social assistance.

Homelessness and the entrepreneurial city

Homelessness is not a new or transient phenomenon, but recently has emerged as a problem affecting different kinds of areas from inner cities to rural areas, and has involved a widening spectrum of the population. A recent *Survey of English Housing* (1995/96) reported on people's experiences of homelessness. Six per cent of respondents reported that they had some experience of homelessness in the last 10 years. Of those aged 16-24 20% said that they had been homeless during the same time period and among lone parents with dependent children the figure was 29% (Green et al, 1997). Although the number of statutory homeless has continued to drop from its peak of 178,867 households in 1991, in 1996 it still represented 131,139 households in Great Britain, higher than any year before 1989 (Wilcox, 1997). Nor is homelessness among single women the 'hidden' homelessness of the past. More women can be seen sleeping rough and, particularly among younger women, there is likely to be greater use made of night shelters, with a rise of 70% in 1995 of women under 21 years old using winter shelters.

Hopper (1991) recognises novel elements of the phenomenon in terms of the scale, the heterogeneity of the homeless population in terms of gender, race and age, and the episodic nature of homelessness. While for Marcuse contemporary homelessness is distinguishable as:

> ... large-scale, permanent and independent of the short-term
> business cycle, a combination never before existing in an advanced
> industrial society. It represents the inability of the market and
> the unwillingness of the state to care for the most basic needs of
> a significant segment of the population ... and their consequent
> complete exclusion from or suppression in the spatial fabric of a
> technologically and economically advanced city. It may thus
> fairly be called 'advanced homelessness'. (Marcuse, 1993, p 359)

As alternative narratives have converged and combined in the
contemporary city, so "economic, political and cultural spaces have been
opened up, resulting in a restructuring of relations of inclusion and
exclusion, of centrality and marginality" (Mommas, 1996, p 196). For
Jessop the "intersection of these diverse economic, political and socio-
cultural narratives" (Jessop, 1996, p 4) has crystallised in the context of
the 'entrepreneurial' city where the processes through which homelessness
occurs and the policy context in which it is maintained are most stark.
The rhetoric of competitiveness, partnership and cohesion has dominated
the discourse at both national and European Union levels. According to
Oatley (1998) urban policy in Britain "has shifted from a welfare approach
dominated by social expenditure to support deprived groups in depressed
areas (1969–1979) to entrepreneurialism aimed at generating wealth and
stimulating economic development" (p 203). Oatley lists a range of
initiatives introduced during the 1990s, from City Challenge in 1991 to
the Single Regeneration Budget which has become the central plank in
the government's regeneration policy, which he claims marked "a paradigm
shift". According to Oatley "These initiatives radically altered the way in
which policies aimed at tackling problems or urban decline and social
disadvantage were formulated, funded and administered" (1998, p x). While
there is nothing new about characterising the city as the site of
entrepreneurialism, what has been radically altered is the intensification
of competition between urban regions for resources, jobs and capital and
the policy agenda which has accompanied this intensification. With the
growing importance of international competition in the global marketplace, which had played a fairly minor role in the Fordist 1950s and
1960s, major cities act as centres of economic, social, cultural and structural
change as the arena is created in which cities promote innovation and
entrepreneurialism in order to secure competitive advantage. The
'managerialism' of the 1960s has given way to what Harvey (1989) refers
to as 'entrepreneurial' urban governance, thus facilitating the

transformation from the rigidity of Fordist production systems supported by Keynesian state welfarism, to a more geographically diverse and flexible form of accumulation. For Harvey, the basis of this new urban entrepreneurialism:

> ... rests ... on a public private partnership focussing on investment and economic development with the speculative construction of place rather than the amelioration of conditions within a particular territory as its immediate (though by no means exclusive) political and economic goal. (Harvey, 1989, p 16)

In both social and urban policy the emphasis is on reducing public services and stressing the role of agencies alternative to local government, and the need for a mix of private, not-for-profit and voluntary inputs. As larger cities endeavour to become transnationally important financial and control centres, urban initiatives concentrate on establishing special corporations for economic promotion in close cooperation with the private sector, thus incorporating elements of deregulation, privatisation and public–private partnership (Fainstein, 1991; Krätke and Schmoll, 1991). So while in the 1960s urban problems of poverty and inner-city decay were met by welfare initiatives and redevelopment, more recently the emphasis has been on growth based on market-oriented solutions and 'wealth creation,' with the consequences that:

> ... the inner city ... becomes a microcosm for growth strategies based on financial services and property development, on deregulation and on polarised labour markets characterised by divergent skills and growing social inequality. (Hill, 1994, p 166)

The affluent consumer and powerful corporations have become the object of urban policy and have, according to Harvey (1989), been subsidised at the expense of local collective consumption for the working class and the poor. The 'public interest' has become subsumed under private interests (Marcuse, 1993), increasing social division as well as reinforcing spatial divisions of consumption. The refurbishment of urban space and emphasis on cultural renewal facilitates gentrification processes and the promotion of consumption palaces, festivals and other leisure and cultural facilities as civic boosterism and place identity have become the "favoured remedies for ailing urban economies" (Harvey, 1989, p 28). As Griffiths (1998) argues "Entrepreneurialism is founded on speculation and risk-taking;

competition by its very nature, throws up winners and losers" (p 43). For the displaced and the poor the 'image of affluence' is likely to offer, at best, the opportunity of low paid, insecure employment and, at worst, the prospect of locating a pitch from which to panhandle for a few hours (see Winchester and White, 1988) before returning to the excluded space of the "multiply divided city" (Marcuse, 1993). Zero tolerance and coercion have become the response to destitution and poverty. Prestigious office locations install deterrents such as sprinkler systems to prevent the homeless from sleeping in their doorways, at the same time as major companies enter into a range of partnerships with voluntary organisations in the spirit of "new philanthropy" (*Housing*, 1991) for the young homeless.

Carlen argues that "at the end of the twentieth century in England the management of homelessness is not merely about housing scarcity but has also become a site of struggle over social change" (Carlen, 1996, p 10). Agencies seeking to work with the homeless have themselves become embedded in the entrepreneurialism of the city. With the emphasis on civic boosterism, according to Ruddick (1996), through their involvement with local growth coalitions in the spirit of public–private partnerships, service providers have, to some extent, become the intermediary in the production of a new social urban space in that they "manage the tensions between the visible impoverishment and global cities" (Ruddick, 1996, p 185).

Hopper (1991), Marcuse (1993) and Carlen (1996) have all pointed to the changing role of government and the nature of the homelessness industry who construct and manage the problem within the narratives of the entrepreneurial city. For Carlen "agency-maintained homelessness" occurs through:

> ... the bureaucratic or professional procedures for the governance of homelessness which *deter* people from defining themselves as homeless; deny that homelessness claims are justifiable under the legislation; or *discipline* the officially-defined homeless into rapidly withdrawing their claims to homeless status. (Carlen, 1996, p 59)

As well as the practices engaged in by local authorities, she highlights the "quality assurance" and "exclusionary categorisation and referral procedures" (p 59) utilised by hostel staff in the selection and management of hostel populations. Hopper (1991) argues that agencies providing services are in fact powerful interest groups in themselves and they manipulate definitions of the problem and change their policies in ways that are most consistent with their continued existence. In Britain, as the providing state has become the enabling state, so attempts have been made to introduce market-based approaches to the delivery of local services. Thus local authorities have developed a strategic role to facilitate services and provision for the homeless through housing associations and non-profit organisations by distributing funds for which organisations have to compete. As service providers "they are the intermediaries through which flow the resources of relief to the homeless, and the people who outline how we should respond to this social phenomena" (Robertson, 1991, p 142). The 'professional' providers, through the bureaucratic process of fund-getting, supply information that appeals to the funding source, encouraging the development of specialised programmes which catalogue the homeless according to a range of individual vulnerabilities. The 'homeless problem' thus becomes defined not in terms of structural causes, but as merely an aggregate of social 'characteristics' symptomatic of underlying causes. The homeless population is thus reclassified as provision fragments and funding focuses on the pathological and individual characteristics of the homeless (that is, alcoholic, mentally ill) to which specialised professional skills are matched to specialised populations. It is the perceived need which becomes the social problem to which specialised caretakers can respond. Not only do these developments influence the labelling and stigma attached to being homeless, but also affect how the homeless person perceives themselves. In order to negotiate the burgeoning networks of agencies the homeless person must (re)classify her/himself into an appropriate category of perceived need.

These processes are particularly apparent in one major government initiative to combat homelessness which has been the Rough Sleepers Initiative (RSI). First initiated in London it is credited with reducing the numbers of central London rough sleepers from 1,000-2,000 in 1990 to around 270 in May 1995. (DoE, 1995). This was accompanied by the Department of Health's Homeless Mentally Ill Initiative (HMII). The government committed £96m for the first phase of the RSI (1990-93) to organise direct access accommodation, advice, outreach work and some permanent housing association lettings. However, the 1995 Consultation Paper reported that:

> ... people continue to sleep out at several main sites, for example, the Strand and the Bullring at Waterloo. Their evident plight is distressing not only for them but also for those who live, work

> and visit the centre of the capital, and it is frustrating for those
> who seek to promote London as a world-class centre for business
> and tourism. (DoE, 1995, p 4)

The initiative was extended for a further period and a greater emphasis
was placed on "those sleeping rough or *with a clear history of sleeping rough*"
(DoE, 1995, p 7; emphasis original). By March 1996 £182m had been
spent on the initiative.

In 1995 the RSI model was extended outside London and local
authorities were required to "quantify the extent of rough sleeping in
their area, and if it existed, to examine its causes" (DoE, 1996, p 21). Only
Bristol was able to 'prove' and document to the satisfaction of the DoE
that rough sleeping was a significant problem and they were awarded
£7.5m in 1996. More recently the RSI has been extended to Brighton,
following their successful bid for capital and revenue funding. It could be
argued that the distribution of funds has been based on a local authority's
expertise in formulating a bid rather than real need. In addition, this
major focus on RSI has contributed to the perception of homelessness as
rooflessness and funding has not been directed towards those people living
in insecure and inappropriate condition. The emphasis on 'rough sleepers'
has been perpetuated by the Social Exclusion Unit, and the Unit has set
itself the target of reducing rough sleepers by two thirds by 2002 (Social
Exclusion Unit, 1998). However, according to the Homeless Network:

> ... it is our contention that without either a continuing supply of
> new accommodation, or a significant reduction in the flow of
> newly homeless people into London, we are likely to see the
> numbers of street homeless people increase sharply over the next
> 18 months. (quoted in Social Exclusion Unit, 1998, p 12)

A recent report has indicated that while for many homeless people (636
or 13%) the resettlement process had had 'positive outcomes' in that the
individuals involved were in non-RSI housing (Dane, 1998), for others
(787 or 16%) the tenancy was considered to have been unsuccessful with
the vast majority ending in abandonment. As one ex-tenant states "When
I left I'd just had enough. It was just a big relief to walk out that door".
For another:

> "... it was like living a shell hermit-like existence. I was lonely,
> didn't have the money to travel into the East End I knew, couldn't

live on my benefits. My referral agency stopped visiting me after six months and my housing association wasn't interested. I knew after six weeks that there was no future in that place for me". (quoted in Dane, 1998, p 15)

Clearly, there could be a number of explanations for these developments. They could be seen as the result of ineffective allocation, management and monitoring strategies adopted by the agencies involved. They could be seen as an example of the contradictions between the images and aspirations of the homeless themselves, and the political and policy narratives instituted by governments, for example, the assertion that "a place in a hostel has to be the start of a process that leads back to the things most of us take for granted" (Social Exclusion Unit, 1998, p 2). They could also be seen as an example of a policy agenda in which the diverse needs, expectations and aspirations of homeless people are subordinated to or subsumed within a strategy of stimulating wealth creation and enhancing competition.

Conclusion

In the context of growing inequality and insecurity, labour market participation has become the panacea for an inclusive society. While the rhetoric of social exclusion has permeated the policy discourse it is not the comprehensive and dynamic approach offered by Berghman (1995), which looks beyond the experiences of work and income which has been adopted. It is a more narrowly applied definition which is encapsulated in the emerging model of citizenship and welfare. There has been a changing balance between rights and responsibilities and between the state and civil society. Work appears to be replacing welfare while social rights focus on contractual relations and coercion.

The policy responses to increasingly visible destitution and homelessness in British cities are an indication of the changes mentioned above. The Social Exclusion Unit has shown little concern with tackling the multifarious processes through which people find themselves homeless. Instead, as cities seek to compete in the international arena, the image of people sleeping in the streets contradicts and undermines the strategies of competitiveness, partnership and cohesion. Thus, it is those sleeping rough who have become the object of a narrowly defined set of policy solutions aimed mainly at restoring legitimacy in the entrepreneurial city. The definition of inclusion perpetuated by the government combined with the reformulation of welfare and citizenship rights will do little to stem the flow of homeless people, nor to support and maintain those attempting to reconstruct a life off the street. This unidimensional construction of social rights and emphasis on entrepreneuralism and competitiveness may benefit some. However, it is unlikely to be a context for developing a policy and institutional framework through which homeless people can achieve forms of social inclusion which are both appropriate and sustainable. As Power et al (1999) argue, factors perpetuating the homeless life-style might begin with lack of accommodation but there are other interrelated and complex factors, such as marginalisation, insecurity, identification, vulnerability, lack of choice, isolation and lack of income/employment. The narrow interpretation of social exclusion evident in current policy does not connect with the multidimensional nature of contemporary homelessness, nor utilise the existing social networks and (limited) resources which exist among the homeless themselves. Within the current mode of integration there is little likelihood of addressing the homelessness issue and it would appear that at the end of the 20th century the most extreme manifestations of social exclusion – homelessness – will continue to be a feature of British cities.

References

Abrahamson, P. (1997) 'Combating poverty and social exclusion in Europe', in W. Beck, L. van der Maesen and A. Walker, *The social quality of Europe*, Bristol: The Policy Press, pp 145-76.

Allen, J. (1998) 'Europe of the neighbourhoods: class, citizenship and welfare regimes', in A Madanipour, G. Gars and J. Allen (eds) *Social exclusion in European cities*, London: Jessica King Publishers, pp 25-51.

Anderson, I. (1999) 'Social housing or social exclusion', in S. Hutson and D. Clapham (eds) *Homelessness: Public policies and private troubles*, London: Cassell, pp 153-73.

Bagguley, P. (1991) 'Post-Fordism and enterprise culture: flexibility, autonomy and changes in economic organisation', in R. Keat and N. Abercrombie (eds) *Enterprise culture*, London: Routledge.

Beck, U. (1992) *Risk society: Towards a new modernity*, London: Sage Publications.

Berghman, J. (1995) 'Social exclusion in Europe: policy context and analytical framework' in G. Room (ed) *Beyond the threshold: The measurement and analysis of social exclusion*, Bristol: The Policy Press, pp 10-28.

Bowles, A. and Gintis, H. (1982) 'The crisis of liberal democratic capitalism: the case of the United States', *Politics and Society*, vol 1, no 1, pp 51-93.

Bulmer, M and Rees, A. (eds) (1996) *Citizenship today: The contemporary relevance of T.H. Marshall*, London: UCL Press.

Burke, G. (1981) *Housing and social justice*, Harlow: Longman Group Ltd.

Byrne, D. (1997) 'Social exclusion and capitalism', *Critical Social Policy*, vol 17, no 1, pp 27-51.

Callinicos, A. (1992) *Against postmodernism: A Marxist critique*, Cambridge: Polity Press.

Carlen, P. (1996) *Jigsaw: A political criminology of youth homelessness*, Buckingham: Open University Press.

Castles, S. and Kosack, G. (1973) *Immigrant workers and class structure in Western Europe*, London: Harper and Row.

Coates, K. and Silburn, R. (1970) *Poverty and the forgotten Englishman*, Harmondsworth: Penguin Books.

Dane, K. (1998) *Making it last: Report into tenancy outcomes for rough sleepers*, London: Housing Services Agency.

Dean, H. (1999) 'Citizenship', in M. Powell (ed) *New Labour, new welfare state?: The third way in British Social Policy*, Bristol: The Policy Press, pp 213-34.

DoE (Department of the Environment) (1995) 'Rough Sleepers Initiative: future plans', Consultation Paper linked to the Housing White Paper, *Our future homes*, London: DoE.

DoE (1996) 'Rough Sleepers Initiative: the next challenge', Strategy Paper linked to the Consultation Paper 'Rough Sleepers Initiative: future plans', London: DoE.

Esping-Andersen (1993) *Changing classes, stratification and mobility in post-industrial societies*, London: Sage Publications.

Esping-Andersen, G. (1996) *Welfare states in transition: National adaptations in global economies*, London: Sage Publications.

EAPN (European Anti-Poverty Network) News (1997) No 49, June-July, Brussels.

European Commission (1994) *European social policy – A way forward for the Union: A White Paper*, European Communities, Luxembourg: Office for Official Publications available at http://www.eurotext.ulst.ac.uk/policy/social/general/espwptoc.html #x (1:10:98@ 14:20:06)

Fainstein, S. (1991) 'Promoting economic development', *Urban Planning in the United States and Great Planning American Planning Association Journal*, vol 57, no 1, pp 22-33.

Florida, R.L. and Feldman, M.M.A. (1988) 'Housing in US Fordism', *Policy & Politics*, vol 12, no 2, pp 187-209.

Forrest, R. and Kennett, P. (1997) 'Risk, residence and the post-Fordist city', *American Behavioural Scientist*, vol 41, no 3, pp 342-59.

Forrest, R. and Kennett, P. (1998) 'Re-reading the city: deregulation and neighbourhood change', *Space and Polity*, vol 2, no 1, pp 71-83.

Giddens, A. (ed) (1982) *Profiles and critiques in social theory*, London: Macmillan.

Giddens, A. (1991) *Modernity and self-identity: Self and society in the late modern age*, Cambridge: Polity Press.

Giddens, A. (1992) *The transformation of intimacy: Sexuality, love and eroticism in modern society*, Cambridge: Polity Press.

Giddens, A. (1994) *Beyond Left and Right: The future of radical politics*, Cambridge: Polity Press.

Green, H., Keacon, K., Iles, N. and Down, D. (1997) *Housing in England 1995/96. A report of the 1995/1996 Survey of English Housing*, London: ONS.

Griffiths, R. (1998) 'Making sameness: place marketing and the new urban entrepreneurialism', in N. Oatley (ed) *Cities, economic competition and urban policy*, London: Paul Chapman Publishing, pp 41-57.

Harvey, D. (1989) 'From managerialism to entrepreneurialism: the transformation in urban governance in late capitalism', Paper presented to the Vega Symposium, Stockholm, July.

Henderson, J. and Karn, V. (1987) *Race, class and state housing: Inequality and the allocation of public housing in Britain*, Aldershot: Gower.

Hill, D.M. (1994) *Citizens and cities*, Hemel Hempstead: Harvester Wheatsheaf.

Hopper, K. (1991) 'Symptoms, survival and the redefinition of public space: a feasibility study of homeless people at a metropolitan airport', *Urban Anthropology*, vol 20, no 2, pp 155-75.

Housing (1991) 'Doing business with the homeless', May, pp 29-30.

Jessop, B. (1994) 'The transition to post-Fordism and the Schumpeterian workfare state', in R. Burrows and B. Loader (eds) *Towards a post-Fordist welfare state*, London: Routledge, pp 13-37.

Jessop, B. (1996) 'The entrepreneurial city: re-imaging localities, re-designing economic governance, or re-structuring capital?', Paper presented at Urban Change and Conflict Conference, Glasgow, January.

Jordan, B. (1996) *A theory of poverty and social exclusion*, Cambridge: Polity Press.

Kennett, P. (1994) 'Exclusion, post-Fordism and the "new Europe"', in P. Brown and R. Crompton (eds) *The new Europe: Economic restructuring and social exclusion*, London: UCL Press, pp 14-32.

Kennett, P. (1998) 'Differentiated citizenship and housing experience in Britain, Germany and Australia', in A. Marsh and D. Mullins (eds) *Housing and public policy: Citizenship, choice and control*, Buckingham: Open University Press, pp 30-56.

King, D. and Wickham-Jones, M. (1999) 'Bridging the Atlantic: the Democratic (Party) origins of Welfare to Work', in M. Powell (ed) *New Labour, new welfare state?: The 'third way' in british social policy*, Bristol: The Policy Press, pp 257-80.

Krätke, S. and Schmoll, F. (1991) 'The local state and social restructuring', *International Journal of Urban and Regional Research*, vol 15, no 4, pp 542-52.

Lee, P. and Murie, A. (1997) *Poverty, housing tenure and social exclusion*, Bristol: The Policy Press.

Levitas, R. (1998) *The inclusive society? Social exclusion and New Labour*, Basingstoke: Macmillan.

Lister, R. (1990) *The exclusive society: Citizenship and the poor*, London: Child Poverty Action Group.

Lister, R. (1998) *Citizenship: Feminist perspective*, Basingstoke: Macmillan

Madanipour, A. (1998) 'Social exclusion and space', in A. Madanipur, G. Cars and J. Allen (eds) *Social exclusion in European cities*, London: Jessica Kingsley Publishers, pp 75-89.

Mann, M. (1987) 'Ruling class strategies and citizenship', *Sociology*, vol 21, no 3, pp 339-54.

Marcuse, P. (1993) 'What's so new about divided cities?', *International Journal of Urban and Regional Studies*, vol 17, no 3, pp 355-65.

Marquand, D. (1998) 'What lies at the heart of the people's project', *The Guardian*, 20 May.

Marris, P. (1996) *The politics of uncertainty*, London: Routledge.

Marsh, A. (1998) 'Processes of change in housing and public policy', in A. Marsh and D. Mullins (eds) *Housing and public policy: Citizenship, choice and control*, Buckingham: Open University Press, pp 1-29.

Marshall, T.H. (1950) *Citizenship and social class*, Cambridge: Cambridge University Press.

Mommas, H. (1996) 'Modernity, postmodernity and the crisis of social modernization: a case study in urban fragmentation', *International Journal of Urban and Regional Research*, vol 20, no 2, pp 196-216.

Neale, J. (1997) 'Theorising homelessness: contemporary sociological and feminist perspectives', in R. Burrows, N. Pleace and D. Quilgars (eds) *Homelessness and social policy*, London: Routledge, pp 35-49.

Niskanen, W.A. (1971) *Bureaucracy and representative government*, Aldine: Atherton.

Niskanen, W.A. (1973) *Bureaucracy: Servant or master? Lessons from America*, London: Institute of Economic Affairs.

Nozick, R. (1974) *Anarchy, state and utopia*, New York, NY: Basic Books.

Oatley, N. (ed) (1998) *Cities, economic competition and urban policy*, London: Paul Chapman Publishing.

Pleace, N. (1998) 'Single homelessness as social exclusion: the unique and the extreme', *Social Policy and Administration*, vol 32, no 1, pp 46-59.

Power, R., French, R., Connelly, J., George, S., Hawes, D., Hinton, T., Klee, H., Robinson, D., Senior, J., Timms, P. and Warner, D. (1999) *Promoting the health of homeless people*, London: Health Education Authority.

Rex, J. and Moore, R. (1967) *Race, community and conflict*, Oxford: Oxford University Press.

Rex, J. and Tomlinson, S. (1979) *Colonial immigrants in a British city: A class analysis*, London: Routledge and Kegan Paul.

Robertson, M.O. (1991) 'Interpreting homelessness: the influence of professional and non-professional service providers', *Urban Anthropology*, vol 20, no 2, pp 141-53.

Rodgers, G., Gore, C. and Figueiredo, J. (1995) *Social exclusion: Rhetoric, reality, responses*, Geneva: ILO.

Room, G. (1991) *National policies to combat social exclusion*, First Annual Report of the EC Observatory on Policies to Combat Social Exclusion, Brussels: European Commission.

Room, G. (ed) (1995) *Beyond the threshold: The measurement and analysis of social exclusion*, Bristol: The Policy Press.

Ruddick, S. (1996) *Young and homeless in Hollywood: Mapping social identities*, New York, NY: Routledge.

Saraceno, C. (1997) 'The importance of the concept of social exclusion', in W. Beck, L. van der Maesen and A. Walker (eds) *The social quality of Europe*, Bristol: The Policy Press, pp 177-85.

Smith, S.J. (1989) *The politics of 'race' and residence*, Cambridge: Polity Press.

Social Exclusion Unit (1998) *Rough sleeping*, London: Social Exclusion Unit.

Somerville, P. (1998) 'Explanations of social exclusion: where does housing fit in?', *Housing Studies*, vol 13, no 6, pp 761-80.

Sommers, M.R. (1994) 'The narrative constitution of identity: a relational and network approach', *Theory and Ethics*, vol 23, no 5, pp 605-49.

Tricard, J.P. (1991) 'Note de problematique: working papers of the Social Exclusion Observatory, EC Commission', in D. Robbins (1992) *Social exclusion 1990-1992: The United Kingdom EC Observatory on policies to combat social exclusion, European Economic Interest Group*, Lille: Animationa and Research, pp 1-6.

Turner, B. (ed) (1993) *Citizenship and social theory*, London: Sage Publications.

Twine, F. (1994) *Citizenship and social rights*, London: Sage Publications.

Wilcox, S. (1997) *Housing finance review 1997/1998*, York: Joseph Rowntree Foundation.

Williams, F. (1994) 'Social relations, welfare and the post-Fordism debate', in B. Loader and R. Burrows (eds) *Towards a post-Fordist welfare state?*, London: Routledge, pp 49-73.

Winchester, H.P.M. and White, P.E. (1988) 'The location of marginalised groups in the inner city', *Environment and Planning D, Society and Space*, vol 6, no 1, pp 37-54.

FOUR

Homelessness in rural areas: an invisible issue?

Paul Cloke, Paul Milbourne and Rebekah Widdowfield

Introduction

VILLAGERS BUY THEIR TRAMP HIS OWN WOOD

Supertramp Max Smith has been crowned king of the road by kindhearted locals who chipped in £26,000 to buy him his own wood. They raised the cash so the happy hobo can live out the rest of his days under his favourite bush amid 90 acres of ancient forest.... Shopkeeper Graham Dando, 49, said "Everybody knows Max and there's a small network of us who keep an eye out for him each day.... If we don't see him we go and make sure he's all right. That wouldn't happen in the city". (Johnson, 1997, p 10)

According to most popular discourses, homelessness is something that wouldn't happen in the countryside. Just occasionally, however, rural homelessness does hit a headline but then, as with this story from the *News of the World* cited above, normality is soon resumed. Instead of homeless people, rural areas entertain 'happy hobos'. Instead of being socially excluded, the happy hobo is cared for by a supportive community. Instead of being forced to move on, he has his wood bought for him by kind-hearted locals for whom a supertramp somehow fits their romanticised view of the idyllic life-styles of country living. Readers can sleep safe in their beds as their rural idyll is being enhanced by the mysterious romanticism of the somehow ageless tramp, rather than being transgressed by the harsh social reality of homelessness.

In this chapter we want to argue that discourses from governments, academics, news media and many (but not all) voluntary agencies conspire to create the impression that the spatiality of homeless people is entirely encompassed by city limits. People's everyday experiences, both televisual and 'live', have served to assimilate homelessness in city sites/sights, and often to conflate homelessness with concomitant 'urban' issues such as the supposed street criminalities of drunkenness, vagrancy and begging. Without wishing in any sense to deny or undermine the socio-political importance of homelessness issues in the city, we want to argue that homelessness is also important in rural areas, and that its significance requires special emphasis precisely because it is usually hidden from view.

Homelessness and rurality appear to be an anathema, and we want to question why that is so. We suggest that in part, the invisibility of rural homelessness is about the ways in which homelessness is defined and recorded. In part, it has to do with the difficulties of gaining advice in rural areas, the assumed futility of trying to find affordable housing in expensive housing markets, and the reluctance of some rural people to admit that they have a problem. Alongside these issues, we want to explore in particular the ways in which popular cultural constructions of rurality themselves render invisible problems such as homelessness which are counter-cultural to an assumed rural idyll. Finally we want to suggest that static models of homelessness in either rural or urban areas may be misleading, given indicative evidence of the movement of homeless people into, out of and through rural areas. These movements further underline the need to understand connections between rurality and homelessness.

Rurality and homelessness

Our first assumption in this chapter is that homelessness does occur in rural areas, although we readily acknowledge that there has been little specific investigation of rural homelessness and that therefore little is yet known about the nature and extent of the issue. The major study in Britain was carried out by Lambert et al in 1992 using government data relating to households which are accepted as homeless by local authorities in particular areas. Clearly, these data underestimate the scale of the problem, partly because households with legitimate problems of homelessness may not receive priority status from a particular local authority, and partly because some homeless households will not contact the local authority at all. Nevertheless, at that time, some 15,000 people per annum were being accepted as homeless and in priority need by rural local authorities. By this calculation, the rural homeless constituted some 12% of the national total, and rates of homelessness were found to be increasing more rapidly in rural areas than in other areas. This trend was confirmed by an update of the Lambert et al study (Bramley, 1994). The latest such statistics (1996) suggest that rural areas represent 14.4% of the national level, and that in local authorities categorised as 'deep rural', the numbers of people accepted as homeless have increased by 12% since 1992.

These imperfect indicators do point towards the existence of significant levels of homelessness in Britain's rural areas, and such a finding would be in keeping with studies from elsewhere. In Canada, for example, Daly suggests that the general assumption is that there is no homelessness in rural areas, at least in part, because of the adverse climate conditions in winter. However, he argues that "there are many rural people who are homeless or vulnerable because of fires, domestic violence, mortgage foreclosures or evictions from farms and homes" (1996, p 147).

A similar conclusion is reached from a wider body of evidence in the United States (Walmer, 1989; Fitchen, 1991, 1992; First et al, 1994; Lawrence, 1995) with the latter study estimating that rural homelessness constitutes between 15% and 20% of the total numbers of homeless, and that in some states the levels are twice this average.

Our second assumption is that the changing geographies of rural areas contribute directly to conditions in which people become homeless. We do not argue for a separate phenomenon of 'rural' homelessness, in that many of the causal factors of homelessness – family breakdown, deinstitutionalisation, housing insecurity, benefit changes and the like – will be aspatial in derivation. However, the rapidly changing nature of rural areas will often provide a problematic context in which such causes take effect. Recent surveys of rural change and deprivation (see, for example, Cloke et al, 1994, 1995, 1997a) have charted a number of important trends:

- a continuing rationalisation of services, employment and public transport;
- in-migration of adventitious and affluent households which has led to the gentrification of many rural housing markets;
- a marked shrinkage in the stock of affordable rented accommodation in rural areas.

It is in particular the existence of increasingly problematic housing markets which can prompt 'affordability crises' for low-income and no-income households. The assumption in government, press and some academic discourses seems to be that individuals and households who are debarred from gentrified rural housing markets will automatically migrate to urban areas where housing and emergency shelter are more readily available.

This assumption fuels the common perception that if homelessness occurs in rural areas, homeless people somehow 'automatically' up and leave for the brighter lights of the city. As suggested above, this perception is at least partly refuted by statistical evidence of acknowledged homelessness within rural areas.

Our third assumption is that commonly accepted popular discourses of homelessness (as evidenced, for example, in media discussions of the subject) are closely interconnected with the visible forms of rooflessness which tend to be associated with big cities. However, we would want to acknowledge the importance of the problems faced by those experiencing less extreme, yet still very significant, forms of homelessness. These more 'hidden' forms of homelessness occur across a range of geographical areas, but their exclusion from much of the political and academic discourse on homelessness has particular implications for the broader acceptance that homelessness exists in rural areas, where social problems tend in any case to be "out of sight and out of mind" (Scott et al, 1991).

We therefore contend that rural areas will be arenas for these more hidden forms of homelessness. Here, we have in mind people who are not registered with local authority housing departments, or who are registered but who are not prioritised, or who are for a number of reasons 'at risk' of becoming homeless (see Watson and Austerberry, 1986; Watson, 1989; Blasi, 1990; Hutson and Liddiard, 1994). Rural people are not immune from living in insecure, overcrowded or unsafe (both physically and emotionally) accommodation, and significant (but as yet uncounted) numbers of people live in short-term tenancies, seasonal lets, mobile homes, caravans and various forms of unfit accommodation. Others will be living as victims of domestic violence. Yet these forms of homelessness are often hidden from formal definition and/or recognition, and these hiddennesses in turn will discriminate against the recognition of homelessness more generally in rural locations. In this way we can begin to understand how rural homelessness ends up out of the public picture. By defining homeless as roofless, many of the hidden homeless of both urban and rural areas are excluded from view. In urban areas the roofless are captured 'on the street' in the public imagination, and so problems of homelessness cannot easily be denied. Rural rooflessness is far less visible, with rough sleepers keeping 'off the beaten track' in woods, fields, barns and so on rather than locating in places of public congregation. These tactics of blending in are illustrated by a homeless man, who we will call 'David', interviewed in the Taunton area, who talks freely about his sojourns and travels in the countryside:

Q: And where were you sleeping at that point?

David: In the woods, under the stars and the sun.

Q: Did you have a tent or anything?

David: No, no just stayed at [local village], just sleeping in fields because it was mainly like summer and it was hot, I was just lying out on the ground and lying. I'd wake and see a couple of deer walking past me, started to scare the life out of me, but apart from that it was brilliant, it really was....

Q: So how long were you over there for?

David: I don't know, because I just like lost track of time, the days and everything you really do, and I loved it. But then winter started setting in, I mean it was a good five or six months, um, but I was just living. A couple of times I came close to actually getting caught poaching, and then I had to do a runner um, but apart from that, everything was alright. People didn't know me, I was walking like, I was just walking around with my gun in my case....

Q: Did they know you were sleeping rough, sleeping outside?

David: No, no because I had um like camouflaged trousers; I had my boots on from the navy ... I just blended right into the countryside because they didn't think that I was a town person because it was the way I was dressed. So I just blended right in with the country. Sometimes I would walk onto people's property, you know private property, and I'd just carry on walking....

Q: So you didn't just sleep in one particular place?

David: No, I was going all over the place, um I'd walk round like 10, 15 miles a day in the countryside; just carry on walking, walk across main roads, dive through hedges....

> If I see a rabbit I'd shoot it and um, find somewhere that
> was nice and isolated and then start cooking it, and then
> once I'd eaten it stay around for five, 10 minutes, and
> then um destroy the fire, make sure it looked like no one
> had had a fire, and then disappear.

Human agency such as that described here is not a common sight in the countryside. Indeed, country people meeting David would not necessarily know that he was homeless and visitors to the countryside, along with many rural residents, simply would not see him and may well deny his existence. Unlike the 'happy hobo' with which we began, David's tactics involved anonymity: 'blending in', 'doing a runner', making it look as if no one had been there.

We want to argue that tactics of anonymity and invisibility are also employed by people experiencing non-roofless types of homelessness in rural areas. Here we have in mind the socio-cultural barriers which can prevent or hinder people from receiving the assistance they require, and which thus ensure that their homelessness remains hidden. Commentators on rural poverty and deprivation (see, for example, Cloke, 1995; Woodward, 1996; Cloke et al, 1997b; Milbourne, 1997) have suggested that rural people are often reluctant to acknowledge the existence of problematic issues in their communities, and it can be anticipated that this attitude extends to the denial of homelessness. Equally, the people experiencing problems often exhibit a high degree of self-reliance, and dependency on localised informal networks of support. There is often a stigma associated with needing help from 'outsider' professionals and this too, will deter a public acknowledgement of problems associated with homelessness, especially given the fear of being 'othered' in the context of a small, often close-knit, community. These more cultural constructions around rural living and prospects for homelessness lead us further into an understanding of the ways in which the cultural identity of rurality serves more broadly to render problems such as homelessness *culturally* invisible. It is to this issue that we now turn.

Cultures of rurality and homelessness

Part of our understanding of how rurality and homelessness are an anathema draws on wider cultural construction of rurality, rural living and rural homes (see, for example, Cloke and Thrift, 1990; Cloke and Milbourne, 1992) attempting to draw together a wide range of sources which point towards the cultural circulation of 'idyll' as an often overriding characterisation of rural affairs. Essentially, rurality is connected in this way to romantic and nostalgic reminiscences of life in a close-knit community, in an environment which is in harmony with nature, and in an atmosphere of self-reliance and good, old-fashioned values. Rural homes will often be assumed to display traditional forms of domesticity and familism, relying on the role of women as home-makers and community-helpers, and exhibiting house, setting, children and possessions as key cultural capitals which reinforce the idea that rural areas are great places in which to live and bring up children.

Such cultural constructions have long been recognised as mythical (Fabes et al, 1983), and with successive waves of migration of new middle classes into the countryside, changing social practices – such as dual-income earning, the transfer of family and home care to paid employees, and potentially important changes in gendered role-playing – might be thought of as eroding the foundations of idyllic rural homes and places. On the contrary, these in-migrations appear to have bolstered idyll-myths, at least in part because the decision to live in the country will often have involved *buying into* ideas of idyll. The propensity for rural areas to be seen as problem-free zones, therefore, has remained strong, regardless of the public politics of the Countryside Marches into London. Indeed these forms of protest, with their curious amalgam of issues relating to hunting, agriculture and rural services, have served by their silence on social issues such as poverty and homelessness to increase the invisibility of these issues. Equally the 1996 White Paper on the future of the countryside steadfastly refused to acknowledge poverty or homelessness as important problems in rural areas. One can only assume that idyllic constructs of rural hearth and home live on in hegemonic public and state discourses concerning rural areas. Idyll-ised rurality inculcates rural geographical and social space with a mask of problem-freedom which is very significant in the understanding of how and why rural homelessness is not represented in popular discourse.

We argue here that key ideas in socio-spatial theory are helpful in examining more precisely the lack of connection between homelessness and rurality. In particular, we identify a series of strands of work which discuss how social issues are influenced by space and vice versa, and how space can be an active agent in the production of social marginalisation (Philo, 1986). For example, Shields (1991) has described processes of 'social spatialisation' in which places are endowed with particular connotations and symbolic meanings, and by which places are imaged, often to the extent that place-images build up into place-myths, based on widely understood core representations and practices. Places thus become known for 'what goes on' there, and indeed for what does not 'go on'. In this way the imagined geographies of particular places find their way into the everyday practices which occur there. We have discussed, above, the way in which homelessness has been assumed to be an 'urban' problem. Here, then, we can recognise an important differentiation in social-spatialisation, and we can assume that different place-images and place-myths will accept, or reject, the appropriateness of homelessness as an everyday practice. This in turn will be a powerful mechanism, in the spatial differentiation of homelessness as an issue.

This notion of 'appropriateness' is taken up by Cresswell (1996). Drawing on the ideas of Pierre Bourdieu, he describes how particular uses of spaces are deemed appropriate or inappropriate by a naturalisation of common sense. Moreover, boundaries will be erected between common sense notions of appropriate or inappropriate behaviour in particular places, and when behaviour is out-of-place, the transgression of these boundaries will be evident in the common narratives and reflexivities of everyday life:

> **The occurrence of 'out-of-place' phenomena leads people to question behaviour and define what is and what is not appropriate for a particular setting ... although 'out-of-place' is logically secondary to 'in-place', it may come first existentially. That is to say we may have to experience some geographical transgression before we realise that a boundary even existed. (Cresswell, 1996, p 22)**

From here, we can suggest that homelessness seems 'in place' in particular city environments, but will be 'out-of-place' in many places in the countryside. Rural homelessness, therefore, represents a transgression of normal socio-spatial expectations, and rurality marks a boundary between in-place and out-of-place homelessness.

Sibley's (1995) work on the geographies of social exclusion adds to this understanding. He suggests that processes of spatial purification represent an essential feature in the organisation of social space. Not only are boundaries erected between taken-for-granted orthodoxies about what is in-place or out-of-place, but the values expressed in everyday practice and life-style will heighten the consciousness of difference, and sponsor fears over the potential disintegration of these boundaries. There is also a sense in which particular built environments themselves assume a differential symbolic importance in the construction of deviancy:

> **In this way space is implicated in the construction of deviancy. Pure spaces expose difference and facilitate the policing of boundaries ... the exclusionary practices of the institutions of the capitalist state are supported by individual preferences for purity and order. A rejection of difference is embedded in the social system.... (Sibley, 1995, pp 86-7)**

We can, therefore, identify the countryside in general, and specific prestigious rural places in particular, as purified space where boundaries are subject to socio-cultural as well as governmental policing and where a rejection of difference is embedded in the rural social system. Sibley's own work on gypsies and travellers points clearly to the purification of rural space.

Homeless people will not necessarily be physically excluded from purified rural spaces. Ruddick (1996), in a study of young homeless people in Hollywood, discusses how homeless people adopt particular tactics in the spaces in which they find themselves. In rural areas too, homeless people such as David, who we have quoted above, will adopt tactics – in this case tactics of anonymity, invisibility, blending in with the country. In this way they do not challenge their excluded position from purified socio-spatial boundaries. The exclusion, then, is in socio-cultural space first, and the recognition of socio-cultural exclusion results in tactical practices in geographic space.

We recognise the danger of potential over-simplification in these arguments. There are, after all, many different 'rurals' and many different levels of purification. We do, however, believe that any overriding idyllisation of rurality does influence the apparent 'inappropriateness' of issues such as homelessness and people who are homeless in the countryside. Authors in North America have reached similar conclusions in somewhat different circumstances. In Lawrence's (1995) study of rural homelessness in Iowa, for example, he notes that representations of rural space in the USA tend to valorise matters of privacy, property and independence, and that homeless people are positioned in social space such that they challenge these representations. His conclusion is that homelessness is both institutive of and transgressive of the imagined geographies of rural society, not least because it challenges and even violates ideas of self-sufficiency and propertied individualism. Although rural

Iowa is certainly not the cultural equivalent of rural England, nevertheless, here too rural homelessness is seen to occupy spaces for which it was unintended, and thus becomes a challenge to the boundaries of rural socio-cultural space.

However, the overall inappropriateness of homelessness among the rural idyll will work out differently in specific places. For example, in small villages there is usually an absence of on-street representations of homelessness. Homeless people who are not known locally will often, like David, stay away from village centres and facilities, preferring to camouflage themselves in the more open country. People who are known locally, and who are experiencing problems of homelessness, tend to be pigeon-holed in some other way, for example, as experiencing temporary housing difficulties. Consider these three extracts from the stories of very different people each referring to the same Devon village. First, we hear the views of 'Sam', a homeless man brought up in a town some 20 miles away, and unknown in the village:

> "I travelled around loads, and often stayed around [local village]. Didn't dare go into the place even at night 'cos there's always someone looking out for trouble. That's not my place, um I just don't belong in there. I like to be on my own out in the wilds. Just need a bit of shelter where I come and go ... and no one sees me. Can't tell you where – it's private and I don't want to be found out."

Sam, like David, is unknown by residents of the village and likes to keep it that way by steering clear of them. Next we hear from 'Pete', the son of a local family who was 'chucked out' by them at age 17. Pete tried his luck in a local market town, and then returned to the village, sleeping on friends' floors and attempting (unsuccessfully) to squat in an empty cottage:

> "Came back to (the village) and stayed with me mates, but they kept telling me to f*** off after a while. So I has this f***in' great idea, and sits myself outside the f***in' shop with my sign – you know 'homeless and hungry'. People thought that it was f***in' funny, old 'Pete' from the council houses, pretending he's f***in' homeless. The old girl sees me and said that me old man would f***in' belt the hide off of me, so I buggered off again."

Pete's homelessness seems to have been rejected as an issue, and passed off as some kind of joke which seems to have been an easier orthodoxy to accept from someone from 'the council houses' than was the presence of a real live homeless person. These assumptions are given credence by the third interview voice, an elderly parish councillor who we shall call 'Louie':

> Q: Do you know of any problems of homelessness in the village?
>
> Louie: There isn't any homelessness here. We have a good, helpful community. If folks are in trouble we help them.... All the undesirables keep themselves to themselves or move away. We've had some lovely people come to live here.
>
> Q: What would you do if you saw a homeless person in the village?
>
> Louie: Well I'd die of shock, I think. We just don't get that round here – in Exeter maybe but not out here.
>
> Q: What about any housing difficulties?
>
> Louie: Well there's the children of local families, but unless they got a business here they move away anyway, don't they.

From Louie's viewpoint then, homelessness and rurality do not mix. Homelessness doesn't exist, and it cannot be envisaged, other than in the nearest city. Even when transposed as a 'housing' problem, it is envisaged as one which somehow naturally 'goes away'.

These assumptions and practices reflecting the boundaries between in-placeness and out-of-placeness of homelessness in rural areas will not necessarily be matched in other rural places. For example, we have also researched the issues of homelessness in Taunton, a rural service centre of around 40,000 population (Cloke et al, 2000: forthcoming). Here there is some replication of city-space issues, particularly in the conflation of homelessness problems with 'town centre problems' of vagrancy, begging, and drunkenness. However, a concerted effort by local business leaders, local politicians and the police to 'clean up' the streets of Taunton has served to create a 'purified commercial space' in the town centre, with the visibility of homelessness being maintained only in the form of donation boxes in some shops. In addition, homeless people in Taunton have tended to be categorised as either insiders or outsiders, with popular discourses suggesting that it is non-local 'outsiders' who are the main 'problem'. This distinction adds an interesting twist to the idea of being 'out-of-place'. The Devon village and Taunton examples suggest that localised differentiation will be significant, and it is certainly important not to allow overarching factors of rurality to swamp the potential of very different place identities and place interconnections. This issue of connections forms the core of the final part of our chapter.

Rural connections

Thus far, homelessness has been characterised largely in terms of structures of hardship, stigma and socio-spatial differentiation. In this final section we want to explore in a little more detail the idea that homeless people exercise choices, and indeed choose tactics in relation to particular areas. We have been drawn to this idea by a number of sources, including the conceptual and empirical work of Susan Ruddick, discussed above. Another important reminder about the tactics of homeless people is found in Timothy Donohue's (1996) *In the open: Diary of a homeless alcoholic*. Almost by definition not too many diaries of homeless people are published, and Donohue's is a compelling account of experiencing homelessness in America. For much of the time he is based in cities, but he also makes occasional forays into rural areas, and here he describes a small town called Henderson where someone has just handed him a $20 bill.

> **I have to admit that the people of Henderson have been extraordinarily kind and giving. Nowhere else in the country have people approached me with such frequency to offer food, clothes and even money. This might have something to do with the fact that there are not *too* many homeless here. A surplus of that kind will turn people sour after a while ... why do they concentrate themselves into specific areas, provoking the contempt of the local population, and depriving themselves of the goodwill and benevolence that can be evoked only when they are seen on a less frequent basis? (Donohue, 1996, p 184)**

Donohue, and others like him, obviously travel around, and make comparative assessment of places and their reception within them. These movements are not simple trips from the periphery to the centre. They reflect instead more circuitous routes, which permit the rotation of options; reflecting tactics of risk and resource assessment, and of spatial diversification. In his account, a small rural place can be a resource-rich location – for a short while. The very unfamiliarity of his presence seems to engender generosity rather than attempts to police the purification of space. Donohue uses tactics here to choose between options. Doubtless some spaces are more pure than others, and the policing of socio-cultural boundaries varies from place to place, but in his book Donohue gives a clear account of how to use a series of different identities to overcome past misdemeanours as he hitches or buses his way across and around America in his form of tactical movement.

We do not believe that such movements are simply an American phenomenon. Another of our informants on the experiences of homelessness in rural Britain is 'Len' who is in his forties and has been homeless for 20 years or so. Only after chatting to Len for two years on and off at a Bristol night shelter did he reveal that his 'tactics' were patterned around 'circles'. These circles turned out to be fairly regular circuits of movement involving Bristol, Taunton, Salisbury, Reading and other places where shelters and 'street-spaces' were known to be available. Len told us that these urban sojourns were punctuated by sometimes quite lengthy sojourns to what he called 'country places'. Here, according to Len, life was 'quieter' and more secure. He was able to find food and shelter there, and although he felt more under surveillance in the countryside than in the city, he said he knew of 'secret ways' through, which meant that he was not disturbed very often. The country, then, was where Len went for his 'holidays', and he insisted that many other homeless people travelled the same kinds of circles through rural areas.

These circular movements involving different urban and rural spaces were also apparent from encounters with other homeless people in rural areas. For Simon, a homeless man in his forties who was living in a Somerset town at the time of our research, regular movement and short stays in different places represented a crucial part of his life. These movements – involving countryside, towns and cities – maintained feelings of freedom and anonymity, although visits to particular urban spaces were required to access essential health services:

Simon: I own my own life, I've got no bills. I feed my dogs first, then I feed myself, have a drink, have a smoke, drop a tab of acid now and then and, um, look after my children basically. Do you know, when you wake up in the morning and you listen to the birds – if you're in the countryside and you wake up and you listen to, er, sort of wildlife birds, yeah? We wake up in Taunton and listen to like sea-gulls first thing in the morning or in Bristol, down in Devon, Cornwall or whatever. Two weeks ago I was in eight towns in 10 days.

Q: Eight in 10 days?

Simon: Yeah, just thumbing through. Do a bit of begging, get enough for a bottle of cider and something to eat, something to feed the dogs and, er, thumb through.

Q: Which towns were you in?

Simon: I started off in Torquay. I came to Taunton, Bristol, Southampton, Winchester, Oxford – that's my doctor's place. D'you know I can only get one doctor in the whole of the country – Oxford.... The nearest dentist I can get is 22 miles from this town [Taunton].

A further example is provided by Alan, another homeless man in his forties in this same town who had been travelling and living rough since his late teens. Alan was also a recovering alcoholic. He described to one of our researchers how a recent breakdown in a personal relationship resulted in a resumption in his travelling life-style, involving a move away from commitment and a recovery of his own freedom of action. In the following account, we witness again circuits of movements involving rural and urban spaces which are secured through the employment of different tactics:

Alan: Um, when I broke up with _____ after living in a house for a year and a flat ... for a year, it [moving on] was just the most natural thing for me to do. To go back on the road.

Q: Where did you go?

Alan: Um, the first place I went was Oxford. The second was
        Cambridge. From Cambridge I went along to Salisbury,
        I think was the next place. Bedford. Um, then I went
        down to Brighton … then up to St Albans … down from
        St Albans to Exeter, and then from Exeter down to
        Plymouth, and then back again as far as here, yeah.

Q: So how do you come to, I mean, all these different places.
        Do you have a route planned out, or, how do you decide
        where to go and when?

Alan: Well, a lot of it depends on friends I think. You think,
        'I'll go and see so-and-so'…. You know where they are,
        so you just head for there – hiking, bussing, local buses.
        It's cheaper to get lots and lots of local buses rather than
        one national, strangely enough. Um, yeah, I just jump
        around the country like that, picking up Social Security
        wherever you go.

Q: Can you do that easily enough?

Alan: Yeah, it's not a problem – busking, begging, whatever to
        supplement Social Security. Yeah, I suppose it's the sense
        of freedom, you know, being able to choose where you
        want to go when you want to go. It's got a lot to do
        with it. Nobody saying 'you must be here today and
        you must be there tomorrow'.

The evidence of Len, Alan and Simon points to a significant phenomenon
in the interconnection of rurality, movements and homelessness. As we
conclude elsewhere:

> … we want to suggest that homelessness in rural areas may be
> implicated in many more of these movements, connections and
> tactics than might be assumed. There certainly is evidence that
> country people will move to urban centres when they become
> homeless. However, it may well be that a reverse or return
> movement of homeless people can occur as they seek, for example,

seasonal casual work, in tourism or agriculture, or as they sleep on the floor of friends, or as with Les they 'holiday' in the country. These and other possibilities imply that there may be far more homelessness and movement of homeless people to and through rural areas than has so far been admitted. (Cloke et al, 2000: forthcoming)

Our ongoing research confirms this conclusion, and points to the paucity of existing evidence which gives voice to homeless people themselves about their experience of rural spaces and places. Rurality and homelessness may be an anathema according to many public discourses, but in the minds of a significant number of homeless people they conjure up experiences of being 'at home without a home', or being on 'holiday', or 'looking for work', or just travelling through.

Conclusions

We began this chapter with the story of Max, the 'supertramp' or 'happy hobo' who was the seemingly romantic exception to the rule that homelessness does not exist in rural areas. We believe that such stories in the media actually serve to reinforce existing prejudices which sponsor a geographical imagination of homelessness which is confirmed for all practical purposes within city limits. The idyll–isation of rurality in Britain has tended to throw a cloak of invisibility over important social issues in the countryside, of which homelessness is by no means least. In terms of socio–spatial theorisation, such homelessness is out-of-place in the purified spaces of rurality, and the cultural policing of these boundaries in turn prompts everyday practices among homeless people which tend to favour anonymity over active lobbying about the issue. As a result, many rural people experiencing homelessness will avoid the stigma of any official declaration of homelessness involved in seeking advice or registering with local authorities. For some, such advice is in any case inaccessible. Equally, many rural residents will deny the existence of rural homelessness in any form, finding it incompatible with the rural idylls which they have bought into, and where it comes to their attention, employing discursive transformations which pass it off as 'housing difficulties'.

Homeless people travelling into or though rural areas will also employ tactics of invisibility in many cases, and thereby add to the impression that homeless people only reside in big cities. It is our view that the response to homelessness in cities by the state is woefully inadequate, and that but for the Trojan efforts of the voluntary sector there would be little direct response to the needs of homeless people in urban environments. We do not underestimate the need for political re-commitment to dealing with the problems of homelessness where such problems are already recognised. However, faced with such evidence that already exists in relation to rural homelessness (limited though that is), and with the more qualitative ideas explored in this chapter, we cannot escape the conclusion that urgent new policy initiatives are also vital in rural areas. Alongside the commonly acknowledged needs for more truly *affordable* accommodation in rural areas, there is also a dire necessity for shelters, hostels, foyers and halfway houses to be provided in centres serving rural localities. Urban initiatives have leaned heavily on voluntary resources. In rural areas, despite a long-standing heritage of volunteering, voluntary agencies are finding it particularly hard to establish a continuing flow of resources to meet the needs they are already addressing. The anathema of homelessness and rurality does not just have human implications, crucial though these are. There are also key policy implications which can no longer be swept aside on the grounds that 'there isn't any homelessness here'!

Acknowledgement

We gratefully acknowledge the financial support of the ESRC for our research on 'The Homeless Poor In Rural Areas' (R000236567) in which we are investigating the hiddenness of rural homelessness, and the movements of homeless people through and between rural and urban spaces.

References

Blasi, G. (1990) 'Social policy and social science research on homelessness', *Journal of Social Issues*, vol 46, no 4, pp 207-90.

Bramley, G. (1994) *Homelessness in rural England: Statistical update to 1992/ 93*, London: Rural Development Commission.

Cloke, P. (1995) 'Rural poverty and the welfare state: a discursive transformation in Britain and the USA', *Environment and Planning A*, vol 27, no 6, pp 1001-16.

Cloke, P. and Milbourne, P. (1992) 'Deprivation and lifestyles in rural Wales II in rurality and the cultural dimension', *Journal of Rural Studies*, vol 8, no 4, pp 360-74.

Cloke, P. and Thrift, N. (1990) 'Class and change in rural Britain', in T. Marsden, P. Lowe and S. Whatmore (eds) *Rural restructuring*, London: David Fulton, pp 165-81.

Cloke, P., Goodwin, M. and Milbourne, P. (1997a) *Rural Wales: Community and marginalisation*, Cardiff: University of Wales Press.

Cloke, P., Milbourne, P. and Thomas, C. (1994) *Lifestyles in rural England*, London: Rural Development Commission.

Cloke, P., Milbourne, P. and Thomas, C. (1997b) 'Living lives in different ways? Deprivation, marginalisation and changing lifestyles in rural England', *Transactions IBG*, vol 22, no 2, pp 210-300.

Cloke P., Milbourne, P. and Widdowfield, R. (2000: forthcoming) 'Partnership and policy networks in rural local governance: homelessness in Taunton', *Public Administration*.

Cloke, P., Milbourne, P. and Widdowfield, R. (2000: forthcoming) 'Homelessness and rurality: "Out-of-place" in purified space', *Society and Space*.

Cloke, P., Goodwin, M., Milbourne, P. and Thomas, C. (1995) 'Deprivation, poverty and marginaliation in rural lifestyles in England and Wales', *Journal of Rural Studies*, vol 11, no 4, pp 351-65.

Cresswell, T. (1996) *In place, out of place: Geography, ideology and transgression*, Minneapolis, IN: University of Minnesota Press.

Daly, G. (1996) *Homeless: Policies, strategies and lives on the street*, London: Routledge.

Donohue, T. (1996) *In the open: Diary of a homeless alcoholic*, Chicago, IL: University of Chicago Press.

Fabes, R., Worsley, L. and Howard, M. (1983) *The myth of the rural idyll*, Leicester: Child Poverty Action Group.

First, R., Rife, J. and Toomey, B. (1994) 'Homelessness in rural areas – causes, patterns and trends', *Social Work*, vol 39, no 1, pp 97-108.

Fitchen, J. (1991) 'Homelessness in rural places: perspectives from upstate New York', *Urban Anthropology*, vol 20, no 3, pp 177-210.

Fitchen, J. (1992) 'On the edge of homelessness: rural poverty and housing insecurity', *Rural Sociology*, vol 57, no 2, pp 173-93.

Hutson, S. and Liddiard, M. (1994) *Youth homelessness: The construction of a social issue*, London: Macmillan.

Johnson, G. (1997) 'Villagers buy their tramp his own wood', *News of the World*.

Lambert, C., Jeffers, S., Burton, P. and Bramley, G. (1992) *Homelessness in rural areas*, London: Rural Development Commission.

Lawrence, M. (1995) 'Rural homelessness: a geography without a geography', *Journal of Rural Studies*, vol 11, no 3, pp 297-308.

Milbourne, P. (ed) (1997) *Revealing rural others*, London: Cassell.

Philo, C. (1986) *The same and the other: On geographies, madness and outsiders*, Occasional Paper No 11, Loughborough: Department of Geography, Loughborough University.

Ruddick, S. (1996) *Young and homeless in Hollywood: Mapping social identities*, New York, NY: Routledge.

Scott, D., Shenton, N. and Healey, B. (1991) *Hidden deprivation in the countryside*, Brixton: Peak Park Trust.

Shields, R. (1991) *Places on the margin*, London: Routledge.

Sibley, D. (1995) *Geographies of exclusion: Society and difference in the West*, London: Routledge.

Walmer, T. (1989) 'Families with "no place to go" on rise', *USA Today*, 12 December.

Watson, S. (1989) 'Definitions of homelessness: a feminist perspective', *Critical Social Policy*, vol 11, no 2, pp 60-73.

Watson, S. and Austerberry, H. (1986) *Housing and homelessness: A feminist perspective*, London: Routledge.

Woodward, R. (1996) '"Deprivation" and "the rural": an investigation into contradictory discourses', *Journal of Rural Studies*, vol 12, no 1, pp 55-67.

FIVE

A home is where the heart is: engendering notions of homelessness

Sophie Watson

Introduction

Definitions of homelessness and the housing policies which are founded on particular definitions construct some individuals as in need of housing while marginalising others. These definitions are gendered and have served to marginalise women's homelessness at the same time as operating with normative assumptions around the patriarchal family and women's place within it. Over time these normative assumptions have shifted and so too has the social and political/economic context in which they are embedded. The first part of this chapter will look briefly at the history of women's homelessness, and the reactions it produced. In the course of the discussion these interrelationships will become clear.

The rest of this chapter is divided into three sections. Part of my argument is that women's experiences of homelessness, like other homeless groups, cannot be separated from the vexed question of the meanings and definitions of homelessness. The gender connotations of homelessness are considered through analysing homeless women's experience as well as the official definitions and categories. These understandings of homelessness have to be situated also in the social, economic and political conditions which precipitate some households into homelessness, and these too change over time. The second section thus considers some specific causes of women's homelessness as well as the broader social, economic and housing context. In the last part of the chapter I draw on recent post-structuralist and feminist thought to engage in a more speculative discussion of the importance of challenging homelessness at the level of the social imaginary and discursive practices. For homelessness as a gendered experience to be addressed, fundamental shifts in social relations as lived, represented and imagined will need to take place.

Women and homelessness: exploring the past

In the 19th century, despite the traditional image of the male vagabond and wanderer, many women were to be found in the casual wards, lodging houses, or working in domestic service due to a lack of alternative forms of independent income. Victorian morality and family values were deeply threatened by the presence of women in what were seen as dens of iniquity. In 1851 Mayhew railed:

> ... the indiscriminate admixture of the sexes among adults, in many of these places, is another evil. Even in some houses considered of the better sort, men and women, husbands and wives, old and young, strangers and acquaintances, sleep in the same apartment and if they choose, the same bed. (Quennell, 1949, p x)

In this period then, notions of moral depravity pervaded notions of women's homelessness.

By the turn of the century throughout the social and political spheres there was growing concern that women's issues were ignored, forgotten or invisible. Thus concern emerged through feminist speakers who challenged the ways in which women were marginalised in all spheres of life from politics to education. More specifically, feminists concerned with the housing problem argued vociferously that women's homelessness was not recognised, not addressed and was underestimated (Higgs and Hayward, 1910). There were some material reasons for this underestimation of women's homelessness, apart from the broader political and social context, such as the practice of women dressing as men, a lack of early census-taking methods, and the social disapproval of women living outside traditional families or wandering the road. Like today, many of the women who were prostitutes were forced into this work through homelessness:

> Although the history of homeless women is intertwined with that of two non-sexed phenomena – begging and vagabondage – it is closely related to one activity men generally do not share to the same extent as women – prostitution. This was almost always an option open to a destitute woman. (Golden, 1992)

Thus it is no surprise to find that in estimates of women's homelessness, like Webb's in 1935, women constituted only 2-3% of the 200,000 unattached migrants. Such perceptions of women's homelessness meant that the provision of accommodation for homeless women was marked from its early days by its shortage relative to the provision for men, on the one hand, and by a different set of moral codes, on the other. In the late 19th century, for example, hostels were established by the Salvation Army to rescue young women from prostitution.

Women on their own who had stepped out of the confines of the traditional nuclear family and motherhood, through choice or necessity, were long regarded with both suspicion and hostility; it is only recently that this has begun to change. Golden (1992) makes the interesting point that the reason the London County Council was reluctant to provide lodging houses for women was that giving them beds would have made them visible and belonging to society in a way that could not be tolerated. Ada Chesterton put it this way: "The most abject specimen of man is quite welcome if he has pence to pay.... But in the case of women there is the rooted belief that they must be bad lots or they would have a home" (Golden, 1992, p 223). From philanthropists such as Ada Chesterton and Octavia Hill through to feminist activists in the 1970s and 1980s there have been persistent efforts to raise the profile of single homeless women and to challenge the dominant assumption that women constitute a small proportion of the single homeless.

Though feminist and community campaigns over nearly three decades have shifted the terms of the debate and policies for the homeless, homelessness definitions and policies still operate on a gendered terrain in which women's housing needs and experiences remain marginalised. Part of the difficulty in theorising homelessness derives from the question of homelessness as defined by objective criteria and categories as opposed to subjective experiences on the one hand, and stereotypical constructions on the other. While it may be straightforward to determine who falls in and out of categories of need as defined by government policy, it is harder to unpack this more fluid terrain of meanings and discursive practices. Again this is an area where gender matters, since historically women's voices and experiences have been less often recognised. As many feminist theorists have argued (Pateman, 1988; Barrett and Phillips, 1992) categories that are accepted as universal or neutral – such as the individual or citizenship – are far from that; rather they speak to men's subject positions and experiences.

Definitions and meanings of home and homelessness

Meanings are not fixed but are continually contested, formed and reformed in the context of political, social, cultural and economic struggles.
This is particularly true for homelessness where homeless groups must
continually struggle to be incorporated into policy discourses in order to
have their needs met. Homelessness is a category which has shifted
dramatically over time and space. In other words it is an historically and
culturally specific phenomenon and a relative concept, like poverty
(Townsend, 1979), where people make judgements about their own
deprivation on the basis of what they see around them. Individuals have
fantasies and imaginary formulations about how other people live in the
world and these are mapped onto, and constituted by, a collective imaginary
in each society which is specific to a particular time and place. Castoriadis
describes it this way:

> **The construction of its own world by each and every society is,**
> **in essence, the creation of a world of meanings, its social**
> **imaginary significations, which organise the (pre-social,**
> **biologically pre-given) natural world, create a social world proper**
> **to each society (with its articulations, rules, purposes etc), establish**
> **the ways in which socialised and humanised individuals are to be**
> **fabricated, and institute the motives, values and hierarchies of**
> **social (human) life. (Castoriadis, 1991, p 42)**

Thus, how homelessness is understood in each society reflects the ways
in which that society is organised, and in a patriarchal society, these are
necessarily gendered.

Part of the difficulty of defining homelessness lies in the concept of
'home' as distinct from 'house'. Houses are relatively easy to reduce to
the notion of dwelling, the material or physical structure that provides
shelter, but homes are not. Given the traditionally dominant association
of women with the family, with the domestic and the private arenas,
home is likely to have particularly strong gendered connotations and so
also is homelessness. If a woman's place is in the home, where is she
without it?

The interviews with homeless women in *Housing and homelessness*
(Watson and Austerberry, 1986) certainly revealed affective responses
around the notion of home which confirmed this point. Many of the
women interviewed associated the home with family, privacy, and a sense

of emotional and social well-being. Women traditionally have tended to socialise at home more than in public spaces like pubs and clubs, and thus the home is conceived as a site of social relations. 'Home' in the research was variously described as "happiness with your husband going out to work, and you're at home doing the shopping and cooking, and you can come home, sit down, watch tele and have a cup of tea"; or as a "place where I can choose the decor, and where who comes is my choice only. It's essential to women. You don't really feel a woman without a nest. It's the expansion of your personality. Its just such a joy to arrange things" or "my own little place where I can buy things and make it nice, where I could invite my friends back for a cup of tea". Socially constructed in the context of a patriarchal society these notions may be, yet gendered expectations are internalised by women themselves, as well as others, so that such symbolic meanings matter nevertheless.

Homelessness for women was thus an absence of home in precisely these terms:"homelessness is no control over the decoration and furniture", "nowhere to rest yourself privately. It affects people, not seeing your friends, not being able to do your own thing and cook your own food", "homelessness is connected with the divorce", "homelessness is feeling nameless. I feel I don't exist, I'm just a thing. That's what I feel like living here". Yet despite these more textured definitions of homelessness which emerged in the context of an in-depth strategy of interviewing, for many of the women the definitions of homelessness they carried with them were predominantly masculine:

> **Homelessness is little old men going around with bags over their shoes. So to that extent I don't think of myself as homeless. Shelter bills – the stereotype. But the only reason I'm not actually homeless is because the people I'm staying with are too middle-class to fling me on the street. (quoted in Watson and Austerberry, 1986, p x)**

Tomas and Dittmar (1995), nearly a decade later, found a different response in their interviews with 12 women who regularly used a day centre in Brighton. Only three of the 12 homeless women could confidently define any difference between house and home, expressing difficulty with the question itself. For these women housing was about safety and security and homelessness was thus the lack of these. The notion of home as a place of psychological meaning was largely absent. Whether this represents a shift in the homeless female population or reflects a different group of homeless women is hard to know. Given feminist challenges to gendered representations in many spheres, greater public participation of women in work and politics, increased visibility of homeless women as sellers of *The Big Issue* in the intervening period, one could conjecture that the homeless female population may well have changed (as we explore below) and the definitions of homelessness given may thus also have shifted. The meanings of homelessness are inherently unstable.

Complex and subjective definitions of homelessness do not, though, lend themselves to policy. How indeed could subjective experiences get interpolated into policy discourse and with what effects? Regulations, standards and definitions of necessity have to be equitable, consistent and objective. In a housing market defined by the shortage of low-cost accommodation, there simply is no possibility of allocating housing on the basis of subjective definitions of need. Women's own sense of themselves as not fitting the image they carry of homelessness, which is nearly always masculine, serves to undermine defining themselves as such and potentially reinforces a passivity and inability to do anything about it. Need does not always get translated into demand. To put it another way, dominant masculine discourses are demobilising to those that cannot recognise themselves within them. The same processes occur when white norms and discursive practices act to marginalise black subjectivities. As one woman interviewed put it:

> **I think one ought to say one's homeless and then you try and do something about it. I mean until I think of myself as homeless, I won't do anything. I used to think of homelessness as someone on a street corner – and because I had friends – I didn't think of myself as homeless. But in fact I've been homeless for a long time, in that I've never had a place I could call my own. (quoted in Watson and Austerberry, 1986, pp 106-7)**

This woman's experience illuminates another aspect of the relative and gendered nature of homeless definitions. That is, if the structurally different positions and also subjective experiences of each member of the household in relation to the home are taken into account, one individual in a household may be potentially homeless according to a broad definition of the term, while another is not.

There is thus a conundrum at the heart of analysing women's homelessness and that is the interlocking of three connected and almost inseparable layers: visibility/invisibility, estimated significance of the problem and its definition. The crucial point is that each of these terms, if you like, determines the other. If homelessness is defined in terms of men's experiences and practices or men's subjectivities then women's homelessness becomes invisible. If it is invisible it is not counted and therefore it is underestimated. Research and also political action in the arena of women's homelessness has had to grapple with this problem for a long time. First the issue of homelessness has to be established as existing, and then drawn out of the shadows and illuminated before anything can be done to address it. Madeleine Drake's research on the single homeless conducted for the Department of the Environment in 1981 (DoE,1981) provides a useful illustration. The survey was intended to be a comprehensive survey of the single homeless. The research was conducted at a range of sites traditionally used by the single homeless – namely large hostels and night shelters. From interviews in these places the research concluded that more than four fifths of the single homeless population were men. There was no explicit recognition that many of these hostels either excluded women entirely or were not used by women because they were male dominated spaces. Findings such as the fact that women were more likely to have office jobs than men could entirely be explained by the fact that the sample of women were drawn from up-market hostels which cater for white-collar workers, while the men were drawn from direct access hostels where employment was no criterion for acceptance.

It was this research which provoked my own early investigation of the issue. As a coordinator of a large homeless organisation for women in London, which was always overflowing at the seams and where new women presented themselves whenever empty places became available, I had an intuitive sense that there were more homeless women than the Department of the Environment research suggested. The research problem was how to show this and then how to conceptualise it. In two studies (Austerberry et al, 1984; Watson and Austerberry, 1986), using different methodologies, it became clear that the extent of women's homelessness was at least as great as men's, if not greater. Our own analysis of data collected by an advice agency for the single homeless found that the ratio of female to male inquiries was four to one. A study some years later found that of the 10,000 calls in 1988, 60% were from women (HAS, 1989). The point is that it is those statistics which register homelessness before it is institutionalised in hostels, on waiting lists or other forms of provision which are likely to give us the most accurate picture of homelessness. When considering any estimate of women's homelessness

– or the prevalence of homelessness among any other groups – one has to ask the question as to how the figure was derived. The differences in methodologies or definitions used can account for the variances in estimates. In the United States, for example, figures range from 300,000 to more than 2.5 million homeless men, women and children (Martin, 1988, p 33). These arguments are now well recognised in the academic literatures on homelessness, but there is still a tendency, in the media for example, to publish figures rather indiscriminately, and for the issue to remain under-theorised, particularly in government-commissioned reports (Neale, 1997).

The specificity of women's homelessness

The inability to gain access to housing is fundamentally related to income, although issues of discrimination and prejudice also play a part (Watson and Austerberry, 1986; Watson, 1988; Sexty, 1990). In many ways, women are no different from other low-income or marginalised groups for whom there is an inadequate supply of secure and affordable accommodation, though single parents are a particularly vulnerable group. But women are further disadvantaged in their access to housing due to their domestic responsibilities and generally lower incomes. There are also reasons why women become homeless which are gender specific, and why their experiences once homeless differ from men's in a host of ways.

To elaborate first on women's employment, income and housing, despite some shifts in labour force participation and some changes in the patterns of domestic work, women still take the major responsibility for the care of children and dependants and are thus marginalised in the labour market. This is global phenomenon. In Britain the average full-time female wage is still approximately four fifths of that for males and many women work part time: 90% of part-time workers are women. If we look at the global picture, 70% of the world's 1,300 million poor are women (UNDP, 1995). In the United States, for example, 44% of single mothers are defined as in poverty with another 14% on the margins of poverty (Sprague, 1991). In many countries the practice of taking male income as the basis of minimum income for access to subsidised housing disadvantages women-headed households. As Borja and Castells (1997) point out, the criteria for eligibility for subsidised housing are often based on regular income from formal employment militating against women's access. The implications of this for women are discussed by Aliyar and Shetty (1992). They describe a housing programme implemented in Solanda, Ecuador. Its goal was to house 6,000 low-income families. Only 175 of households who were supported were headed by women, and the authors emphasise that had the general eligibility criteria been applied then the great majority of these could not have had access to housing.

Housing supply and provision has not kept pace with demographic changes and this affects women particularly. While the traditional family remains dominant ideologically the reality is that its significance worldwide is decreasing. This dramatic shift has occurred as a result of a number of factors. At the level of the social, there is no doubt that changing educational, employment and housing possibilities and the women's and gay liberation movements have shifted social attitudes such that less people are rushing into marriage, and if they do, it is at a later age. More people are choosing to live alone or cohabit, with or without children, in heterosexual or gay relationships. In 1994-95 in Great Britain more than a quarter of households consisted of one person living alone which is almost double the proportion in 1961 (CSO, 1996). At the same time, when relationships break down there is less and less stigma associated with divorce, with one in 2.8 marriages in Britain now ending in divorce.

Thus in the UK the traditional nuclear family now accounts for less than a third of all households. The growth in lone-parent households (90% of which are headed by women) is the most striking demographic shift of the last two decades, increasing from 8% in 1971 to 22% in 1991. Research conducted by the London Housing Unit showed that single parents were more than eight times more likely to become homeless than other households (quoted in Brotchie, undated). Single parents, especially women, are very dependent on local authorities for their housing. One year after divorce, where this took place between 1991 and 1993, where the former matrimonial home was owner-occupied, 11% of women were renting from the social sector. For women who are unable to gain access to public housing or housing associations, who are unable to remortgage, or get a mortgage for the first time, after the divorce has been settled, housing becomes a serious problem. Women who have been out of the labour force, or in part-time work, are particularly vulnerable, as are those who separate in middle or older age (Butler, 1994).

These patterns are not unique to England: many countries face similar challenges. According to Moser:

> **It is estimated that one third of the world's households are headed by women. In urban areas, particularly in Latin America and**

Africa, the figure exceeds 50 per cent ... and globally the phenomenon is on the increase. (Moser and Peake, 1987)

Manuel Castells (1997) presents a compelling case for related global shifts which he links not only with social movements but also with the rise of the informational global economy and technological changes in reproduction.

The other major demographic shift which is relevant to women's access to housing is in relation to longevity, with many people living into their eighties and nineties, particularly women. Currently women over pensionable age constitute the largest group of single people at 12%. Older people, and older women particularly, form the largest group in local authority housing – 26% of people over 65 and 27% over 80 are public tenants. Older women who do not have this security are vulnerable to homelessness from family breakdown or disputes with children. Men post-retirement are three times more likely than women to be receiving an occupational pension and women in work at the moment are less likely to be members of a pension scheme suggesting that the problem of women's low income in older age is one which is likely to persist.

Despite these demographic shifts, housing in Britain, as in many countries, has been developed to accommodate the nuclear family household. Thus public housing was primarily built, designed and allocated to households with children, while single people were marginalised. Access to home ownership in many areas is also limited to households with two incomes or single people with high incomes and secure employment prospects – which implicitly has meant that fewer women than men can take on a mortgage. The overall picture, then, is one where women in general are marginalised in their access to housing. The exception to this is in their access to public housing and housing associations – where women who head households with children are eligible for housing through waiting lists or as a homeless household. The decline in the public housing stock has been well documented and has considerably disadvantaged this group in terms of choice and access (Marsh and Mullins, 1998).

Though I have argued so far that women are vulnerable to homelessness for structural reasons, in the last decade an increasing body of evidence has identified psychological factors and a history of abuse and violence as equally important (Brotchie, undated). A study of women at First Base Day Centre in Brighton (Tomas and Dittmar, 1995) found that 58% of all moves made by homeless women were either to escape abuse or as a result of social services intervention to place children in care or in Bed & Breakfast accommodation. This contrasted with a group of housed women interviewed who had made a similar number of moves, but these were predominantly moves associated with employment or personal choice. Joanne Passaro's (1996) study of homeless women on the streets of New York encountered similar stories of abuse. Jean, a panhandler on the corner of Fifth Avenue and Tenth Street described her life:

> **In a manner of speaking I think I've always been homeless for all of my life. The reason for that being that obviously I came from parents but I came from parents who didn't want me ... early on my mother would incite my father and because he didn't have an outlet he would physically take it out on me – throw me, bang my head against the wall, smack me.... I ended up in the streets. (quoted in Passaro, 1996, p 66)**

In the same study, Janet a homeless activist in the Bronx, described herself as:

> **... the child of incest. I was also the child of alcoholics ... I hated my life, I hated myself, I didn't know it at the time. I got married at the age of 17, but by this time already I had two children ... eventually [drink and drugs] led to the disintegration of my marriage, I lost my house, car, bank account, I lost my children, I lost everything. (quoted in Passaro, 1996, p 70)**

There are many such stories in the literature on homeless women, where early unhappy lives led to homelessness as an adult woman. Brotchie (undated) suggests that the high incidence of abuse and violence towards women has an impact on their experience of homelessness. In her view the symptoms of sexual abuse and homelessness – such as insecurity and low self-esteem – are similar and one can often compound the other. The HHELP team in London identified a number of symptoms in homeless women who had experienced abuse: self-harm, low self-esteem, depression and insomnia, mood disturbances, lack of confidence, poor health, anxiety, loss of identity and loss of power.

A cause of homelessness among women and their children that has increasingly been recognised is domestic violence in relations of marriage and cohabitation. In Britain, as a result of campaigns in the 1970s which challenged the myth that battered women had a home to return to, and were therefore not considered to be homeless, feminists and activists succeeded in getting battered women to be regarded as homeless under the 1977 Housing (Homeless Persons) Act. These institutional arrangements are specific to the UK but serve as an example of continuing marginalisation of homeless women's needs despite legislation. Subsequent to the Act it became clear that many local authorities avoided their responsibilities. Binney's (1981, pp 78–85) early study of local authority practice suggested that of 207 applications under the Act, 32% of the women were found not to be homeless, 24% were regarded as another local authority's responsibility, 9% were defined as not in priority need, and 8% were found to be intentionally homeless. Later studies have come to similar conclusions though the local authority reasoning appears to have become more sophisticated (Cowan, 1997, p 117). What is also clear is that there is wide variation in practices across and within homeless persons units (HPUs). Hague and Malos' in-depth study found that HPUs were using a range of techniques, some of which they were unaware of, to avoid their responsibility for battered women (Hague, 1999).

The 1985 Housing Act was expanded to incorporate the notion of threat. Thus, a person was to be defined as homeless "if it is probable that occupation of [the accommodation] will lead to violence from some other person residing in it or to threats of violence from some other person residing in [the accommodation] and likely to carry out the threats" (Section 58(3)(b)). Another important shift was in the recognition that a battered woman and her children may need to be rehoused in a local authority where she had no local connection, rather than being referred back to an alternative authority of prior connection. Thus, the local connection provision could be overridden if the applicant "or any other person who might reasonably reside with him will run the risk of domestic violence in that other district" (Section 67(2)(c)).

The current policy approach in Britain is to foster interagency cooperation in dealing with domestic violence cases. Initially the interagency cooperation arose out of the refuge movement (Cowan, 1997, p 123), where local refuges needed to work with the local authority – particularly to find permanent accommodation – and vice versa. Central government has subsequently become involved in the form of circulars from the Home Office calling, among other provisions, for the police to take a more active role in securing immediate protection for women, for the establishment of domestic violence units, and encouraging police liaison with other agencies (Cowan, 1997). Yet despite developments in interagency working, further research has found that although many housing and social services departments have been involved in the interagency fora, in some areas housing departments were absent despite their responsibilities for acting on homelessness and domestic violence (Hague, 1999).

Once homeless, young women's experience may be quite different from those of men. Thornton's (1990) UK study confirmed this view:

> **Few resort to sleeping rough, for fear of exposing themselves to violence or sexual abuse, and rather than entering the institutional environment of a hostel or boarding house many prefer to make their own temporary accommodation arrangements with family or friends. (quoted in Brotchie, undated, p 3)**

Another traditional way out of homelessness for women is to find employment with accommodation attached – domestic work, childcare, caring for elderly people, nursing, hotel work and so on. The problem, though, is that such employment is usually temporary and with little security of tenure, women can easily be precipitated back into homelessness if another position is not found. As women get older, their vulnerability to homelessness increases. And just as private or hidden forms of homelessness are gendered, so also are the public spaces of the homeless. In the context of New York Passaro (1996) found that:

> **... the staking out of public space in the city is a phenomenon dominated by homeless men. On a day in February 1990, she counted 24 women panhandling or just sitting on the streets between 42nd and 50th streets from the East Hudson to the river and 210 men. By the evening half of the women had gone and 192 men were counted. (Passaro, 1996, pp 83-5)**

The overall picture of women's homelessness is a contradictory one. Are women more or less at risk of homelessness now than they were 20 years ago? Have women's lives become more or less precarious? According to certain measures women have gained greater financial and economic independence. Yet do homeless or potentially homeless women gain from this? Given that the gains in employment opportunities are mainly to the benefit of younger women, it is unlikely that middle-aged and older women who are marginal to the labour market will be any more able to find a job than they were 20 or more years ago. Similarly the cuts in public housing will mean that for many women there are fewer housing options than there once were. Where homeless women's lives may be less at risk is in the sphere of domestic violence and abuse. The reason for this is that there has been a growing recognition of the issue and both the government and voluntary sectors have tried in various ways to address the issue. It could also be argued that as women have become more visible and active in various public arenas, so also the homeless woman on the street is regarded with less fear and hostility than two or three decades earlier. Whether this makes her life less precarious, however, is difficult to assess.

Towards a new social imaginary and new strategies

For all forms of homelessness, there are a range of solutions and approaches. In the British context, these include an extended provision of low-cost accommodation in different forms of social or public housing, a stronger requirement on local authorities to carry out their responsibilities to homeless people as defined by the Housing Act (the treatment of victims of domestic violence being a case in point), a range of social and community facilities for homeless people with special needs, a variety of short- to long-term housing provision to address different forms of homelessness, an extension of schemes such as foyer schemes to link housing solutions with employment to address the complex nexus between homelessness and unemployment, and so on.

The majority of these solutions require expenditure on the part of governments and a commitment at local and central government to properly combating extensive levels of homelessness in this society. But it is also useful to draw on recent post-structuralist and feminist theory to shed a different light on the problem. This might be particularly fruitful given the fact that academic discourse has largely taken on board many of the early feminist arguments. For our purposes here the work of Foucault (1977, 1979) offers some useful insights. First are his notions of power, micro-politics and resistance. A second strand is the more elusive terrain of discursive practices, of the construction of meanings and how subjectivities and individual experiences and a sense of self are constituted within these.

In radical traditions power is conceived as repressive and negative in its effects. Power is postulated as excluding and oppressive and as possessed by institutions or groups of people who use it for their own ends. For the homeless person, according to this model, there is little room for manoeuvre to effect change or to resist, since power is concentrated in the hands of either the capitalist state, institutions or individuals. One of Foucault's major contributions was to challenge this notion of power. In his work power is seen as exercised, not possessed, and as a strategy. Power in this formulation is fluid operating in a capillary-like fashion constituting all social relations. Power is thus not given but is exchanged and is productive in that it constitutes the domain of the social: power relations are everywhere. For Foucault, where there is power there is also resistance. Thus power is not about something done to people over which they have no control. Thus, homeless people can occupy public space, as they do on the streets, organise together to campaign for housing, squat empty houses and so on. In Foucault's terms these local resistances in specific sites are termed micro-politics and represent important strategies for change.

Another key element of Foucault's view of power for social policy is his argument that power and knowledge are intimately connected and intertwined: we cannot think of one without the other. All fields of knowledge are constituted within power relations and all knowledges constitute a field of power. This is particularly relevant to analysing the professions, including the housing professions, and the knowledges on which they are based. This would imply, for example, interrogating the education of housing managers and uncovering the hidden assumptions embedded in the material given to students, and analysing their effects.

Also within post-structuralist thought there is a critique of the attempt to build grand theories and an argument instead that we can only understand the world in partial, specific and local ways. Thus, in relation to housing policy what this means is that we can begin to see housing policy as necessarily contradictory and complex. Some housing policies in some contexts may reproduce capitalist or patriarchal relations, for example. But other housing policies will need to be understood and analysed in different ways using different frameworks of analysis. This means, therefore, paying attention to local contexts and the locally different effects of policies on different groups of people. This approach acknowledges that the world is fluid, changing and inherently complex and fragmented. The implications for the development of effective housing policies are that they should be developed to address the specific needs of particular groups in particular circumstances. This too can be seen as a form of micro-politics. Such a strategy does not preclude the need for universal standards or provisions based on clear criteria of need. What it does, like feminist attempts to break out of the difference versus equality debate, is to bring together notions of universality and particularism to provide a more textured approach to policy formulation.

Our second terrain is that of discourse. Here what is important is how different frameworks of meanings are produced and with what effects. Thus, not only do material practices matter – for example, how homeless people are actually treated – but also how different discourses act to produce certain outcomes. For example, what becomes important is how the Housing Act creates particular notions of homeless people – which marginalise some groups, create others as victims, others as blameworthy and so on. Crucial here is the notion of discursive practices: how are particular discourses mobilised and in what arenas? How can we intervene to change these?

Being homeless is not simply about not having a roof over one's head, as we have seen. What is also important is how homeless subjects are constructed. According to Foucault's view, subjects are both the target of power and its articulation:

When I think of the mechanics of power, I think of its capillary forms of existence, of the extent to which power seeps into the very grain of individuals, reaches right into their bodies, permeates their gestures, their position, what they say, how they learn to live and work with other people. (Foucault, 1977, p 10)

One aspect of this is how homeless people are seen in relation to their very beings as bodies. Wright (1997) makes the point that "people living on the street are not just neutral bodies, but subjugated bodies and resisting bodies moving through, sitting, lying down, and sleeping in, the social-physical spaces of the city, a negative trope for surrounding housed society" (p 58). Homeless people also, he suggests, challenge routine assumptions about 'healthy', 'active', 'hardworking' bodies who are housed, simply by sleeping on the pavement. If we engender this argument, then homeless women's bodies can be seen to represent a challenge to the feminine body, the mother or wife located in the home, cooking in the kitchen, going about her daily domestic tasks. In a sense she comes to be the feared 'other', held up as a counterpoint to happy 'normal' life. As such the homeless woman serves to keep housed women in their place, by her presence she becomes a reminder to all women of what they might become if they step out of line. By sleeping on the street wrapped in a blanket, by bringing her bed into the street as it were, she is also starkly disrupting the public/private boundary on which much planning regulation is based. What we see in a graphic way is the private, and the sphere associated with feminine domesticity and sexuality seeping into the public in disruptive and threatening ways.

As feminist philosophers have argued (for example, Grosz, 1989; Gatens, 1992) the body is not given, fixed and determined but is a terrain where meaning is inscribed, constructed, and reconstituted or the interface of the subject and the social. Many homeless women on the street dress themselves in eccentric clothes, or, if younger, pierce or tattoo their bodies and dye their hair – 'we are not like you' – they seem to be saying. Women's bodies, like black bodies and homeless bodies, are seen and understood through the dominant social imaginary that privileges whiteness and maleness (Wright, 1997, p 68). Homeless bodies in the public imagination are dirty, unhealthy, degenerate, smelly and deviant. Where women in a society signify caring, nurturing, cleanliness, well-kept, groomed and maintained bodies, the homeless woman's body comes to be seen as all the more grotesque.

How homeless bodies are constructed offers an illustration of the way in which negative symbolic representations can serve yet further to marginalise the already marginalised. Space is both produced and consumed within relations of difference where women and black people are often at the bottom of the pile. And these differences, in part, are a product of a social imaginary which classes these categories of people as subordinated. Wright (1997) describes this more intangible way of thinking about space in the following way:

> ... the organisation of societies, of race, ethnic, gender, and class configurations, of social-physical space and temporal organisation, is not conducted strictly along biological or chemical lines, or by the logic of reason, or by a materialist logic of capitalist development, but are the by-products of the organisation of fantasies, of the working of the social imaginary in a dialectical relationship with the material world. (Wright, 1997, p 44)

It is also useful to think about how networks of power differentiate space unequally, or how the social imaginary is translated into spatial hierarchies within which the city becomes socially polarised and fragmented. Who has the power to define and describe and delineate the spaces of the city? How do homeless people get defined as unsuitable and alien intruders into the central spaces of the city? These are the kinds of questions that need to be asked.

In conclusion then, new ways of approaching homelessness, and more specifically the gendered nature of homelessness open up new strategies and possibilities. Part of the process of challenging dominant discourses of homelessness and also its lived materiality, lies in changing the ways in which society is understood, and the ways in which these understandings are translated spatially. This involves resistances at the local level – Foucault's micro-politics – which may be struggles at a particular refuge or hostel or struggles over a segment of abandoned land, or may be resistance to the ways in which particular subjects are constructed in policy discourses, or in the social practices of housing officials, planners, or developers. Given that gender is constructed in a host of ways in this society, combating women's homelessness requires flexibility and innovative approaches. It also requires change on a diversity of shifting terrains from the provision of housing to the construction of meanings and dominant images. A recognition of this complexity is important to any more general analysis and intervention in the homeless arena.

References

Aliyar, V. and Shetty, S. (1992) 'Shelter policy: implications for women in development', in M. Dandekar (ed) *Shelter, women and development: First and Third World perspectives*, Ann Arbor, MI: George Wahr.

Austerberry, H., Schott, K. and Watson, S. (1984) *Homeless in London 1981-91*, London: STICERD, London School of Economics.

Barrett, M. and Phillips, A. (1992) *Destabilising theory*, Cambridge: Polity Press.

Binney, V., Markell, G. and Nixon, J. (1981) *Leaving violent men*, Women's Aid Federation, England.

Borja, J. and Castells, M. (1997) *Local and global*, London: Earthscan.

Brotchie, J. (undated) *No place like home*, Brighton and Hove: Homeless Womens Project.

Butler, S. (1994) *Middle aged, female and homeless: The stories of a forgotten group*, New York, NY: Garland Publishing.

Caplow, T. (undated) 'Homelessness', in D. Sills (ed) *International encyclopaedia of the social services*, London.

Castells, M. (1997) *The power of identity*, Oxford: Blackwell.

Castoriadis, C. (1991) 'Le délabrement de l'Occident', *Esprit*, December.

Cowan, D. (1997) *Homelessness: The (in)appropriate applicant*, Aldershot: Ashgate.

CSO (Central Statistical Office) (1996) *Social trends*, London: HMSO.

DoE (Department of the Environment) (1981) *Single and homeless*, Report by Madelaine Drake, London: HMSO.

Foucault, M. (1977) 'An interview', *Radical Philosophy*, no 16, pp 10-15.

Foucault, M. (1979) *History of sexuality, vol 1*, London: Allen Lane.

Gatens, M. (1992) 'Power, bodies, difference', in M. Barrett and A. Phillips (eds) *Destabilising theory*, Cambridge: Polity Press, pp 120-38.

Golden, S. (1992) *The women outside: Meanings and myths of homelessness*, Berkeley and Los Angeles, CA: University of California Press.

Grosz, E. (1989) *Sexual perversions*, Sydney: Allen and Unwin.

Hague, G. (1999) 'Women and domestic violence policy', in S. Watson and L. Doyal (eds) *Engendering social policy*, Buckingham: Open University Press, pp 131-48.

HAS (Housing Advice Switchboard) (1989) *Annual Report*, London: HAS.

Higgs, M. and Hayward, E. (1910) *Where shall she live? The homelessness of the woman worker*, London: P.S. King and Son.

Marsh, A. and Mullins, D. (1998) *Housing and public policy: Citizenship, choice and control*, Buckingham: Open University Press.

Martin, M. (1988) 'Homeless women: an historical perspective', in R. Beard (ed) *On being homeless: Historical perspectives*, New York, NY: City Museum.

Moser, C. and Peake, L. (1987) *Women, human settlements and housing*, London: Tavistock.

Neale, J. (1997) 'Homelessness and theory reconsidered', *Housing Studies*, vol 12, no 1, pp 47-63.

Passaro, J. (1996) *The unequal homeless: Men on the streets, women in their place*, London: Routledge.

Pateman, C. (1988) *The sexual contract*, London: Polity Press.

Quennell, P.C. (1949) 'Mayhew's London', in P. Quennell (ed) *Selections from 'London labour and the London poor' by Mayhew, H.*, first published 1851, London: Griffin, Bohn & Co.

Sexty, C. (1990) *Women losing out:Access to housing in Britain today*, London: Shelter.

Sprague, J.F. (1991) *More than housing: Lifeboats for women and children*, Boston, MA: Butterworth.

Tomas, A. and Dittmar, H. (1995) 'The experience of homeless women: an exploration of housing histories and the meaning of home', *Housing Studies*, vol 10, no 4, pp 493–517.

Townsend, P. (1979) *Poverty in the United Kingdom*, London: Allen Lane.

UNDP (United Nations Development Programme) (1995) *Human development report*, New York, NY: Oxford University Press.

Watson, S, (1988) *Accommodating inequality*, Sydney: Allen and Unwin.

Watson, S. and Austerberry, H. (1986) *Housing and homelessness:A feminist perspective*, London: Routledge.

Wright, T. (1997) *Out of place: Homeless mobilisations, subcities, and contested landscapes*, Albany, NY: State University of New York Press.

SIX

Theorising homelessness and 'race'

Malcolm Harrison

Introduction

The recognition of diversity has become a hallmark of today's social sciences, with an increasing awareness of variations in identities, ethnicity, and life-styles. Faced with this variety, observers may have become more reluctant to generalise about housing options and constraints for households. Yet beyond the level of individual or small group experiences – however varied – lie longstanding patterns and mechanisms of relative inclusion and exclusion. Homelessness among black minority ethnic households reflects and illustrates these patterns. This chapter will seek to locate and appraise the diverse specificities of daily experience alongside a broader analysis of structural or institutional forces. It will also note that activists are well aware of the broad causative forces involved, and have challenged institutional practices that generate or reinforce exclusion.

We will begin by indicating the meaning attached below to the term 'homeless', and will also anchor our account by noting how very significant homelessness is for black minority ethnic communities. The chapter will then turn to the issue of causation, offering a model of exclusion which includes racialisation and other 'structural' factors, but also acknowledges diversity. Following this, some aspects of experiences for black people are explored further, emphasis being placed on choice, diversity and stereotypes. We then consider institutional roles, including agency responses. Finally, conclusions are drawn. Homelessness for minority ethnic households is very much part of a larger pattern of constraints and options. Despite the diversity of household experiences involved, stratification and racialisation remain important for that overall pattern. In a climate where images sometimes have as much impact as realities, governmental responses do not seem to recognise the full nature or extent of minority ethnic homelessness. Yet there has been a strong current of resistance and criticism from the grass roots, with a very definite awareness of shared problems and of the importance of broad socio-economic issues.

In this chapter reference will be made to 'black minority ethnic' (or 'black and minority ethnic') in order to cover a large range of groups seen as differing from the majority white populations. This follows a convention used at present within housing practice in order to simplify discussions. The terms minority ethnic or black are also used in this inclusive way from time to time below, largely in order to vary the text; for present purposes the former is not meant to refer to white minority groups. In addition, in some places in the chapter a narrower definition of 'Black' is drawn on, in line with practice in analyses of specific sets of data by ethnicity or ethnic origin.

Meanings and impact

If homelessness means the lack of a home in a reasonably full sense of that term, then our concern cannot be only for those who have no shelter. We must also consider people who suffer severe involuntary sharing and overcrowding, who lack control over their accommodation, or who are insecure or threatened. A 'home' is a dwelling that provides opportunities for independent living, serves social functions, and ideally is bound up with or facilitates productive social relationships. Consequently, people who are involuntarily dependent on refuge or hostel space, or living temporarily with friends, may be acknowledged as homeless alongside others who are without even temporary fixed abode.

There have been many definitions and typologies of homelessness, and some good analyses of causation (for an overview see Johnson et al, 1991). Yet it still remains difficult to find a reliable estimate of numbers of homeless black people, especially if we define homelessness broadly. Nonetheless, we do know that the issue is highly significant for black minority ethnic households, although inadequately acknowledged in research literature until relatively recently (see Johnson et al, 1991, pp 19 and 29). Greve refers to a "surge in homelessness among ethnic minority groups", beginning in the early 1960s, and points out their over-representation among homeless families and young single persons in London and other large urban areas (Greve, 1997, p xvi). It is the UK's capital city that has often received the most attention. Commenting on black housing needs in London, Lemos (1995, p 18), states that the "weight of evidence that black people are more likely to be homeless and to wait longer to be rehoused either permanently or temporarily is overwhelming". The phenomenon, however, is national rather than confined to London. Not surprisingly, homelessness status has become important among minority ethnic households being offered housing association accommodation (see Harrison et al, 1996, pp 74-6).

Moving beyond the broad category of black minority ethnic households, some recent commentators have focused on specific groups. Davies et al dealt with homelessness among young people from black and minority ethnic communities, indicating the seriousness of the problem (1996, p 86). Although there were deficiencies of available data, they felt that factors which had exacerbated the problem had been growing. Kemp has noted the situation of young black women, referring in his work to the experience of "treble discrimination and disadvantage" (that is, being under 25, female and black), and has also supplied some interesting figures on people sleeping rough (1997, pp 80-1, 86). Turning to ethnicity or household origin, we need to be aware of analyses of differences between minority ethnic groups. Burrows has noted that the experience of homelessness has been greatest among heads of households identifying themselves as 'Black'; almost 14% of these heads of households had experienced homelessness (1997, p 57). In contrast, the proportions of those experiencing homelessness among households with heads identifying themselves as 'Indian', 'Pakistani' or 'Bangladeshi' had apparently been below the average for the population as a whole (but we must not interpret this by adopting a simple stereotype about ethnicity). Burrows (who draws upon governmental survey data) indicates that although the overwhelming majority of people experiencing homelessness were 'White', the 'risk' of having experienced this form of social exclusion was greatest among members of the 'Black' population. A 'Black' head of household was over three times more likely to have experienced homelessness than a 'White' head of household.

A model of exclusion

Approaches to causation should take account both of 'micro' levels of household experience, constraint and choice on the one hand, and of broader patterns, practices and institutional structures on the other. Elsewhere, the present writer has proposed the notion of 'difference within difference' to signify recognition of diversity and 'agency' at 'micro' levels, within the wider frameworks created by structural forces that differentiate larger groupings across society (Harrison, 1998). Studies about minority ethnic homelessness show the importance of an understanding of both (or multiple) levels, and of the interactions between these.

Our simple model will use three starting points: structural and demographic forces; racialised practices and events; and household strategies, preferences and constraints. Demographic factors are mentioned here as part of the broad picture (alongside structural forces), and include trends in population and household formation that may have increased the pressures for overcrowding and sharing, and the needs or demands for dwellings in particular places. Allied issues are the changing tendencies for young people to leave home, and growth in numbers of households headed by single parents. Any of these factors may have important implications for homelessness, if there are shortages of affordable accommodation or other problems limiting access. Structural factors are taken to include those relatively longstanding socio-economic forces and institutional arrangements that condition circumstances and opportunities for households, and give rise to or reflect broad patterns of stratification. Although the implication here is of factors that have some continuity over time, 'structure' is not necessarily unchanging, or entirely independent of other 'variables' (such as grass-roots political activity or emergent cultural practices). Furthermore, structural factors themselves overlap and may mutually affect one another, operating sometimes in an apparently 'seamless' manner. This chapter does not attempt a systematic or ordered disaggregation of such factors (although particular factors are referred to), nor is any general set of 'rules' proposed by which to predict (in advance of specific circumstances) the expected relative impact of identifiable structural factors as against individual household strategies. Precise outcomes and impacts are likely to be contingent, to some degree, on time and place, and the room available for household manoeuvre will vary. One possibility, however, is that for many people there are presently greater risks and more precariousness at the level of individual experience than in the past, as the structural context has been changing. In Britain the organisation of welfare state services and Income Support certainly has been shifting in significant ways, while the interactions of state and markets in the employment and investment spheres have been having profound effects on people's security and opportunities (see Chapter Two for an extended discussion). It might be argued that the losers have included many people within minority ethnic communities, where employment decline has been paralleled by some reductions in available services and benefits. In any event, we should include broad labour market, social welfare and housing market factors under the institutional or structural heading, as well as matters related to class. In addition we need to note that the law and order system and allied mechanisms for dealing with social 'irregularities' may have a differential impact on communities, and direct potential consequences for homelessness. For instance, if disproportionate numbers from minority groups serve custodial sentences or are taken into care, this may have a subsequent impact on black people's relative ability to obtain adequate housing. Steele has noted that the most vulnerable black homeless young people are those leaving care, prison or mental health institutions; they tend to drift into homelessness (1997, p 4).

Homelessness may be seen as one part of a chain of experiences, being influenced by and in turn influencing other events. Visible homelessness on the streets may be thought of as the most obvious manifestation of poor conditions experienced by a wide range of households (and especially low-income ones), rather than an entirely discrete phenomenon. Any general framework for explaining homelessness has to acknowledge labour market factors and patterns, since the power to secu   ,ood dwelling is often likely to reflect incomes and employment   s. Connections between the economic and housing opportunitie: ouseholds may be mediated, muted or amplified by welfare state ir   ions, but ability to pay generally remains very significant. While fa·   ۱reakdown or some other immediate trigger might be one precip·   ; factor at a specific stage, it is the supply of and access to afforda·   ousing which remain crucial. Like other households, most homel   inority ethnic people may be keen to have permanent accommodatı٥   ;ee, for instance, Steele, 1997, p 31). Supply is affected by housing market conditions, and access by incomes, availability of capital, and the activities of housing providers. This is a situation affecting black and white households alike, although not necessarily in an even way.

For black minority ethnic households, it seems that to some extent a pattern of disadvantage in employment is matched by disadvantage in general housing conditions, although with variations between different groups and communities (for a recent account of conditions and trends see Lakey, 1997). The operation of housing markets (including the social rented sectors) has been crucial, and outcomes for minority ethnic households have included poor quality houses, shortages of appropriate dwellings, inadequate amenities, and overcrowding. Overcrowding has had immediate implications for homelessness, and has reflected the interaction of low incomes and high housing costs with demographic trends and family or cultural needs. An important Commission for Racial

Equality report on Tower Hamlets in the 1980s indicated that a main reason for homelessness there was the ejection of applicants from overcrowded households, often preceded by very long periods of severe overcrowding. Only when the situation had become "completely intolerable" did a family present itself as homeless (Commission for Racial Equality, 1988, p 25). Overcrowding levels may have decreased somewhat nationally (see Lakey, 1997, p 223), but the issue nonetheless remains important.

Burrows points out that the experience of homelessness is "profoundly related to social class" (1997, p 58), and he appears to imply that in statistical terms it is factors such as living in an urban area, being economically inactive, or living within a particular type of household – rather than ethnicity per se – which influence homelessness (p 64). His comments correctly draw attention to key forces at work, but clearly there are interactions between ethnicity and racisms on the one hand, and factors like unemployment, uneven development of local economies, or low pay on the other. In effect, labour market and housing experiences are very uneven as between ethnic groups, partly because racisms are interwoven into socio-economic and institutional arrangements in highly significant ways. This brings us to the issue of racialised practices and events.

Racialisation may permeate institutional as well as individual behaviours, and racisms persistent over time may have the weight of an established 'structural' factor with a degree of independent significance. For instance, adverse stereotypes and images of black people have been long-lived, and one view might be that these are maintained as elements within 'regimes' of racialised representation, expressed through mass media, hostile political and social movements, and other outlets. These images can align with individual prejudices and general ideas about issues like 'respectability', adding racialised notions of risk minimisation to the preconceptions of some landlords and housing intermediaries (cf Harrison, 1995, p 72). Racist ideologies and discourses may influence policies and practices. Prejudice can also be manifested in racist intimidation, violence or harassment, potentially constricting a household's choice of residential area or dwelling. Racism of this kind is thought to have direct impact in terms of agencies' under-recognition of the extent of homelessness among black people, since it is a disincentive to take-up of services and may lead to homelessness being less obvious than for white people. An anticipation of racist hostility is based on harsh reality; for instance, it has been noted that black young people leaving care may suffer racism when homeless (see Francis, 1993). None of our comments, however, should be taken to imply that racisms can be simplistically analysed in housing, and complications across the boundaries with ethnicity and nationality are likely. Drawing on work by Jeffers and Hoggett, we may acknowledge that it is hard to employ a single model of racism "that would encompass the variety of injuries that people [have] suffered", since the real world is painfully complex (see Jeffers and Hoggett, 1995, p 332). Even so, racisms do play a big part both in the practices of institutions and in the calculations of individuals.

When it comes to economic disadvantage, black minority ethnic labour market participation has been crucial, and hall-marked by negative discrimination, low pay and limited prospects. In effect, the daily operation of labour markets reflects not only class-linked stratification, but also divisions founded on racisms. This is not to deny variations linked with locality or ethnicity. Summarising on employment, within the recent Policy Studies Institute study, Modood notes employment's centrality for issues of life chances and equality, but also indicates that differences between minority groups are as important as points of commonality (1997, p 84). Nonetheless, the data show continuing adverse overall patterns which we can interpret as being related to racialisation. For instance, on unemployment, "ethnic minority young people consistently have higher rates than the white population" (p 90). Interestingly, the same study shows that perceptions that employers discriminate may have strengthened (pp 130-5).

Racisms have been significant in helping to produce the adverse housing outcomes already noted above, not only indirectly through the impact of the world of work, but also directly through the practices of providers. The record of several local authorities in allocating accommodation for minority ethnic households has been criticised (for instance, Phillips, 1986; Henderson and Karn, 1987), and responses to homelessness have often been seen as inadequate or racist. Alongside more direct negative discrimination, a lack of cultural sensitivity can be interpreted as a feature of a racialised service or response, and we add some further points on this later in the chapter.

The third element in our model is the dimension of household strategies, preferences and constraints. This is dealt with more fully below, but we need to acknowledge now that each household may have different experiences and resources, despite the significance of commonality at the broad level of racism and economic disadvantage. Even so, there may also be patterns within the broader structural framework as far as specific ethnic, age, gendered or locality-based categories are concerned. Strategies and constraints for women and men may differ, and household composition will affect available options.

To summarise, the argument here is that a good description and explanation of housing exclusion processes would require reference to labour and housing market factors, to the relative socio-economic status and resources of groups, to household and community change, to racialised practices, and to the impact of individual and group choices and constraints. As an aspect of relative exclusion from the comforts of life, homelessness generally needs to be set in the context of socio-economic disadvantages and difficulties, rooted in broad structures, yet with its details shaped through individual accident, difficulty and intent. Interactions between household diversities and structural factors (including racisms persisting over time) give rise to patterns of specific homelessness experiences. Figure 6.1 summarises key elements in these interactions.

Experiential diversity

Households vary greatly in their composition, resources, housing conditions and histories. Their preferences, experiences, actions and reactions may be discussed in relation to three key issues in particular. Firstly, there is the role of choice, resistance and 'non-participation'; secondly, the issue of diversity and culture; and thirdly, the question of stereotypes and images. We will comment on each of these in turn.

Choice, resistance and non-participation

Households act as social agents, albeit socially constrained, and vary in the extent of their choices. Individual and collective resources may be crucial when people wish to resist or offset the impact of the 'day-to-day injustices' which are so important (cf Neale, 1997, p 43). A model needs to include elements of individual strategy, resistance, and – for some at the interface with housing agencies – refusal to participate in white-led 'solutions'. Part of homeless people's potential resources may be the accommodation available through housing agencies, but cultural insensitivity and racist histories may reduce the value of what is on offer for potential users. People may be reluctant to approach agencies because of the prospect of then experiencing the impact of individual and institutional racisms. Among the young, low expectations of assistance may develop, with agencies perceived as uncoordinated, unwelcoming or lacking in sensitivity (see, for instance, O'Mahony and Ferguson, 1991,

Figure 6.1: Interactions between 'structural' factors and experiential diversity leading to minority ethnic homelessness

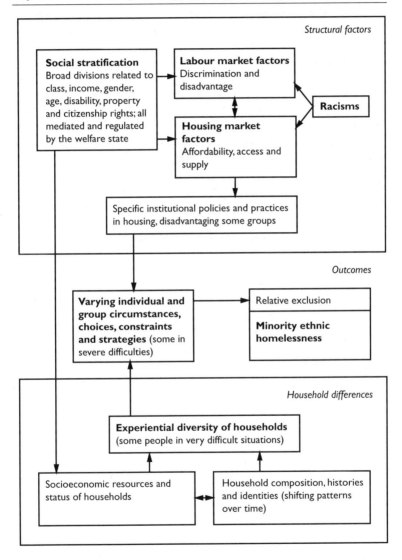

p 8; Steele, 1997, pp 5-6). It has been argued that homelessness has a greater impact on black people than on their white counterparts, because of racism and discrimination within private, public and voluntary sectors (see O'Mahony and Ferguson, 1991; Bulgin and Julienne, 1995). Minority ethnic homeless people have faced constrained choices, been denied access, experienced harassment, and been asked to meet requirements not asked of white people (such as providing passports: see Hendessi, 1987; Commission for Racial Equality, 1988, p 24). Black people's resource position when agencies 'intervene' is therefore different from the outset.

One outcome is that minority ethnic homeless people may be reluctant about approaching or remaining in white-run facilities such as hostels or refuges (see Hendessi, 1987, p 33; O'Mahony and Ferguson, 1991, p 7). They may be wary of discrimination within accommodation, of being placed in the wrong localities (Steele, 1997, p 40) (where they may feel at risk), and of police harassment. There may be reluctance to use the provision that is available for people sleeping rough, such as winter or night shelters, yet clear risks if out on the street. There may be worries about sharing, yet for young people a perception that most accommodation on offer is shared (Steele, 1997, pp 4, 40, 22). Agencies' lack of cultural awareness can be a very direct problem, as with inadequacies over dietary provision, or where there is a feeling that a council does not understand a culture and therefore underestimates the urgency of a situation. For instance, one informant in Steele's Nottingham study, criticised council delay, noting that they "don't understand the culture" and that it was "very shameful for me and my children to live in a hostel" (Steele, 1997, notes to Table 26).

Summarising, we should think in terms of important differences in the ways that homelessness is experienced (Ye-Myint, 1992, p 6; Davies et al, 1996, p 87; cf Bulgin and Julienne, 1995), perhaps reinforced by differences in use of available services, which may be under-used by minority ethnic households. There may be similar reasons for white and black households becoming homeless, but certain causative forces and subsequent adverse events may be intensified for the latter (cf Steele, 1997, p 4).

Not surprisingly, black homeless people may sometimes turn to friends rather than white-run agencies. There is also likely to be some preference for black-run hostels (Davies et al, 1996, pp 10, 88), although a shortage of these. Appropriate staffing can be crucial. This is illustrated well by an instance reported in 1997 as part of the work for an MA at Leeds University by Ali Soyei; one fieldwork respondent stated that if a hostel had not been run by 'brethren', he would not have gone there.

Racist practices have also been challenged directly in a variety of ways. Being aware both of the broader issues and of the immediate institutional barriers to effective provision, activists have sometimes sought to establish alternative forms of support outside the white-run 'mainstream'. One collective response here can be the setting up of separate agencies to meet the housing and allied needs of minority ethnic groups, and to keep the issues on the public agenda. The black voluntary housing movement has been one route for achieving these goals. Some black-run housing associations began partly as a response to homelessness, and the issues have often been stressed or highlighted in the movement's literature. The concerns have been evident, for instance, in contributions in the Federation of Black Housing Organisations' early Newsletter and in subsequent issues of *Black Housing* (December 1987, June and December 1989, March/April 1994, August 1995, February and May/June 1996, etc). Individual black-led housing associations have encouraged or sponsored initiatives, enquiries and publications, most notably the survey-based report from Ujima and Barnardo's (O'Mahony and Ferguson, 1991). This highlighted the increase of homelessness among young people, and indicated that Ujima had seen over 3,000 new applicants under 25 years old in the year ending December 1990 (p 2). There is clearly a strong awareness among activists and minority ethnic housing professionals both of the specific details and of the broader causative factors, such as shortage of affordable housing, the impact of racism, unacknowledged needs, cultural insensitivity among 'mainstream' providers, and issues of control of resources. Being on or near to the 'front line' has not led to a loss of vision about the broader questions or possible solutions.

Diversity and culture

It has become customary for scholars to acknowledge the implications of family and cultural situations differing from a supposed white 'norm', but the agenda is complex. Minority ethnic groups are themselves diverse, and differences related to ethnicity may be interwoven with the other variables of religion, age, gender and impairment. The specific character of needs or stresses may seem intensified or even unique for a group. For instance, there may be difficult problems for young Asians if they reject cultural and family traditions and become very isolated (Steele, 1997, p 4), or probems may arise when parents return to a country of origin

(O'Mahony and Ferguson, 1991, p 6). Or particular family and cultural processes may press upon some Asian women, who may be reluctant to seek help for a range of reasons (for examples, see Dibblin, 1991, pp 12-13; Steele, 1997, p 39). A woman who has left the family or matrimonial home may sometimes appear as 'an outcast' with few networks or sources of accommodation (see *Black Housing*, 1995; Steele, 1997). Steele also refers to the apparently specific problems of "young people from mixed race families" (p 39).

Despite the distinctiveness of these and other circumstances, however, there is an intersection between local or specific preferences, cultures, conflicts, life-styles, and structural factors, as we have already indicated. Consequently, while recognising the significance of ethnicity and culture, it is very important not to substitute new behaviourist stereotypes for old ones based on crude black/white distinctions, with the new ones based on assumptions about static cultural differences and notions of distinctive family issues such as Asian inter-generational or gender-based conflict. Stereotypes of this kind can lead to a blaming of 'victims' or relatives, when discussion is focused on an issue like youth homelessness. It is essential in an analysis not to be deflected by over-stating the significance of culture or ethnicity as independent causal factors. Young people from minority communities, for instance, may be vulnerable economically because of lack of opportunities to compete effectively in labour markets orientated to profits and exploitation, where job choice may be influenced by area decline and racist employment practices. This may restrict their capacity for independent living, forcing upon some a choice between a parental home with severe frictions, temporary refuge with friends, or some other precarious solution.

Culture certainly plays a part in how problems manifest themselves, and the advantages of a culturally sensitive response are clear. Single homelessness among minority groups, for instance, may be exacerbated because it is 'hidden', 'invisible' or unrecognised, partly for cultural reasons (O'Mahony and Ferguson, 1991, p 5). Perhaps cultural factors may play a part when individuals fall into precarious circumstances, become trapped, share rather than living on the streets, or find temporary solutions. Undoubtedly, culture will frame certain kinds of resources available to people, and could affect their 'bargaining power' (cf Johnson et al, 1991, pp 18-20). Yet this must not be given exaggerated significance in an analysis. Economic resources and institutional structures remain the dominant long-term determinants of eventual housing outcomes.

Women's circumstances require further mention, since they may differ from those of men (see for instance Dibblin, 1991, p 29). There will also be variations between the experiences of women from different communities and settings (for an overview on black women see Dhillon-Kashyap, 1994). Some specific differences from men have been noted in particular studies of minority ethnic homelessness. Davies et al found a difference in the accommodation cited by women and men as their last home (1996, p 24). Steele noted that men were more likely to have no fixed abode and to be staying with friends, while women were more likely to be living in other forms of temporary accommodation and living with parents (Steele, 1997, p 3). Policy responses and grass-roots initiatives have acknowledged key issues affecting some women, as in the setting up of women's refuges targeted on suppo rting people from specific communities (for some discussion of refuges see Mama, 1989). Domestic violence or abuse are clearly immediate causal factors that may affect women from many backgrounds, including young black women (Hendessi, 1987, pp 32-3; O'Mahony and Ferguson, 1991, p 6; Steele, 1997, p 20). Culturally insensitive services may have exacerbated matters (for instance, if children have been expected to interpret for third parties in a context of domestic dispute). Nonetheless, both direct racism and structural issues around low incomes and access to affordable dwellings must be kept in mind too.

Stereotypes and images

Images and stereotypes about homelessness can badly mislead. As Boulton notes, the "image of a homeless person as a middle aged white man with an alcohol dependency problem is still prevalent" (foreword by Boulton in Ye-Myint, 1992). It may be assumed in politics, government or parts of the mass media that single homelessness is about white males, and that black people have alternative sources of accommodation (cf SHIL, 1988, p 27). There has been insufficient recognition that homelessness affects women, and that single homelessness is not necessarily a primarily white phenomenon (see SHIL, 1988, p 9). The idea of hidden or invisible homelessness has already been mentioned above. It can be used by writers to emphasise that minority ethnic homeless people may be under-represented among those who come forward for official assistance, and that the extent of their problems is unacknowledged. (Parallels may be drawn with the situations that have faced some women; see Watson and Austerberry, 1986, p 18). It could be argued, however, that alternative descriptions (such as unrecognised homelessness) are preferable to the phrase hidden homelessness, if the latter terminology might be taken to justify inaction. Noting the growth and devastating effects of so-called hidden homelessness, Ye-Myint points out that in her study no one *was* hiding, but that there was a refusal to see them (Ye-Myint, 1992, pp 2, 7; cf Ford, 1997, pp 89, 104-6). The key point, however, is that homelessness images and official data may understate the significance of the issue for minority ethnic households. There are good reasons for some minority ethnic households in urgent need not joining the queue for officially-sponsored assistance alongside white people, as we indicated above. For certain groups there are additional factors, in that official responses may be obstructive, deliberately unsupportive, or threatening. Hendessi suggests that for some migrants and refugees it is a case of "out of sight – out of mind" (1987, pp 13-22). It should also be remembered that there are in any case many 'concealed' (or potentially separate) households in minority ethnic communities, given the extent of overcrowding and the difficulties of reunifying households (for instance, see Hillaac, 1995). Furthermore, the politics of under-recognition may be significant not just because of misleading images, but also insofar as voice and visibility may be positively interrelated.

When minority ethnic homelessness *is* recognised, further myths come into play. For instance, reference may be made to 'misfits', or to drug and alcohol dependency (for the actual situation see Davies et al, 1996, p 9). In reality low income may be a far more salient factor, allied with such immediate matters as private landlords' prejudices and requirements (or adverse reactions to people on Income Support), against a backcloth of shifts in benefits and local housing supply conditions (see, for instance, Hendessi, 1987; Steele, 1997, pp 24-5). Some young homeless people may actually be studying at colleges (Steele, 1997, pp 2 and 14). Indeed, Davies et al's report noted that young black single homeless people tended to be more optimistic about their futures than did young white people (1996, p 39). The former might be determined not to be seen as having hit 'rock bottom', more commonly reported themselves as physically and mentally well than did white respondents, and were less likely to have seen a mental health professional. They appeared to have had greater self-esteem (see pp 33, 38, and 87). Mistaken assumptions may also be made about ethnicity or gender, with possible consequences for agency responses. Contrary to prevailing images, homelessness definitely does affect some young Asian people (Steele, 1997), including young women.

Institutional frameworks, behaviour and responses

Institutional characteristics and practices can be viewed as a set of structural factors, with both negative and positive aspects. On the one hand there has been a record of racism at various levels within governmental and other housing suppliers, but on the other some attempts to respond to the problems of black homeless people. In specific terms the legislation itself frames and constrains what support can be offered for those in crisis, and limits the targeted categories. Rather than addressing affordable housing supply in a serious way, national homelessness policy has placed more weight on a traditional welfarist approach of selective aid linked to personal disaster or demonstrable failure to obtain decent accommodation, qualified by notions of who is 'deserving' in terms of intentionality and local connections. The official test of success in this context has had to be the degree to which the most deserving and needy are reached by safety-net services, instead of the extent to which homelessness is prevented from arising in the first place. Some minority ethnic households have been reached by safety-nets, while others have not. The 1977/85 system apparently catered positively for people escaping racial abuse, as an aspect of the special reasons which might make people 'vulnerable' (see Pleace et al, 1997, pp 3-4), but immigration and asylum issues provided bases for some far less positive official standpoints during the Conservative periods of office. An influential theme was that people might come to the UK and become dependent on public funds or services, yet might be seen as relatively undeserving because of national origins. Rules on eligibility have not only affected asylum seekers, but also families seeking to re-unify (see Johnson et al, 1991, p 19). On the latter, cases in Tower Hamlets have become well-known. Moore et al, for instance, refer to the "cause célèbre" concerning the declaration of families as intentionally homeless because they had left their UK homes to bring their families from Bangladesh (1995, pp 24-5; for separated families see also Commission for Racial Equality, 1988).

At local level, housing agencies have had a degree of discretionary power, in strategy and in implementation via gatekeepers. General criticisms of responses to homelessness have included arguments about agencies themselves maintaining homelessness, and about issues of deterrence, discipline and denial limiting recognition (see Carlen, 1994). Homeless people may feel that they are stigmatised as "defective citizens" (Steele, 1997, p 42). At their most damaging, practices have been evidently discriminatory (see Commission for Racial Equality, 1988). Individual experiences of adverse treatment need to be understood against the general background of rationing problems in local authority housing (Lidstone, 1994), the lack of provision of appropriately-sized units, the lack of staff with useful language skills, the importance and interpretation of intentionality, and the use of criteria such as prioritising of rehousing applications from sons and daughters of existing tenants.

When it comes to proactive responses to homelessness itself, there still seems to have been a rather muted response from local agencies in the 1980s, provoking accusations of a 'half-hearted approach' to monitoring (see SHIL, 1988, p 27). Nonetheless, there was at that time some support for community groups, specific targeted projects, and so forth (pp 21-4), and this has continued. In recent years, obvious negative discrimination in housing agency practices may have become harder to find, as minority ethnic needs have become more recognised. In some instances, prioritising of homelessness cases by local authorities might even appear to have worked to the advantage of minority ethnic housing applicants (who thereby might be apparently over-represented), although the quality of accommodation offered has remained a problem (Jeffers and Hoggett, 1995, pp 326-7). Even so, cultural insensitivity and inadequate recognition have remained key issues. Ye-Myint's study of non-priority homeless people indicates a refusal of policy makers, agencies, or funders to recognise the scale of problems faced by black and minority ethnic communities (1992, p 2), with the Rough Sleepers Initiative not benefiting them sufficiently (p 4). In general we can suggest that although increased cultural sensitivity has become more recognised as a key to positive change, this is hard to achieve without greater resources. Severe funding problems may arise with ad hoc initiatives, which can end up being "stifled because of lack of resources" (SHIL, 1988, p 26). Making mainstream services more sensitive remains difficult, although provision of better information can be relatively inexpensive, and tactics such as employing more outreach or support workers with appropriate language skills could help. Capital expenditure remains a difficult issue, in terms of quantity and destination. There is no guarantee that new high-profile initiatives will reach minority ethnic clients (for instance, for foyers see Quilgars and Anderson, 1997, p 223).

On the cultural dimension a word of caution is also needed. While cultural competence is now seen to be necessary in public services, the local management of ethnic differentiation cannot be a substitute for tackling racism or economic disadvantage (cf Harrison and Law, 1997, pp 293-4). There has been a danger of this happening through the emphasis on culture and ethnicity. Mama has referred critically to the "culturalization of race", and indicated that the power of funding can ensure the "reproduction of a particular racial politic". Perhaps it has sometimes become politically easier to promote specific communities' cultural preferences selectively (as 'special needs') than it has been to pursue equal opportunities and improved general services (see Mama, 1989, p 43). There clearly could be difficult tasks for agencies in balancing cultural sensitivity with continuing recognition of broader issues and needs.

Conclusions

Homelessness for minority ethnic households is part of something much larger, and is not a fixed state into which a statistically-calculable group has fallen. There are degrees of severity of the experience, which is itself very varied and influenced by personal events, but it must be understood as part of a broader pattern of housing constraints and options. Becoming homeless is more likely to arise from a series of events and surrounding circumstances than simply from one precipitating factor on its own. Changes in the welfare state have increased the fragmentation and precariousness of urban life, while uneven economic development has meant that people's strategies must operate in localities with very varying employment prospects and market conditions. Household experiences have been much affected by the shifting context, especially insofar as the level of risk associated with many choices is perceived to have increased. The processes of economic and institutional change have had complex relationships with ethnic differentiation, but on the whole minority ethnic households do not seem to have found their opportunities and resources substantially improved in relative terms by the national economic and welfare strategies of the 1980s and 1990s.

The adverse outcomes experienced by black minority ethnic households have not really been recognised fully by governments; nor have the forces of causation been acknowledged adequately. The way issues have been perceived and discussed has often been in danger of reflecting neither data nor experience, but images, as part of a racialised regime of representation and stereotyping. Perhaps this regime – although we must not be too deterministic – might have been at its strongest when ethnicity has been interlocked with issues of immigration or asylum. Certainly, though, racisms have helped structure debates, official responses and senses of priority and urgency nationally and locally. Neither governmental outlooks nor media representations of 'race', however, are unchanging (for the latter see Law et al, 1997). On their part, many housing activists have fought to set the record straight, and to keep the issue of the control of housing resources by black minority ethnic people themselves at the heart of the policy debate. They have understood the importance of the goal of a good supply of affordable and accessible dwellings, and the role of minority ethnic management in providing culturally sensitive facilities. The successes and official recognition of the black voluntary housing movement are testimony to the determination of activists to keep the key issues in view.

We will end with an old-fashioned and perhaps unfashionable conclusion. An analysis of social stratification remains crucial to understanding processes and patterns of relative exclusion, and homelessness should not be analysed as if it were separate from this. Racisms are not necessarily independent of institutional behaviour, stratification and economic power, but nonetheless have had a range of semi-independent effects in housing arenas. There is so much continuity in this that racisms need to be dealt with as part of the major structural forces that shape outcomes as well as being influential for grass-roots behaviour. The experiences, cultures and strategies of households are extremely important, but individuals and groups do not always operate on grounds of their own choosing. Although this chapter has developed an account that is specific to minority ethnic groups in particular, the kind of explanatory 'model' outlined here has, perhaps, wider applicability. Homelessness – despite the potential importance of immediate local 'triggers' such as intergenerational conflict – is the rather large tip of an iceberg of disadvantage, best understood in terms of patterns of relative or differential inclusion and exclusion, within a welfare state that regulates opportunities and itself contributes to the production and reproduction of social divisions.

References

Black Housing (1995) 'Project profile: Sahara, an oasis for black women fleeing domestic violence and oppression', *Black Housing*, vol 11, no 3, August, p 13.

Bulgin, S. and Julienne, L. (1995) 'Black people and homelessness', *Black Housing*, vol 11, no 3, August, pp 8-10.

Burrows, R. (1997) 'The social distribution of the experience of homelessness', in R. Burrows, N. Pleace and D. Quilgars (eds) *Homelessness and social policy*, London: Routledge, pp 50-68.

Carlen, P. (1994), 'The governance of homelessness: legality, lore and lexicon in the agency-maintenance of youth homelessness', *Critical Social Policy*, Issue 41, vol 14, no 2, pp 18-35.

Commission for Racial Equality (1988) *Homelessness and discrimination*, London: Commission for Racial Equality.

Davies, J. and Lyle, S. with Deacon, A., Law, I., Julienne, L. and Kay, H. (1996) *Discounted voices: Homelessness amongst young black and minority ethnic people in England*, Sociology and Social Policy Research Working Paper 15, Leeds: University of Leeds.

Dhillon-Kashyap, P. (1994) 'Black women and housing', in R. Gilroy and R. Woods (eds) *Housing women*, London, Routledge, pp 101-26.

Dibblin, J. (1991) *Wherever I lay my hat: Young women and homelessness*, London: Shelter.

Ford, J. (1997) 'Mortgage arrears, mortgage possessions and homelessness', in R. Burrows, N. Pleace and D. Quilgars (eds) *Homelessness and social policy*, London: Routledge, pp 88-108.

Francis, J. (1993) 'Hide and seek', *Community Care*, no 994, 25 November, pp 18-19.

Greve, J. (1997) 'Preface: homelessness then and now', in R. Burrows, N. Pleace and D. Quilgars (eds) *Homelessness and social policy*, London: Routledge, pp xi-xvii.

Harrison, M. (1995) *Housing, 'race', social policy and empowerment*, Aldershot: Avebury.

Harrison, M. (1998) 'Theorising exclusion and difference: specificity, structure and minority ethnic housing issues', *Housing Studies*, vol 13, no 6, pp 793-806.

Harrison, M. and Law, I. (1997) 'Needs and empowerment in minority ethnic housing: some issues of definition and local strategy', *Policy & Politics*, vol 25, no 3, pp 285-98.

Harrison, M., Karmani, A., Law, I., Phillips, D. and Ravetz, A. (1996) *Black and minority ethnic housing associations: An evaluation of The Housing Corporation's black and minority ethnic housing association strategies*, Source 16, London: The Housing Corporation.

Henderson, J. and Karn, V. (1987) *Race, class and state housing: Inequality and the allocation of public housing in Britain*, Aldershot: Gower.

Hendessi, M (1987) *Migrants – the invisible homeless: A report on migrants' housing needs and circumstances in London*, London: Migrant Services Unit, London Voluntary Services Council.

Hillaac (1995) *Somali housing needs in Sheffield*, Sheffield: Hillaac Housing Association with Community Operational Research Unit, North Sheffield Housing Association Ltd and Sheffield City Council.

Jeffers, S. and Hoggett, P. (1995) 'Like counting deckchairs on the Titanic: a study of institutional racism and housing allocations in Haringey and Lambeth', *Housing Studies*, vol 10, no 3, pp 325-44.

Johnson, B., Murie, A., Naumann, L. and Yanetta, A. (1991) *A typology of homelessness*, Discussion Paper 3, Edinburgh: Scottish Homes.

Kemp, P. (1997) 'The characteristics of single homeless people in England', in R. Burrows, N. Pleace and D. Quilgars (eds) *Homelessness and social policy*, London: Routledge, pp 69-87.

Lakey, J. (1997) 'Neighbourhoods and housing', in T. Modood, R. Berthoud, J. Lakey, J. Nazroo, P. Smith, S. Virdee, and S. Beishon, *Ethnic minorities in Britain: Diversity and disadvantage*, London: Policy Studies Institute, pp 184-223.

Law, I. with Svennevig, M. and Morrison, D. (1997) *Privilege and silence: 'Race' in the British news during the General Election campaign*, Leeds: 'Race' and Public Policy Research Unit, University of Leeds.

Lemos, G. (1995) *Communities within communities*, London: NFHA.

Lidstone, P. (1994) 'Rationing housing to the homeless applicant', *Housing Studies*, vol 9, no 4, pp 459-72.

Mama, A. (1989) 'Violence against black women: gender, race and state responses', *Feminist Review*, no 32, Summer, pp 30-48.

Modood, T. (1997) 'Employment', in T. Modood, R. Berthoud, J. Lakey, J. Nazroo, P. Smith, S. Virdee and S. Beishon, *Ethnic minorities in Britain: Diversity and disadvantage*, London: Policy Studies Institute, pp 83–149.

Moore, J., Canter, D., Stockley, D. and Drake, M. (1995) *The faces of homelessness in London*, Aldershot: Dartmouth.

Neale, J. (1997) 'Theorising homelessness: contemporary sociological and feminist perspectives', in R. Burrows, N. Pleace and D. Quilgars (eds) *Homelessness and social policy*, London: Routledge, pp 35–49.

O'Mahony, B. and Ferguson, D. (1991) *Young, black and homeless in London: The reality behind the myth*, London: Ujima Housing Association and Barnardo's.

Phillips, D. (1986) *What price equality?*, GLC Housing Research and Policy Report 9, London: Greater London Council.

Pleace, N., Burrows, R. and Quilgars, D. (1997) 'Homelessness in contemporary Britain: conceptualisation and measurement', in R. Burrows, N. Pleace and D. Quilgars (eds) *Homelessness and social policy*, London: Routledge, pp 1–18.

Quilgars, D. and Anderson, I. (1997) 'Addressing the problem of youth homelessness and unemployment: the contribution of foyers', in R Burrows, N. Pleace and D. Quilgars (eds) *Homelessness and social policy*, London: Routledge, pp 216–28.

SHIL (Single Homelessness in London) Anti-Racist Sub-Group (1988) *Single homelessness among black and other ethnic minorities: Local authority policy and practice*, London: SHIL.

Steele, A. (1997) *Young, drifting and black*, Nottingham: Homeless Support Centre, Nottingham City Council.

Watson, S. and Austerberry, H. (1986) *Housing and homelessness: A feminist perspective*, London: Routledge.

Ye-Myint, C. (1992) *Who's hiding ?*, London: No Fixed Abode.

SEVEN

The criminalisation of homelessness, begging and street living

Gary Fooks and Christina Pantazis

Introduction

The concept of risk has long since developed from an abstraction solely concerned with attempting to predict the consequences of modern society to one which is now used to articulate them (Douglas, 1992). This is no less true in the context of studies on homelessness where the concept of risk generally finds its expression in two related but ultimately distinct ways. The first sense concerns the risk of becoming homeless such as when we are told that the young are more at risk of homelessness than the old, that in England as a whole the risk of experiencing homelessness over the last 10 years is about 4.3% and that a black head of household is over three times more at risk from experiencing homelessness than a white head of household. The second concerns the risks inherent in and attendant on homelessness; exemplified in the finding that single homeless persons are at greater risk of poor health than the general population (see, for example, Bines, 1994; Burrows, 1997; Kemp, 1997; Pleace and Quilgars, 1997).

Risk, although rarely explicitly, is therefore an important and much used medium of ostensible explanation and articulation in the discussion of homelessness. What is more significant in the context of this discussion, however, is not the pervasive use of risk, but rather how the use of risk converges to at once produce and reinforce the status of the homeless population as a population of victims. More specifically, the homeless are primarily presented as suffering in two principal ways – first as a simple result of being homeless and then again for experiencing the problems that are attendant on homelessness, such as malnutrition and premature death (Keys and Kennedy, 1992; Grenier, 1996). This depiction of homeless people as victims, although predominant, is not, however, complete, but rather is subject to one important exception, namely those narratives that relate to homelessness and crime.

When this dimension of homelessness is typically represented the relationship between homelessness and the risk of victimisation is inverted (see, for example, Baron and Hartnagel, 1998; McCarthy and Hagan, 1991; Rothman, 1991). The homeless person as a victim, in other words, tends to disappear and instead the emphasis is placed on the risk to the 'respectable' public of criminal victimisation from the homeless. This is not to say that the depiction of the relationship between the homeless and criminal victimisation is monolithic. There are some notable exceptions. Not only are the homeless sometimes portrayed as the victims of crime by the 'respectable' and homeless population alike, but also as the architects of crimes against other homeless people (see, for example, Carlen, 1996; Spurling, 1998). Nevertheless, the most widely reproduced image of homelessness and crime, especially in the news media, not only involves the depiction of the homeless person as an architect, rather than an object, of crime but, more significantly, as a victimiser, and not a victim, of the 'respectable' population.

What this chapter aims to explore is some of the implications for this dual use of risk on policing strategies of the homeless. The discussion looks at Charing Cross Homeless Unit – a dedicated unit of police officers which is gradually finding itself being approved as a model of good practice for the future of homeless policing. It contains a number of interviews with police officers at the Unit, including the Operational Head, and an Inspector from a neighbouring police Division. It also incorporates some of the findings of ongoing fieldwork involving the observation of policing practice on the streets. Specifically, the authors observed the work of two of the Unit's officers policing the Division on foot. And finally, it also includes a discussion based on interviews which were undertaken with a sample of voluntary organisations, working with and on behalf of homeless people, who had contact with the Charing Cross Homeless Unit.

The homeless population: crime, victimisation and the meaning of homelessness

The various ways in which the concept of risk manifests itself in the discussion of homelessness is ultimately an expression of different aspects of the meaning of homelessness[1]. As with all terms, homelessness has a multiplicity of potential meaning, dependent, in part, on the context in which it is used in the present and, in part, on the contexts in which it has been used in the past (Volosinov, 1929 [reprinted 1986]). Yet, homelessness seems to be a particularly complex term, made up of diverse and conflicting elements. This is in part due to the flexible nature of its definition (Widdowfield, 1998). This chapter uses the term homeless to refer strictly to those sleeping rough[2] because of the priority given to rough sleepers by the police in our study, but even among the officers we studied different definitions seem to be in use in different contexts[3]. Problems of definition deepen when one begins to consider popular euphemisms for homeless people such as beggars. Contrary to popular belief not all homeless people beg (Anderson et al, 1993). Likewise, not all people who beg are homeless (Management Information Unit, 1997). Moreover, homelessness needs to be distinguished from 'street living' as this may also involve those people who actually have accommodation but whose daytime activities (eg, drinking, sleeping) are largely spent on the streets. While the considerable number of competing definitions of homelessness partially explains the complexity of the term, it is, in fact, beyond the definition of the term (in the context of representations of the relationship between homelessness and social order) that the true diversity of meaning of homelessness becomes apparent. More importantly, when the meaning of homelessness in this context is examined, a number of productive lines of enquiry into understanding the policing of the homeless and explaining the relative success of competing strategies of policing the homeless are opened up.

The deserving and undeserving homeless: victim or criminal?

As we have already observed, homelessness has become intimately bound up with the concept of the victim. The attendant rise in structural explanations of homelessness in which, for example, shortages in the housing supply have been emphasised at the expense of individualised explanations focusing on personal failure and inadequacy has, however, meant that it is not simply as victims that the homeless have come to be conceived but, more significantly, as victims of circumstance (Drake et al, 1982; Carlen, 1996, p 27; Pleace et al, 1997, p 2). It is important, however, not to overstate the significance of this association[4]. Beyond academia explanations of homelessness that stress individual pathology, and emphasise homeless people as problems as opposed to having problems, compete far more vigorously with structural theories for acceptance. In particular, the depiction of the criminal homeless, in contrast to the criminally victimised homeless, has become deeply etched into the lexicon of journalists, police and politicians. This is of interest for two related but ultimately separate reasons.

In the first instance, it appears to misrepresent the true position – especially in the context of people who beg. Evidence in respect of aggressive begging, for instance, suggests that someone who begs is twice as likely to be verbally abused or kicked than to beg aggressively (Moore et al, 1995, p 221)[5]. Thus, homeless people are primarily depicted as criminals, as opposed to victims of crime, even when it seems that they are more likely to fall victim to crime than to commit it. However, it is not the accuracy of the depiction that is most striking, but rather the fact that it has such resonance in the first place. How do the homeless population come to be represented as criminal – a label of censure aimed at securing mass intolerance – when the predominant image of the homeless emphasises their status as victims that by contrast invites empathy and, therefore, tolerance?

The answer, in part it seems, is that the homeless, *qua* homeless, are not directly represented as criminal. Instead, the criminal homeless are described as beggars, aggressive beggars or squatters – negative signifiers with deep historical roots (see, for example, Chambliss, 1969; Stedman Jones, 1971). The importance of these signifiers is that they draw attention away from the material circumstances of the homeless, the source of their suffering, and direct it onto the threat that the homeless, and the forms of behaviour they are associated with, present to the social order[6]. The effect, in other words, is to produce a 'debate closure' in which only certain dimensions of homelessness are discussed. While the importance of negative signifiers to setting the terms of debates must not be underestimated, their use has clearly not eliminated the underlying tension that exists between both competing narratives. The following political exchanges around homelessness in the mid-1990s illustrate this perfectly.

The mismanagement of vilification

In 1994 the Prime Minister, John Major, claimed that the "sight of beggars was an eyesore which could drive tourists and shoppers away from cities", that begging was "offensive" and "unnecessary" (Major cited in Watson, 1994) and that rough sleeping was simply another life-style choice[7].

Significantly, Major's attempt to intervene in the debate over the popular causes of homelessness – by emphasising choice and, therefore, blaming the homeless for their situation – was largely unsuccessful, prompting the weak Tory administration of the mid-1990s to search for new objects of vilification around which middle-England could unite. Other strains of homelessness had been singled out before, demonised in political debate and the news media and censured in legislation – like the squatters and hippy convoys in the 1994 Criminal Justice and Public Order Act, and asylum seekers in the 1996 Asylum and Immigration Act (see Cowan, 1997). Others, like single mothers, were to follow (see Cook, 1997). On this occasion, however, the homeless as an undifferentiated mass seemed resistant to a sustained attack culminating in legislation[8].

This response to a deliberate attempt to mobilise support against rough sleepers affords a valuable insight into the meaning of homelessness. It is not that the homeless are wholly insulated from political assault, but more that they are not a group that can be unambiguously attacked or censured. This is precisely because the image of homeless as victims of circumstance has become such a resonant theme within discourses of homelessness that it has come to form part of what it means to be a homeless person and, therefore, part of the meaning of homelessness. As Tony Blair, then leader of the opposition, said in response to Major's comments, there was "an element of those people out on the streets who are homeless and destitute for reasons that are tragic rather than reasons they have caused themselves" (Blair cited in Travis and Meikle, 1997). The impact of this association between homelessness and the concept of the victim of circumstance on party political dialogue has been uneven. One of its effects has been to enable the homeless as an undifferentiated mass, but only as an undifferentiated mass, to be presented as some of the most vulnerable, blameless and deserving of the poor. Jack Straw, for instance, accused Major of climbing "into the gutter alongside the unfortunate beggars themselves", adding that it was "outrageous" that he should "attack the victims of his party's policies over the past fifteen years" (Straw cited in Howarth, 1995). Another effect, encountered to some extent by Major, is also illustrated by the fact that Tony Blair was, in essence, forced to issue a retraction in *The Guardian* after having stated that it was "right to be intolerant of people homeless on the street" (Blair cited in Travis and Meikle, 1997)[9]. In short, the overarching effect of this association appears to be that, in certain contexts, homelessness is resistant to attempts by politicians from imposing their meaning, and therefore their preferred solutions, on the problem.

Blair's comments are important for the simple reason that they tend to suggest that the political lexicon of the Labour Party at once embraces the image of the homeless as victims and victimisers. In fact, it appears that government policy explicitly moves forward on this basis; revolving around a view of the homeless as, on the one hand, people who need to be cared for and protected while, on the other, controlled because the behaviour they are associated with is perceived as antagonistic and threatening to the rest of society. This is illustrated in the *Report on rough sleeping* by the Social Exclusion Unit. In the foreword to the report, Tony Blair, now as Prime Minister, wrote that rough sleeping "is a source of shame for all of us" and that its elimination was necessary for the welfare of rough sleepers. To this effect, he claimed that there were "good reasons for aiming to end rough sleeping. It is bad for those who do it, as they are intensely vulnerable to crime, drugs and alcohol, and at high risk of serious illness, and premature death." In the same context, however, he added that "rough sleeping is bad for the rest of society", explaining that "[m]any people feel intimidated by rough sleepers, beggars and street drinkers, and rough sleeping can blight areas and damage business and tourism" (Social Exclusion Unit, 1998, p 7).

This tension is crucial to understanding not only government policy, but also some of the current trends in homeless policing which are beginning to receive political approval. The following discussion examines the tension between the care and control of homeless people by focusing primarily on the Charing Cross Homeless Unit. One of the aims of this discussion is to illustrate how the effectiveness and legitimacy of particular methods of policing depend upon the way in which this tension is incorporated into the strategies, procedures and working practices of the police. What our examination of the Homeless Unit suggests is that the effectiveness, and sustained legitimacy of, intensive policing strategies of the homeless depend on two broad characteristics. First, a real commitment to a truly multiagency approach and, second, the imposition of a highly structured and legalistic approach to policing that overtly eschews the social disciplinary forms of policing that are commonly practised in relation to the homeless population (see, for example, Choongh, 1998).

The Charing Cross Homeless Unit

The Charing Cross Homeless Unit was established in the early 1990s, and is currently one of only two such units in the country[10]. Located in the heart of central London, it deals with more homeless people than any other police Division in the United Kingdom (Police 1). It comprises six officers and has four major objectives: first, to deal with crime committed by and against the homeless; second, to deal with rough sleepers who are vulnerable because of their age or physical or mental health; third, to refer rough sleepers to agencies who can provide them with support with a view to finding them accommodation; and fourth, to liaise with and meet outside agencies and charities who deal with the homeless. The size of the Unit and the fact that there is only one other like it in the United Kingdom belies its potential significance. Already, the work of the Unit has begun to attract close attention from beyond the geographical boundaries of the Division. Not only have other police forces within the United Kingdom expressed an interest in adopting some of the methods of the Unit (Police 1), but the various task forces established by government to address rough sleeping in particular, and social exclusion in general, also seem to have been impressed by the Unit's work. This has even extended to the Unit's current operational head receiving an invitation to serve on the Social Exclusion Unit.

The origins of the Unit stretch back to the late 1980s – a period during which, according to the police, a gang of young homeless men in central London were "prey[ing] on the weaker, more vulnerable sections of the homeless community" by extorting money, food, clothing, drugs and other valuables – colloquially known as "taxing" (Police 1). In conjunction with local authorities, the private and voluntary sectors approached the police to explore ways of resolving the "taxing" problem (Police 1). Operation Burlington, the collaborative operation that emerged from these discussions, resulted in the successful conviction of the gang, and the eventual demise of "taxing" (Police 1).

The success of Operation Burlington served to guarantee the police's commitment to the new set of relationships and alliances that had been forged during the Operation. Such a valuable and effective set of relationships could not, it seems, be squandered (Police 1). Not only had Operation Burlington enabled the police to protect a new, vulnerable generation of young homeless people who were moving into and through London, but, just as importantly, it had also helped the police to penetrate what was regarded as an uncooperative alliance between the voluntary sector and homeless population; a group identified within police culture in general, and the Division in particular, as a notable source of social disorder and crime (Management Information Unit, 1997; Choongh, 1998, p 627).

While the trust between the police and other agencies was fragile at first, the police soon began accepting invitations to "the various meetings, consultative meetings, that dealt purely and simply with the homeless and homeless issues" – their involvement growing from being initial passive observers to eventual active participants (Police 1). This continued support for a multiagency approach – reflecting a general trend within policy (Bennett, 1994; Stephens and Becker, 1994) – was not wholly unqualified. It did, however, eventually lead to the Unit being established on a permanent basis and also fed into real changes in the practice of policing the homeless in the Charing Cross area.

Among other things these changes involved a conscious effort to empathise with the aims of the voluntary sector and a newly found respect for the restrictions under which they operated. The officers working within the Unit, for instance, acknowledged that the voluntary sector could not be regarded simply as a source of information for the police – a view, it seems, that contradicted the prevailing occupational ethos of the police at the time. As one police officer explained:

"... we realised that some of the things that we demanded, or felt that we could demand from the public couldn't be given, because they had a responsibility of confidentiality to their clients. And they also felt if they were dealing with their clients on the street where the crime happened, then that wouldn't necessarily be to do with them, their business. And police had difficulty understanding this." (Police 1)

The Unit's support for closer cooperation with voluntary sector organisations also involved an attempt to modify and extend policing practice to assist those organisations wherever possible. As one police officer put it "we began to identify tasks that we could perform for the voluntary agencies which made their life easier" (Police 1), such as ensuring that homeless people with mental health needs are sectioned with appropriate sensitivity and tracing homeless people whom the voluntary sector have lost track of (Police 1; Voluntary 2).

Significantly, this strategy of facilitating the day-to-day work, as well as the medium and long-term objectives, of the voluntary agencies has also involved a more flexible approach to core policing functions. An important example of this includes the practice of suspending the execution of arrest warrants for minor offences like begging or drunkenness at the request of voluntary organisations where an arrest would undermine the process of finding accommodation for the arrestee (Police 1). This adaptation of conventional policing procedures, in exceptional circumstances, produces clear benefits to the voluntary sector; preventing months of hard work in securing accommodation for the homeless person from being delayed and possibly frustrated (Voluntary 2).

More significant, however, is its value to the police. This is not simply because it encourages good relations between the two but it also avoids the danger, inherent in conventional policing methods, of policing practice actually exacerbating, rather than ameliorating, the homeless problem in the Division, thereby taking scarce resources away from other policing functions. As one police officer commented:

> "... the police had operated a system whereby many of the sort of itinerant groups that were on the street, they had a revolving door policy, they'd arrest them for minor offences, four hours in the cells, they'd come out again. Nothing was being achieved by this, it was a drain on police resources, it wasn't cost-effective, and sometimes it could actually have a detrimental effect on the rehabilitation of the person who they'd bring in from the street, if some of the outreach was working for them." (Police 1)

This last quote, emphasising the priority of reduction, is particularly significant. As will become apparent below, reduction is not simply a strategy of the Homeless Unit, but a central one. More to the point, how reduction is realised and articulated is central to preserving working relationships with the voluntary sector, and therefore to the continued legitimacy (and continuation) of intensive methods of policing.

The Unit, the reduction of rough sleeping and 'zero-tolerance'

Although reduction is just one of four of the Unit's objectives, it tends to be represented as the paramount objective of the Unit. In fact, at one level it seems possible to explain the origins and continuing operation of the Unit solely in terms of it being an effective strategy for reducing rough sleeping in the Charing Cross Division. Conventional policing practices, as we have seen, are redesigned so as not to impede the reduction of homelessness. Similarly, interagency cooperation, the Unit's fourth objective, is, in part, designed to facilitate the process of referring rough sleepers to agencies who can help them to find accommodation, the Unit's third objective. The precise extent to which all the Unit's stated aims are subsumed within and dictated by the objective of reduction is, however, unclear. One police officer gave an indication that facilitating reduction of rough sleeping was the primary goal of the Unit, explaining it as the sole reason for interagency cooperation:

> **"Well our remit is to try and reduce homelessness. Now you can't reduce homelessness by a revolving door system.... The only way to reduce homelessness is through a joint effort, whereby we work with the agencies in order to try to achieve a successful outcome." (Police 1)**

The Unit's emphasis on reduction was also used to place its operation beyond the traditional goals of policing in the context of a broader movement to eradicate homelessness. As one police officer explained, "in the long term, our aim is the same as the voluntary agencies and the same, if you like, as the Social Exclusion Unit – to eradicate homelessness" (Police 1). Notwithstanding the multiple objectives of the Unit, in other words, the reduction of homelessness seems to find itself singled out and promoted as the overarching objective. Nonetheless, it is important not to conceptualise the imperative of reduction as an end in its own right. On the contrary, reduction is not pursued as an end in itself any more than it is pursued as part of a broader movement to eradicate homelessness. Instead, it is better to understand reduction as part of a wider policing strategy through which the problems posed by a large homeless population can be minimised in a politically acceptable way.

There is nothing particularly surprising about this. The Unit is staffed by police officers. Moreover, the Unit's stated aims include the need to deal with crimes committed by and against the homeless. What is interesting, however, is that the Unit's representation of the importance it attaches to reduction suggests that the imperative of crime control is, to a large extent, subordinate to it. Whether this is deliberate or an inadvertent effect of how the Unit presents itself is unclear. What is clear, however, is that the politics and techniques of reduction seem to be central to understanding the significance of the Unit. More specifically, the form that reduction takes and how this is understood is central to explaining how a group of officers, dedicated to policing the homeless, is able to at once command the support of the voluntary sector and avoid being characterised as a medium of urban cleansing. How do the police negotiate the consent of key parts of the community when the polarised image of homelessness (as a simultaneous source of victimisation and crime) makes their demonisation, and therefore control, so problematic? To begin to understand this it is first necessary to understand the particular problems that reduction poses for conventional styles of policing.

Promoting the reduction of rough sleeping above all other considerations is uniquely problematic for the police in general who represent a far clearer articulation of state power than, for example, the welfarist proposals of the Social Exclusion Unit. An undue emphasis on reduction might expose them to criticisms of harassment or, worse still, pursuing a deliberate policy of clearing the streets. The danger of this has been recognised by the police themselves who have realised the serious implications of police-led forms of reduction in the context of the association[11] between homelessness and social victimisation; expressing concerns over being associated with a generalised clamp-down on the homeless. According to the Community Affairs Editor of *The Guardian*, for example, a Home Office review of the vagrancy laws "prompted fierce opposition" from the police because it proposed a "lock them up and hose them down" solution to a "social problem" (Meikle, 1995). Thus, despite occasional experiments with street clearing on a localised basis, at a policy level at least, the police seem to understand the dangers that reduction poses for police legitimacy – an integral part of contemporary policing that constantly needs to be generated and regenerated through the media of police practice and its representation.

At a more local level, however, the position the police take over the reduction of rough sleeping is more ambiguous. No Metropolitan Division, it appears, formally acknowledges that its officers have followed a strategy aimed at eliminating rough sleeping in a locality through conventional policing methods. This is true of both the Homeless Unit and also, it seems, of other Divisions in the Metropolitan District including, significantly, those Divisions that have experimented with 'zero-tolerance' policing. This is surprising considering that, as a result of its association with policing in New York under William Bratton, the label of 'zero-tolerance' has, among other things, become a code for a clamp-down on street life and, therefore, the visible homeless (see Brogden and Nijhar, 1997).

This apparent disjunction is more readily understood when one considers that those Divisions in the Metropolitan District which have tried 'zero-tolerance' seem at first to have invited comparisons with New York, only to later deny the strict relevance of the label or to contest its meaning. The best examples of this have occurred in the context of Operation Welwyn and, the less ambiguously entitled, Operation Zero-Tolerance which both took place in the King's Cross area of London.

The comments of the local police commander who oversaw Operation Zero-Tolerance give a particularly clear insight into the police's ambivalent relationship with 'zero-tolerance'. He at once conceded that the label was a mistake because of its associations with 'zero-tolerance' policing in New York, but also that it was a powerful soundbite which drew attention to what the police were actually trying to do even though, he claimed, that, unlike New York, the consent of local groups and elected representatives had been secured (Superintendent David Smith cited in Rose, 1997). Significantly, although King's Cross was fast developing a reputation among the visible homeless as a hostile environment (see, for example, Chaudhary and Walker, 1996), he added that the Operation "wasn't about moving the homeless out of doorways but dealing appropriately with criminal offences" (Superintendent David Smith cited in Rose, 1997).

The apparent pressure to disassociate 'zero-tolerance' from the process of policing the homeless, but not necessarily the crimes they commit – the focus on the class of offence, rather than offending class – is deeply enmeshed with the notion of the homeless as the classic victims of circumstance. The effect is to shift the emphasis away from the identity of those subject to police force onto the purpose of, or motivation for, police intervention – a focus, in other words, away from the homeless person as the victim of circumstance onto the homeless person as vagrant, beggar, aggressive beggar or squatter.

The problems of having to constantly justify methods of policing the homeless by publicly negotiating an acceptable route through the polarised meaning of homelessness is not one that the Homeless Unit encounters. The Unit simply dismisses the relevance of "zero-tolerance" altogether. As one police officer said "this thing ... zero-tolerance ... we don't agree with" (*Police 1*). The significance of this outward repudiation of 'zero-tolerance' goes beyond the mere rejection of an ambiguous label, or even a style of policing, but rather relates to the broader system of ideas and justification of which it is part – a system of ideas in which the use of conventional policing methods as a viable means of either reducing or controlling the homeless population are rejected out-of-hand. This rationalisation finds expression in many ways. Foremost among these is the emphasis placed upon the voluntary sector and other statutory agencies as the principal forces in reducing homelessness:

> "... we can't provide a house, we can't provide, you know, many
> of the services that are provided. All we can ensure is that the

> services which can provide a successful housing outcome are given every opportunity and afforded every facility in order to be able to achieve that preferred outcome, whether it be through step housing or whatever.... Police can't deal with homelessness on their own." (Police 1)

The Unit's insistence that the police can only ever perform a supportive role in reducing homelessness across Divisional boundaries, in a sense, simply represents an acknowledgement of the limitations of any policing strategy that falls short of the extreme coercion necessary to permanently remove the homeless from the streets[12]. However, at the same time it also produces several benefits for the Division beyond the Unit's genuine, but unverifiable, expectation that it is the best way of reducing homelessness. In particular, shifting the focus away from the police not only disperses, and therefore reduces, the police's responsibility for the homeless problem, but it also subordinates the role of force, symbolised by the police, in eliminating homelessness. In effect the care and control dilemma faced in the context of policing King's Cross is neutralised as a result of its structural incorporation into policing practice.

This process – the apparent subordination of force through partnership – is deceptively elaborate. It is not only integral to the Unit's continued characterisation as a model of good practice, but also central to the actual realisation of the model itself. Partnership ultimately involves compromise – a relational process that at once involves and attracts the support of the very voluntary sector organisations upon which the model and its representation depends. What is important, however, is not so much the process of compromise in itself, but rather how the process of compromise and its motivations help us to understand its extent and the relationship between the police and the homeless that this implies.

The Unit, care and welfare: a police force for the homeless?

At one level the Unit's related strategies of explicitly displacing responsibility for the reduction in homelessness onto the voluntary sector and statutory agencies and also rejecting 'zero-tolerance' can be explained as part of a long-term trend[13] driven by the twinned demands of effectiveness and efficiency. To this effect, the police claimed that the Unit's policing strategy was more effective than 'zero-tolerance', or similar styles of policing, since clearing the street would not necessarily solve the problem as the homeless would simply drift back again (*Police 1*). At another level, however, the Unit explains its decision to assume a supportive role – enmeshed with the rejection of 'zero-tolerance' and the abandonment of other traditional forms of policing – in terms of the language and motives of welfare. For instance, the Unit deliberately promotes the fact that it works with and for the homeless, and not simply against them, emphasising its unique approach in not only responding seriously to complaints of crimes against the homeless but also in giving the homeless a voice within the police. As one police officer explained, contrasting the Unit's policy of support to alternative methods of responding to crimes against the homeless:

> **"They also felt that because they were homeless they were looked upon generally as down-and-out by the vast majority of the public and by the police, it has to be said, that they wouldn't be believed when they made an allegation of crime, or that crime wouldn't be properly investigated, because, you know, 'no fixed address', who would find them? Who would know where they were, how would they be contacted?" (Police 1)**

The Unit's unusual emphasis on safeguarding the welfare of the homeless, through close collaboration with the voluntary and other statutory agencies, ultimately plays an important part in characterising the Unit as a police force for the homeless. As one police officer put it to a man found begging on the street who had not come into contact with the Homeless Unit before: "We're a cross between police officers and social workers, we investigate crimes against the homeless and by the homeless. We're on your side really. If you're fair with us, we're fair with you." (Observation 2). The extent to which the Unit's officers present themselves as being involved in a qualitatively different enterprise from conventional policing even goes beyond the suggestion that the Unit has evolved into a new hybrid configuration of those organisations responsible for the homeless. To this end, it was suggested that the Unit's dedicated officers served as moral entrepreneurs holding the line between two opposing cultures – the housed and the homeless.

> **"... round about the end of the '80s, you have this gulf between the social services, and the police, with very little cooperation on either side ... the police ... were working the 'revolving door' system, and the knee-jerk reaction, if you like, to the requests or**

> the demands of normal society, through tenants associations and business groups, etc, or consortiums.... On the other hand there was this group on the street, which were generally put down if anything went wrong and there happened to be one of them close by, 'well, it's got to be them', because they're the ones there. And nobody really bothered to look into – well, look very much further for anti-social behaviour. So we decided the only way that we could build up the confidence of the people on the street, having done so with the help of the outside agencies ... was to continue along that vein." (Police 1)

This attempt to break with the past and mediate rather than respond to the demands of 'normal society' was, according to the police, based upon the Unit's privileged insight, as a dedicated group of police officers, into what really worked. Since, although "everybody ha[d] a problem with homelessness" and "would like to see homelessness eradicated for different reasons", the Unit's strategy recognised that rough sleeping could not be eradicated or cleared completely but only contained (Police 1). At one and the same time, however, the representation of the Unit as a police force for the homeless just as much as it is a force for policing the homeless can be conceived as an attempt to present its work as the ultimate form of inclusion – where, rather than simply being policed, the homeless of the Charing Cross Division could now expect to command the support of the police in the same way as the 'respectable' population. As the police stressed, the homeless had "the right to be treated as you would treat any other person in society" (Police 1).

There is a profound irony in this representation of the Unit's policing strategy as an innovative attempt to invert the conventional effects of policing – a major component of social exclusion. The irony is that despite its welfare-based approach, despite the close relationships it has forged with the voluntary sector and other statutory agencies and despite its repudiation of 'zero-tolerance' and conventional policing, its methods appear no less intrusive than other policing strategies and it is more this, in the context of its emphasis on partnership and welfare, that distinguishes the Unit from other Divisions in the Metropolitan area.

The Homeless Unit and 'zero-tolerance'

The most effective way of illustrating the full extent of the Homeless Unit's intrusion into the lives of people sleeping rough in Charing Cross is to compare the ratio of the Unit's officers to rough sleepers with the number of officers per head of population in other areas and forces. When one considers that the number of rough sleepers in Charing Cross rarely, if at all, exceeds 200[14], this means that the police–rough sleepers ratio in Charing Cross is remarkably low – about 1 in 30 in summer, dropping to 1 in 10 in winter[15]. This compares with an average of one officer for every 416 people in England and Wales and 281 for the combined Metropolitan Police District and City of London force – the area with the highest concentration of police per head of population in England and Wales (Prime et al, 1998). This means that during the summer months when the ratio in Charing Cross is at its highest there are about nine times more officers policing the visible homeless in the Charing Cross area than there are officers policing the rest of the population of London[16].

The fact that there is such a high proportion of officers relative to rough sleepers does not in itself mean that the homeless of Charing Cross experience an unusually punitive regime of policing. It may, for instance, simply be an observable effect of the resource intensive methods required to direct the rough sleeping population to sources of food or shelter. This interpretation cannot be wholly discounted since the Unit's brief commits it to a wide range of functions such as tracing young missing persons and organising the clearance of areas prior to them being cleaned by the City's refuse services. What is clear, however, is that these low ratios are not benign. On the contrary, they provide the infrastructure necessary to realise a policing strategy in which rough sleepers, and people involved in activities which are commonly associated with homelessness such as begging and street drinking, are more at risk from becoming the objects of formal police powers than either the 'respectable' population or even, possibly, homeless persons subjected to more conventional styles of policing in other Divisions.

The scale of the police's intrusion into the lives of the homeless in the Charing Cross Division is difficult to fully appreciate. As a matter of policy the Unit makes contact with every new person who sleeps rough or spends their day within the Divisional area. As one police officer put it: "we introduce ourselves" (Police 1). The purpose of this introduction is justified in terms of the express or implied interests of the homeless. The introduction is generally intended to provide the police with the opportunity to inform the homeless that, "if they've got any problems then they come through us" (Police 1). It is also justified on the basis of assisting the voluntary sector in keeping track of their clients. This, however, is not always the case. Sometimes the Unit's policy of introduction is used as a basis to threaten some people with more formal action – as a way of introducing them, in other words, to the Unit's policy on begging.

> "... in order to warn them or arrest them for begging, we've got to see them do it. And if we haven't seen them do it, then we'll, what we call a gypsy's warning, where we'll sit down and say look if you start begging, we'll be back whatever. You know, and generally they take the gypsy's warning." (Police 1)

The fact that the officers from the Unit not only presume familiarity with homeless people but also regard it as a positive aspect of their work suggests, as Bittner once put it, that rough sleepers are not so much denied a right to privacy, but rather seen as not having any privacy (Bittner, 1969, p 147). As an example of police intrusion, however, the Unit's policy of blanket 'introductions' is far less significant than the Unit's rates of arrest for people of 'no fixed abode' and the related category of people who beg.

Arresting statistics

The number of arrests of homeless people and the related, but not co-extensive, category of people who beg across the Charing Cross Division is striking. Of the 8,033 arrests made in the Charing Cross Division for all offences between 1 June 1996 to 31 May 1997, for example, 433, or 5%, were for begging. Not all people arrested for begging, however, were homeless. In fact, only about three quarters, 77%, of those arrested for begging were of 'no fixed abode'[17] – an imprecise category that includes rough sleepers, those in hostel accommodation and anyone who wished to conceal their address. The arrest of people of 'no fixed abode' who beg in the Charing Cross Division, however, is still significant at over 4%. Even more remarkable, however, is that 1,384 arrests, or 17%, were of people of 'no fixed abode'. Significantly, most of these arrests, 79% in total, were for begging, drunkenness and other 'minor offences'. This left only 21% of arrests against the homeless for 'more serious criminal matters', compared with 55% over the Division as a whole – a striking differential considering that the homeless and people who begged were far more likely to be either charged, cautioned or warned and far less likely to have no further action taken against them (Management Information

Unit, 1997). Homeless people, in other words, not only seem to be subjected to a far greater risk of formal intrusion from the police, but are also, at greater risk of both arrest and charge for far less serious offences.

This last proposition raises several questions. Principle among these is whether the Unit's arrest and charge rates reflect real rates of offending and, if not, whether the extent to which recourse is made to the police's formal coercive powers is greater than that of neighbouring Divisions. The most obvious problem involved in acquiring precise answers to these questions is that there are no reliable estimates of the number of homeless people who are of 'no fixed abode' in the Charing Cross Division over any given length of time[18].

Even in the absence of meaningful comparisons with other Divisions, the emphasis that Charing Cross' arrest and charge rates seems to place on homeless crime is difficult to ignore. There may be problems in unravelling the precise implications of the figures, but as a measure of the wholesale criminalisation of an entire population their significance is difficult to deny. This is especially the case when one considers that the seemingly high rates of arrest and charge are not attributable to a small recidivist group of arrestees. As many as 85% of those either arrested for begging or, once arrested, found to be of 'no fixed abode' were only arrested once with over 10% being arrested between two and four times and only four people of 'no fixed abode' being arrested over five times (Management Information Unit, 1997). The exercise of formal police powers against those of 'no fixed abode' in Charing Cross, in other words, is dispersed throughout that population – a pattern that does not appear, on the basis of the available evidence, to be repeated throughout criminal justice (see, for example, Maguire, 1997; Phillips and Brown, 1998)[19].

The following discussion attempts to explore the pattern and dynamics of this dispersal by examining the relative merits of three possible ways of interpreting the figures. The first, which is qualitatively different from the second and third, maintains that the extent of homeless crime and begging as measured by formal police intervention corresponds to 'real' relative rates of offending. The second and third reject the proposition that the criminalisation of the homeless is primarily determined by, or a response, to real relative rates of offending. The second contends that the Division's recorded rates of arrest and charge are exceptional; that they are not only greater than those of other neighbouring Divisions, in other words, but are also a product of the techniques used to police the homeless and begging within Charing Cross. The third centres on the proposition that the Division's arrest and charge rates, although not commensurate with real rates of offending, are comparable with those of other Divisions in the Metropolitan District. The implication of this interpretation is that the Unit's claim to be as much a police force for, as opposed to against, the homeless has little or no effect on the general vulnerability of homeless people to criminal justice intervention.

As the discussion progresses it will emerge that despite apparent differences between conventional policing techniques and the Unit's policing strategy, in respect of the exercise of formal police powers differences are minimal. Moreover, if anything the available evidence suggests that the Unit's strategy is predicated on higher levels of formal intrusion. This is not to say that the Unit's strategy is no different from conventional policing. Quite apart from the suggestion that the Unit's strategy is, in many respects, more intrusive, its close relationship with the voluntary and statutory sector is distinctive. However, although the Unit's multiagency approach is interesting as another example of the contemporary trend towards multiagency based solutions to social problems (in which the police participate), its true significance seems to reside in the way in which the operational proximity of the Unit to other institutions has enabled it to secure acceptance of, and therefore gain consent for, what is largely, in terms of the exercise of formal police powers at least, a conventional policing strategy.

Homelessness: a criminogenic or criminalised condition?

The process of assessing whether high relative rates of arrest and charge are better explained in terms of policing strategies, rather than higher relative rates of homeless criminality, is extremely problematic. This is in part due to the intractable problems of measuring real rates of crime. There is insufficient space to rehearse the arguments over the accuracy of methods of crime measurement (for a fuller discussion see Coleman and Moynihan, 1996) or to consider the problems that the concept of crime itself poses to the measurement of criminal behaviour as an independent reality beyond the formal processing mechanisms of criminal justice (see, for example, Kitsuse, 1962; Becker, 1963). Suffice to say there is the possibility that the Division's ostensibly high levels of arrest and charge correlate with equally high rates of offending. This is the implication of much of the criminological literature. As Baron and Hartnagel have observed, "past research suggests [the homeless] population is heavily involved in criminal activity" (Baron and Hartnagel, 1998, p 166). There are certainly very real pressures on homeless people to commit crime – a point explored by Carlen whose study of youth homelessness suggested that much of the crime committed by homeless people is survivalist in nature (Carlen, 1996). Not surprisingly the police themselves subscribe to the view that the level of police intrusion reflects real relative rates of offending. "If", as one police officer told us, "a [homeless] person commits a crime, then we deal with that person as we deal with any other member of the community" (Police 1). On closer inspection, however, there is evidence to suggest that arrest and charge rates were not an oblique effect of real relative rates of homeless crime, but rather were the result of selective enforcement – the policing of a suspect population[20].

To begin to understand this proposition, it is first important to appreciate that the enforcement of the law is an uneven process. This is not to say that policing is a completely random process, simply that policing, and the exercise of police discretion, is highly contextualised. Police officers are, among other things, responsive to setting and organisation; selecting, classifying and sorting suspects on the basis of police-driven criteria (see McConville et al, 1991, pp 14-24). A good example of this is the dramatic decline in recorded offences of 'indecency between males' in the late 1950s and 1960s – a direct result of changes in police behaviour in anticipation of the legalisation of homosexuality (Walker, 1971). That police discretion is context dependent is no less true of the police of the Charing Cross Homeless Unit. Officers from the Unit respond to homeless people differently in different contexts and also differently compared to how other officers respond to non-homeless people. The Unit's policy of introduction, for instance, is reserved for the homeless and people who spend their days on the streets. Likewise, the police actively look for homeless people when out on the beat. Their movements, in effect, are ordered according to the conventional 'hang-outs' of the homeless – places which provide entertainment (such as the street performers of Leicester Square), privacy (such as back alleyways or the front of premises obscured from view by scaffolding and other building works) or shelter (the entrances to underground and overground railway stations). This selective response seems to extend to the exercise of formal police powers. The fact that people of 'no fixed abode' are more liable to be arrested and charged for less serious offences within the Charing Cross Division is particularly important to this effect; raising a presumption that the resources devoted to policing the homeless are deployed, among other things, to subject them to greater formal forms of intrusion than non-homeless people for reasons other than real relative rates of offending.

Other explanations, it should be noted, do exist. One explanation that cannot be wholly discounted is that homeless people are more inclined to commit minor, rather than major, offences and do so at an alarming rate. The fact that as much as 17% of arrests were of people of 'no fixed abode' in an area that includes Leicester Square, Covent Garden and Charing Cross and that the rate of charge post-arrest is higher, however, suggests otherwise. It is important to stress that, in the absence of meaningful comparisons where variables such as age, offence type and previous convictions are controlled, there is only a suggestion to this effect. The higher rate of charging may, for example, be explained in terms of a higher rate of previous convictions or cautions which, according to the most recent Home Office Circular on the matter, should serve to set additional limits on the use of a caution rather than charge and prosecution (Home Office, 1994). The significance of potentially higher rates of previous cautions or convictions, however, is itself equivocal. The terms of the 1994 Home Office Circular on cautioning, for instance, provide that cautions can be considered where the instant offence is trivial. When one considers that 77% of arrests of people of 'no fixed abode' were for begging, drunkenness and other 'minor offences' (such as public order offences), it appears that many of the offences that people of 'no fixed abode' are arrested for are expressly recognised in the 1994 Circular as offences in respect of which a second caution can be administered. Moreover, it is also important to note that minor offences like begging and drunkenness are precisely the type of offences that first become subject to criminal justice intervention as a result of police initiative, rather than citizen reporting; suggesting that higher rates of previous cautions and convictions may also be as much a product of police discretion and behaviour as they are real rates of offending.

Police discretion, in short, appears to be exercised in a way that selects the homeless into, rather than out of, the criminal justice process, except in those exceptional circumstances where the imperative of reducing homelessness is best served by suspending formal intervention as in the case of failing to execute arrest warrants. An understanding of the reasons behind the apparent direction of this process of selection is important to assessing whether Charing Cross' arrest and charge rates are higher than neighbouring Divisions – an important first step to exploring the effect of the Unit on formal criminal justice intervention against the homeless. At one level, there are a number of structural factors that expose the homeless to a greater risk of arrest, and therefore charge, that cannot be attributed to the policing methods of the Unit. The homeless, for example, are geographically exposed to the process of criminalisation. As

McConville et al have observed, "it is easier to police public than private spaces, and so those people who inhabit the former ... are most 'at risk'" (McConville et al, 1991, p 17). The law itself, or more specifically the police's power of arrest granted by section 25 of the 1984 Police and Criminal Evidence Act, is also drafted in a way that is enabling of formal police intervention. The power can only be exercised if any one of several arrest conditions is satisfied. Among other things, these conditions include the situation where the name and address of a suspected person cannot be ascertained for the purpose of serving a warrant – a condition that seems to justify the use of arrest for homeless people in almost all circumstances (notwithstanding the demand for reasonable suspicion) irrespective of the seriousness of the offence. Notwithstanding the effect of these structural considerations on the Division's arrest and charge rates, however, its seemingly high levels of arrest and charge also appear to be traceable to the existence of the Homeless Unit itself, and, in particular, the policing methods of the Unit.

There is some suggestion that the Unit presides over a policy of intrusive formal intervention – little different from those methods that have been described as 'zero-tolerance'. As one officer explained, despite the unusually close links that had been forged with social services, they were not "a soft option" as their "strict policy on begging" demonstrated (Police 1). The policy is restricted to begging and sets out in clear terms the circumstances in which an officer should arrest and charge someone for begging. It involves a formal warning for a first offence of begging, arrest and caution for a second and prosecution for all subsequent offences. An indication of how this policy compares with the approach that other Divisions take to arrest and charge was given to us by one officer who revealed that the Unit's approach to begging was a "pro-arrest policy" which "was the closest you could get to zero policing without calling it zero-tolerance policing" (Observation 1). The officer added that the policy was so strict that the Division was in danger of driving homeless people into other Divisions. The term 'zero-tolerance', we were told, was only avoided as a matter of convention because it was too loaded with meaning and, therefore, politically expedient not to mention it (Observation 1). This does not by itself demonstrate that the Unit's policy of formal intervention for begging is more than or even as strict as other Divisions and therefore likely to result in higher or comparable arrests and prosecutions. On closer inspection, however, this does seem to be the case.

Other Divisions, including those who have in the past practised 'zero-tolerance', seem, as a matter of routine (as opposed to during specific operations), to leave the decision to individual officers, rather than requiring them to follow a strict policy. As an Inspector from a neighbouring Division, whose officers had been involved in Operation Welwyn, told us:

> **"It would be the officer's decision, the officer dealing with it at the time, it would be his personal decision how he's going to deal with [the matter] ... they would not be directed that they have to make an arrest." (Police 2)**

The effect of desisting from formally attempting to direct how individual officers exercise their discretion – either in the context, or outside, of specific operations – is difficult to determine. Notwithstanding the fact that the existence of a strict policy is not the same thing as its implementation, the available evidence suggests that the absence of a strict policy produces lower levels of formal intrusion – in the context of begging at least. Research undertaken by Crisis throughout Central London, for instance, recorded that the general experience of the police among people who begged was that if, when asked to move, they did so and were polite in the process, a caution or arrest would rarely follow (Murdoch, undated). This experience seems to be confirmed by the Inspector quoted above who argued that a rigid policy of arrest was more resource intensive and, therefore, not justified on the basis of the seriousness of the offence.

> **"... we haven't actually developed a policy for that problem ... because it hasn't emerged as a problem of significance that requires a detailed strategy to deal with it. You know, a formal warning, a caution and then a prosecution. Because our resources are getting so limited. What we have to look at are offences that are actually going to cause serious concern to people." (Police 2)**

The Inspector's reservations about a pro-arrest policy against people who beg, it should be added, was as much a function of the difficulties in getting results as it was an effect of attaching greater concern to more serious offences. The principal obstacle, he informed us, was in obtaining evidence for begging. Since a police officer would commonly have to actually witness the offence, the CCTV cameras, which had proved highly effective in the context of other offences in the King's Cross area during and since Operation Welwyn, were unable to provide the necessary evidence any more effectively than uniformed officers patrolling the area. This, he argued, was because uniformed officers were commonly identified by people suspected of begging long before they were able to get near enough to witness evidence of the offence. The extent to which the Inspector's comments reflect the reality of policing people who beg is difficult to determine; what seems significant, however, is that the same problem does not arise for the Unit's plain clothed officers – a decision ostensibly taken to secure the trust of the homeless population of Charing Cross.

The Unit's adoption of a pro-arrest policy seems to present a confusing paradox. The fact that the homeless people with 'no fixed abode' appear to be at greater risk of formal police intervention than the non-homeless population, and possibly even than homeless people in other Divisions, suggests that the Division's[21] apparently high homeless arrest rates are either better explained in terms of the Unit's dedication to policing the homeless, or its policy on begging, or both. At best it appears that a policing strategy emphasising care, and therefore suggestive of a benign effect on arrest and charge rates, has no effect on homeless arrest rates, and therefore no effect on the fact that the homeless are arrested in part because of their homelessness. However, rather than acknowledging that these arrest rates contradict the Unit's emphasis on welfare and its position as a police force for, just as much as against, the visible homeless, the Unit, in fact, represents them as complementary.

The Unit's refusal to acknowledge the contradiction may seem difficult to understand. It may seem even more unusual given that one officer argued that the high arrest figures were a simple product of the fact that the Unit operated within a conventional policing culture which was evaluated on the basis of conventional policing criteria – arrests, in other words. As a police unit dedicated to the homeless its performance could only be demonstrated by arresting them. This, the officer concluded, probably explained why other Divisions in the Metropolitan area had lower arrest figures for begging since, as they had other targets to meet, such as mugging or robbery, the homeless in those Divisions tended to be moved on rather than arrested, allowing resources to be diverted to these, more serious, offences (Observation 1).

Notwithstanding the power of ostensibly incongruent performance indicators to dictate policing practice, one police officer nonetheless insisted that this peculiar and unusual extension of police intervention was justifiable in terms of the Unit's mission statement despite the equal priority that this gave to crimes against the homeless. To this effect, it was claimed, that the criminalisation of the homeless was necessary to prevent their criminal victimisation – explaining, "begging leads to aggressive begging, leads to the formation of taxing" (Police 1).

The suggestion that a person begging is likely to progress to aggressive begging and subsequently to more serious forms of crime such as 'taxing' has no basis in empirical observation. Moreover, on closer examination, it appears as much to be a justification of convenience – which, in effect at least, serves to preserve the image of the Unit as just as much a police force for the homeless as against them. The image, which has several components, can be misleading. An examination of one of these components illustrates the point.

One police officer explained that although the Unit 'policed' the homeless it also 'defended' them. One of the first points to appreciate is that the Unit's success neither implies nor depends upon the devotion of equal resources to the investigation of crimes against the homeless and by the homeless against the housed and 'respectable'. The organisational priorities and distinguishing features of the Unit, in addition to how it is formally represented, at first suggest otherwise. To this effect, the Unit places great store by the fact that its officers wear casual clothes and put considerable emphasis on knowing the visible homeless by name. These two departures from conventional practice were said to have been instrumental in enabling the Unit to break down the historic distrust between the police and homeless. More specifically, it was suggested that the homeless were, as a consequence, more prepared to report crimes to the police and that officers were better able to investigate crimes and prepare them for court. The closer relationship between the Unit's officers and the homeless better enabled officers to trace witnesses, who went only by their nicknames, and increased their commitment to ensuring that homeless witnesses arrived on time and sober to give evidence in court (Police 1). The results of these changes, however, have been mixed. Although in a small number of serious cases there has been some success, in general the distrust remains as does the reticence of the homeless in coming forward to report crime. As one officer said, "despite what's written in the mission statement about crimes by and crimes against we mainly deal with crimes committed by the homeless against the 'respectable' population" (Observation 1).

Intrusion into the lives of the homeless, in other words, is not only direct and unrelenting, but also seems to be unmitigated by any appreciable improvement in police protection. At the most basic level, homeless people who are of 'no fixed abode' – especially, it seems, those who beg – are forced unwillingly into frequent confrontation with the police. As one officer put it, begging was a repetitive 'game they play': a trade off between enjoying the proceeds of six days of begging at the expense of an inevitable arrest, a day remanded in custody and a 'small fine'. It is important to add that trivialising arrest belies the fact that homeless offenders who fail to pay their fines can find themselves facing several months in prison (see, for example, O'Hagan, 1998), and that this basic pattern of formal intrusion is possible precisely because of the existence of a well-resourced, dedicated unit.

Conclusion

This chapter has explored the tension between the care and control of homeless people by looking at the Homeless Unit – a dedicated unit of police officers based at Charing Cross.

The Unit's emphasis on the care and protection of homeless people is wide-ranging and encompasses a number of related, but ultimately discrete, elements. This emphasis must be set against the Unit's need to control the homeless, particularly the visible homeless, and the activities commonly associated with them, such as begging and street drinking. This control is achieved in a number of different ways. Chief among these, however, is the use of conventional police powers or, to be more precise, the power of arrest and charge.

Notwithstanding the Unit's interest in care and welfare, the effect of the existence of a dedicated Unit of officers, it seems, is that the homeless in the Charing Cross area experience a higher level of intrusion into their lives. The policy of 'blanket' introductions, which is designed to systematically introduce newcomers in that area to the functions of the police, ensures that no rough sleeper or person involved in activities such as begging will go for very long without coming into contact with the Unit's officers. Significantly, the policy is unique to the Metropolitan District. Although implemented in a civil manner, without, it seems, undue provocation or assault, it represents a potent symbol of the status of privacy in the relationship between the police and the homeless. It demonstrated the routine nature of contact between the police and the homeless people of Charing Cross and, therefore, the right of the police to closely survey and regulate the lives of the homeless – a right confirmed in practice in the context of the Unit's pro-arrest policy for begging offences.

Despite the Unit's expressed repudiation of 'zero-tolerance', its policy on begging bears a close resemblance to the basic premises of 'zero-tolerance' in Britain (Bratton et al, 1997). Both attempt to clamp down on offences which are regarded as non-serious, both operate on the assumption that the tight control of the disorderly leads to wider benefits in social control. In fact the Unit's pro-arrest policy may represent a more intrusive threat to the lives of the homeless in London than strategies that have hitherto been described as 'zero-tolerance' policing. This is because, unlike Operation Welwyn, for instance, the execution of the Unit's pro-arrest policy, like its operation, is continuing; producing the seamless criminalisation of homeless people.

The policy is justified by the Unit on the premise that begging "leads to aggressive begging, leads to the formation of taxing" (Police 1) – an ambiguous proposition that can be interpreted in two particular ways. One interpretation is that locations where people beg will soon attract aggressive beggars, and consequently people intent on 'taxing'. This is a variant of the broken windows thesis (see Wilson and Kelling, 1982) – and at once feeds into and implies 'zero-tolerance' policing strategies. There is, however, no empirical evidence to support this particular argument. An alternative interpretation of the police officer's comments is that there was – in the case of this group – a progress from them begging through to taxing. There is no empirical evidence to support this argument either. However, it is this argument which the Unit puts forwards to explain the emergence of taxing in Charing Cross.

What this clearly illustrates, if one accepts that the Unit was established to end 'taxing', is that the tension between the care and control of homeless people was an organising feature of the Unit's operation from the outset (Police 1; Observation 1). According to the officers of the Unit, the Unit was set up to defend homeless people who were vulnerable to becoming the victims of the group's taxing activities, but this, unusually, was a method of defence that involved the criminalisation of a substantial part of the homeless population – a form of crime prevention, in other words, by way of mass criminalisation.

This justification does not simply reveal the tension between the care and control of the homeless, but more importantly the difficulty in determining where care ends and control begins. This is not so much because the two are difficult to disentangle, but more that, at least in the above context, care is control. The police, in other words, seem to have few reservations about employing unusually coercive means of control to produce care ends. It is a paradox that the Unit has yet, it seems, to recognise. In fact, it is a paradox that few seem to recognise in view of the support that the voluntary sector lends the Unit. The explanation for this paradox is unclear: it resides somewhere in the mystifying and seductive effects of the concessions the Unit makes to conventional policing and its general multiagency approach to policing. What is clear, however, is that the Unit must tackle it if it is to become a Unit that can truly represent itself as a police force that is genuinely responsive to the needs of homeless people.

Acknowledgements

The authors would like to thank the editors, and Dave Cowan, Courtney Davis and Anna Fooks for their comments on earlier drafts of the chapter.

Notes

[1] Although homelessness is something ultimately, but not entirely, distinct from homeless people (either statutory or non-statutory) or rough sleepers, it is primarily used here to describe the homeless population as well as the relation of homelessness.

[2] While begging and street living are considered as activities which are associated with the condition of homelessness. They are, in other words, perceived to be part and parcel of the 'homeless problem'.

[3] For the purposes of calculation and formal classification, homelessness either meant rough sleeping (Police 1) or being of 'no fixed abode' (Management Information Unit, 1997).

[4] The present appeal of structural explanations is a relatively recent phenomenon (Pleace et al, 1997, p 2). It is neither a permanent fixture of academic, political or popular cultural landscapes, nor has its adoption as a preferred method of explaining homelessness been absolute. In fact, within academic discourse it generally co-exists within explanatory accounts which also draw upon individualised explanations of homelessness (see, for example, Dant and Deacon, 1989).

[5] This contrast is all the more remarkable in view of the low threshold at which the definition of aggressive begging was set in the study from which this finding was taken – a highly relative term which was taken to

include the passage of passers-by being blocked so that he or she had to move to one side (Moore et al, 1995, p 221).

[6] This process is exemplified in its clearest form, in the following extract from the *Daily Mail*, written by Simon Heffer:

> **In theory, no one need sleep in shop doorways. We have a welfare state that is, by comparison with many civilised countries, positively luxurious.... Motives other than sheer poverty seem to account for a significant part of the problem. They are motives – crime, dropping out, or exploiting gullible tourists by begging – that deserve a response of 'zero tolerance'. Most of us want these people removed from the streets, not least because the trend towards aggressive begging infringes the civil liberty of ordinary people to go about their lawful business unmolested. (Heffer, 1997)**

Heffer's assertion of an almost natural association between sleeping rough and crime is striking, although not entirely uncharacteristic, in its breadth. He cites crime as a cause of homelessness, suggests the existence of an organic link between sleeping rough and aggressive begging, itself a crime, and his use of "ordinary" and "lawful" serves as an implied contrast with the deviant and unlawful homeless. Although Heffer's location of crime as a cause of homelessness is unusual, among some journalists the close link he draws between homelessness and crime is not. A correspondent for the BBC, for instance, claimed that New York's 'zero tolerance' approach towards 'vagrancy', and not crime in general, had been responsible for the dramatic reduction in the City's crime problem, making New York an ideal place for shoppers from Britain to purchase Christmas presents (BBC, 1998).

[7] Although it may not be immediately apparent that to emphasise choice is, in effect, to locate the causes of homelessness within the moral and social deficiencies of the homeless themselves, the two are deeply enmeshed. This is illustrated in the following leader from the *Mail on Sunday*:

> **Similar muddled thinking confuses the controversy about homelessness. The overwhelming majority of those sleeping rough are not homeless in the traditional sense. They haven't been evicted by wicked landlords or seen their homes flooded or**

burnt. The notion that hard-stretched local authorities should provide council houses for asylum seekers who flock into Britain from abroad or over-age runaways is nonsense. Research shows that many of those allegedly homeless have refused hostel accommodation, don't like sharing with others, resent authority and rules, and are pernickety about the type of accommodation they are offered or where it is located. However ultimately self-destructive such attitudes might be, it is their freedom of choice and there is absolutely no reason why the rest of us should feel guilty or put our hands ever deeper in our pockets. (*Mail on Sunday*, 12 January 1997)

[8] According to *The Guardian* it was only after Jack Straw's speech in autumn 1995, urging a crack down on "aggressive beggars, winos and squeegee merchants" that there was serious discussion in cabinet about government policy on this issue. Michael Howard, the then Home Secretary, was said to have advocated the reform of vagrancy laws which became known in Whitehall as the 'sluice 'em down' policy to force beggars off the streets. This, however, was reported to have been blocked by David Curry at the Department of Environment (Travis and Meikle, 1997).

[9] Blair presented his retraction as a clarification, claiming that he was referring not to the homeless, but to homelessness (Blair, 1997). This, however, tended to contradict the full text of the interview which read:

Obviously some people will interpret this in a way which is harsh and unpleasant, but I think the basic principle is here to say: yes it is right to be intolerant of people homeless on the streets. But the way to deal with that is you make sure that when those people come off the streets that you're doing the other part of the equation. You're providing them with somewhere to go. (Blair cited in Macaskill, 1997)

[10] The other homeless unit is in Manchester.

[11] Albeit a complex and ambiguous one.

[12] For an account of such a policy see Foote (1969).

[13] In the 1970s Archard observed that the trend among "legislators and policy makers" was to "redefine vagrancy in favour of a medical and social work strategy of control, and thereby replace the dominant criminal label attached to it" (Archard, 1979, p 19).

[14] According to the head of the Unit, the Division "average[s] between 163 to 180 rough sleepers" in summer and 60 to 62 in winter when the winter shelters are open. This does not mean that the number of people who would otherwise be rough sleepers in winter do not spend their days on the streets. The figure is lower in winter because the count takes place in the early hours of the morning and because of the opening up of the winter night shelters.

[15] These ratios are based upon the police's own imperfect estimation of the rough sleeping population which is also used by the Rough Sleepers Initiative (see note 14).

[16] The fact that the Homeless Unit seems to concern itself with street living in general which may, or may not, include homeless people is probably offset by the fact that regular uniformed officers of the Charing Cross Division also concern themselves with the rough sleeping population.

[17] See note 18 for a discussion of and problem with the meaning of 'fixed abode'.

[18] This is, in part, due to the highly flexible nature of the term. Homelessness, as we have observed earlier, means different things in different contexts and to different people. The vague and flexible nature of the term is reflected in police practice. Although the Unit's periodic estimates of the 'homeless' population in the Division are regarded among the voluntary and statutory sectors as the most reliable available figures, they are inadequate as a denominating unit for the purpose of calculating offending rates among the homeless population of the Division. This is because these estimated are of rough sleepers and not of people of 'no fixed abode' – the basic unit used in the Division's statistics. Moreover, people of 'no fixed abode' is itself unsatisfactory since it may include people who, on any measure, are not homeless, but simply wished to conceal their address. And finally, even if a reliable estimate of the number of people of 'no fixed abode' for any given period of time were available,

comparisons with other Divisions would not be possible since Charing Cross is the only Division to collate their arrest and charge figures with respect to a person's housing status.

[19] Strict comparisons are difficult to make. The reasons for this are numerous. Among other things, the Division's figures relate to arrestees (as opposed to those charged or convicted) and only record arrests in the previous 12 months. The best available comparisons are either of offenders (although see Phillips and Brown, 1998) or relate to previous convictions (usually for standard list offences) with no time restriction.

[20] Hillyard's (1993) work on the Prevention of Terrorism Act illustrates that some populations can, in political and legal contexts, be readily constructed as criminal, or potentially criminal, therefore fusing enforcement of the law and the control of populations.

[21] On the basis of the available data, assessing the extent to which the Unit enforces its own policy with a view to isolating its contribution to the arrest of the homeless in Charing Cross although not fraught with problems is certainly not problem free. Across the Division it appears that non-Unit officers are more inclined to ignore begging offences than their colleagues in the Unit. The Division's annual analysis of homeless and begging arrest statistics, for example, recommends that to improve the police's response to begging offences and offences committed by people of 'no fixed abode', patrolling officers should be encouraged "to deal with all instances of begging that come to their notice and not to 'turn a blind eye' if they are already assigned", save where "other matters were pressing" (Management Information Unit, 1997). The Unit's officers, on the other hand, seem more inclined to adopt a strict approach to the enforcement of its arrest policy. Although the evidence is not conclusive, what evidence there is is highly suggestive. Not only does the Unit present a firm and consistent policy on arrest as instrumental in achieving its objectives, but its officers work under the assumption that arrests are the only measure of their effectiveness as a Unit (see below). This is not to say that the Unit's enforcement of its arrest policy is absolute. On the contrary, during our research the police took no formal action against a woman who, although begging, had also been recently assaulted by her former partner. Bruising from the attack was clearly visible. The officers did not even mention the possibility of formal action in the future, choosing instead to concentrate their inquiries on the earlier assault with

a view to safeguarding the woman's welfare and reassuring her that a formal complaint would be dealt with seriously.

The problems involved in isolating the Unit's contribution to the Division's arrest rates for begging and of people of 'no fixed abode' are also numerous since the Division does not collate its statistics in a way that allows the Unit's arrest behaviour to be isolated and examined. This is not to say that the Division's figures are unable to provide any insight into the impact of the Unit on arrest rates. In practice, there appears to be a relatively strict division of labour between the Unit and other officers from the Division. The significance of this in terms of the application of the Unit's policy is difficult to ascertain. Notwithstanding the fact that most officers patrolling the Division are not part of the Unit, its significance is probably less than immediately apparent, since non-Unit officers tend to leave the homeless to the Unit, save where immediate action is necessary (*Police 1; Observation 1*).

References

Anderson, I., Kemp, P. and Quilgars, D. (1993) *Single homeless people*, London: HMSO.

Archard, P. (1979) 'Vagrancy – a literature review', in T. Cook (ed) *Vagrancy: Some new perspectives*, London: Academic Press, pp 11-28.

Baron, S. and Hartnagel, T. (1998) 'Street youth and criminal violence', *Journal of Research in Crime and Delinquency*, vol 35, no 2, pp 166-92.

BBC (1998) *BBC News at One*, 16 December.

Becker, H. (1963) *Outsiders*, New York, NY: Free Press.

Bennett, T. (1994) 'Recent developments in community policing', in M. Stephens and S. Becker (eds) *Police force, police service*, London: Macmillan, pp 107-30.

Bines, W. (1994) *The health of single homeless people*, York: Centre for Housing Policy, University of York.

Bittner, E. (1969) 'The police on skid-row: a study of peace keeping', in W. Chambliss (ed) *Crime and the legal process*, New York, NY: Dryden Press, pp 135-54.

Blair, T. (1997) 'War on the streets', *The Guardian*, 8 January.

Bratton, W., Mallon, R., Orr, J. and Pollard, C. (1997) *Zero tolerance: Policing a free society*, London: IEA Health and Welfare Unit.

Brogden, M. and Nijhar, P. (1997) 'Rediscovering the residuum – zero tolerance and reconstituting the control of the poor', in L. Lundy, M. Adler, S. Wheeler and J. Morison (eds) *In search of the underclass*, Working Papers from the SLSA One-Day Conference in Queen's University, Belfast: Law Faculty, Queen's University, pp 17–22.

Burrows, R. (1997) 'The social distribution of the experience of homelessness', in R. Burrows, N. Pleace and D. Quilgars (eds) *Homelessness and social policy*, London: Routledge, pp 50–68.

Carlen, P. (1996) *Jigsaw: A political criminology of youth homelessness*, Buckingham: Open University Press.

Chambliss, W. (1969) 'The law of vagrancy', in W. Chambliss (ed) *Crime and the legal process*, New York, NY: Dryden Press, pp 51–63.

Chaudhary, V. and Walker, M. (1996) 'The petty crime war', *The Guardian*, 21 November.

Choongh, S. (1998) 'Policing the dross: a social disciplinary model of policing', *British Journal of Criminology*, vol 38, no 4, pp 623–34.

Coleman, C. and Moynihan, J. (1996) *Understanding crime data*, Buckingham: Open University Press.

Cook, D. (1997) *Poverty, crime and punishment*, London: Child Poverty Action Group.

Cowan, D. (1997) *Homelessness: The (in)appropriate applicant*, Aldershot: Dartmouth.

Dant, T. and Deacon, A. (1989) *Hostels to homes? The rehousing of single homeless people*, Aldershot: Avebury.

Douglas, M. (1992) *Risk and blame*, London: Routledge.

Drake, M., O'Brien, M. and Biebuych, T. (1982) *Single and homeless*, London: HMSO.

Foote, C. (1969) 'Vagrancy-type law and its administration', in W. Chambliss (ed) *Crime and the legal process*, New York, NY: Dryden Press, pp 295–329.

Grenier, P. (1996) *Still dying for a home: An update of Crisis' 1992 investigation into the links between homelessness, health and mortality*, London: Crisis.

Heffer, S. (1997) 'Should the workhouse come back for people like this?', *Daily Mail*, 8 January.

Hillyard, P. (1993) *Suspect community*, London: Pluto.

Home Office (1994) 'The cautioning of offenders', Circular 18/94, London: Home Office.

Howarth, D. (1995) 'Straw and the sun-dried tomatoes', *The Guardian*, Letters page, 7 September.

Kemp, P. (1997) 'The characteristics of single homeless people in England', in R. Burrows, N. Pleace and D. Quilgars (eds) *Homelessness and social policy*, London: Routledge, pp 69-87.

Keys, S. and Kennedy, M. (1992) *Sick to death of homelessness*, London: Crisis.

Kitsuse, J. (1962) 'Societal reaction to deviant behaviour: problems of theory and method', *Social Problems*, vol 9, no 3, pp 347-56.

Macaskill, E. (1997) 'Blair opts for zero tolerance', *The Guardian*, 7 January.

McCarthy, B. and Hagan, J. (1991) 'Homelessness: a criminogenic situation?', *British Journal of Criminology*, vol 31, no 4, pp 393-410.

McConville, M., Saunder, A. and Leng, R. (1991) *The case for the prosecution*, London: Routledge.

Maguire, M. (1997) 'Crime statistics, patterns and trends: changing perceptions and their implications', in M. Maguire, R. Morgan and R. Reiner (eds) *The Oxford handbook of criminology*, 2nd edn, Oxford: Clarendon Press, pp 135-88.

Mail on Sunday (1997) 'Why should we bankroll beggars', 12 January.

Management Information Unit (Charing Cross Divisional OCU) (1997) *Homeless and begging arrest trend analysis, 1/6/96 to 31/5/97* (unpublished).

Meikle, J. (1995) 'Police fears help block beggar plan', *The Guardian*, 6 September.

Moore, J., Canter, D., Stockley, D. and Drake, M. (1995) *The faces of homelessness in London*, Aldershot: Dartmouth.

Murdoch, A. (undated) *We are human too: A study of people who beg*, London: Crisis.

O'Hagan, A. (1998) 'Billie's story', *The Guardian*, 9 July.

Phillips, C. and Brown, D. (1998) *Entry into the criminal justice system: A survey of police arrests and their outcomes*, Home Office Research Study 185, London: Home Office.

Pleace, N. and Quilgars, D. (1997) 'Health, homelessness and access to health care services in London', in R. Burrows, N. Pleace and D. Quilgars (eds) *Homelessness and social policy*, London: Routledge, pp 149-58.

Pleace, N., Burrows, R. and Quilgars, D. (1997) 'Homelessness in contemporary Britain: conceptualisation and measurement', in R. Burrows, N. Pleace and D. Quilgars (eds) *Homelessness and social policy*, London: Routledge, pp 1-18.

Prime, J., Taylor, P. and Waters-Fuller, J. (1998) *Police service personnel: England and Wales, as at 31 March 1998*, Home Office Statistical Bulletin, Issue 17/98, London: Government Statistical Service.

Rose, D. (1997) 'From zero to nothing', *The Observer*, 12 January.

Rothman, J. (1991) *Runaway and homeless youth*, New York, NY: Longman.

Social Exclusion Unit (1998) *Rough sleeping – Report by the Social Exclusion Unit*, London: The Stationery Office.

Spurling, L. (1998) *The victimisation of homeless people*, http://www.cf.ac.uk/uwee/cplan/enhr/files/Spurling-L.html.

Stedman Jones, G. (1971) *Outcast London*, Oxford: Oxford University Press.

Stephens, M. and Becker, S. (1994) *Police force, police service*, London: Macmillan.

Travis, A. and Meikle, J. (1997) 'Parties squabble over street cred', *The Guardian*, 8 January.

Volosinov, V. (1929) (reprinted 1986) *Marxism and the philosophy of language*, Cambridge, MA: Harvard University Press.

Walker, N. (1971) *Crimes, courts and figures: An introduction to criminal justice statistics*, Harmondsworth: Penguin.

Watson, R. (1994) 'Major's war on the beggars', *Bristol Evening Post*, 27 May.

Widdowfield, R. (1998) 'The limitations of official homelessness statistics', in D. Dorling and L. Simpson (eds) *Statistics in society*, London: Arnold, pp 181-8.

Wilson, J. and Kelling, G. (1982) 'Broken windows', *Atlantic Monthly*, March, pp 29-38.

EIGHT

The homelessness legislation as a vehicle for marginalisation: making an example out of the paedophile

David Cowan and Rose Gilroy

> One of the delegates, a Bakers' Union shop steward, who had lost his job in one of the big mergers of the local bakeries, got up and said.... "It's the morality of housing that we're after. Society is a chain, and the strength of a chain is its weakest link, and the wealth of a society is the wealth of its poorest members.". (Benn, 1990, p 15)

Introduction

Nowhere are the Orwellian characteristics of access laws more apparent than in the formulation and implementation of the homelessness legislation in England and Wales. Even though the UK is in the process of implementing a variant on the European Convention of Human Rights, this will not guarantee a 'right to housing'. Indeed, talk of 'rights' in this context is misconceived because the homelessness legislation has "always required us to oppress the homeless by making *moral judgments*, not about their housing need, but about *why* the homeless become homeless in the first place" (Cowan, 1997a, p 21). The homelessness legislation, therefore, provides a shroud which legitimates the exclusion of substantial numbers from housing.

The importance of morality, both within the legislation as well as to its interpretation, should not shock us. The rationale for the harshness of the Poor Law regime(s) was that those who required state support were, in some way, undeserving. Under one version of this legislation, undeservingness was part of the public humiliation of poverty – recipients of Poor Law relief were forced to wear the letter 'P' on the right shoulder of their uppermost garment (Cranston, 1985, pp 34-43). With this in mind, it is surely significant that the two defining periods in the making of the modern homelessness legislation – 1976-77 (culminating with the 1977 Housing (Homeless Persons) Act) and 1993-96 (1996 Housing Act, Parts VI and VII) – have taken place against a backdrop of a broader societal concern about the relationship between the creation of, and response to, poverty. Parliamentary debates surrounding the 1977 Act must be read in the context of the "extensive and hysterical" media coverage of the case of Derek Deevy, the supposed "King Con" of a broader problem of welfare scroungerphobia (Golding and Middleton, 1982, p 61). Similarly, Parliamentary debates surrounding the 1996 Housing Act, Parts VI and VII, must be read in the context of ill-founded concern that single mothers became pregnant to jump the housing queue (DoE, 1994; on this issue, see generally Cowan, 1998). Again, this was perceived as the pinnacle of a much broader complaint about the 'problem' of welfare, in which claimants are regarded in some way as fraudulent (see DSS, 1998 for current discussions of welfare 'fraud').

This background provides one of the central contexts in which local authorities are required to interpret the legislation. A further broad context has been the changing patterns of the housing (quasi-) market, which could not have been foreseen when Stephen Ross MP put forward his Housing (Homeless Persons) Bill to Parliament. The impact of the subsequent Thatcher–Major era and beyond has been to exacerbate inequalities in each sector of that market (summarised in Bramley, 1993, p 129). Thus, local authority officials are forced into ever-harsher interpretations of the homelessness legislation because of the supply-side failure. Yet, this failure is spatially, qualitatively and temporally differentiated, which in turn legitimates different levels and types of decision making between and within local authorities (Loveland, 1995). In this context, attempts to realise the 'goal' of equal decision making through the Code of Guidance (envisaged in DoE, 1989) have foundered (compare the 'rule of law' concept that the law should be applied equally to all: Dicey, 1902; cf Cotterell, 1992, pp 152 et seq).

Meshing with debates about the legitimacy of bureaucratic discretion (Franklin and Clapham, 1997), there has been a long-term controversy about the role and relevance of formal law over and above the 'local law' (Mashaw, 1983). By 'formal law' is meant the homelessness legislation itself, Statutory Instruments, and Code(s) of Guidance, together with the enormous number of judicial decisions which have arisen out of it. The law is now so complex that the leading text covering it stretches to 278 pages (Arden and Hunter, 1997), and in places the law is also contradictory.

Not surprisingly, therefore, Loveland's in-depth study of three local authorities' implementation of the legislation in 1989-90 found widespread *ultra vires* decision-making practices. He concluded that "legalism is an intruder in the administrative arena. It does not prescribe administrative behaviour, but challenges it. It does not facilitate the decision-making process, rather it gets in the way" (Loveland, 1992, p 22).

Broader socio-legal research has labelled this as a regulatory trilemma: "Law is either ignored by the system, or it destroys the system's traditional norms of behaviour; or is itself disintegrated by the pressures imposed on it by the political and social systems" (Teubner, 1987; Black, 1996). This derives from the belief that law has become self-referential ("decisions refer to rules and rules to decisions": Teubner, 1984, p 295), which has fuelled talk of a "crisis in regulatory law" (Teubner, 1984, p 295). This broader work enables us to ask the question whether the law *should be* directive of alternative, autonomous systems guiding the administrative process. A recent study of administrative processes in one authority subjected to considerable judicial inspection found that officers regarded the law as malleable, so that, in part, "the sense which the officers have of *how* to secure a decision which fits with the [officer's] initial perceptions has been informed in part by their experience of judicial review" (Halliday, 1998b, p 207). In addition officers "required [applicants] to be squeezed into the intelligible format of an either/or dichotomy" (Halliday, 1998a) – a classic statement of law's binary divide, that is, lawful/unlawful, legal/ illegal etc. So, the law denies the applicant's ability to tell their housing history, as well as legitimating the 'gut feeling' of officers about individual applicants. Indeed, a feature of recent socio-legal research has been the finding that the 'gut feeling' or instant moral judgement has determined the assessment as well as the techniques deployed within the assessment process (see also Sainsbury, 1992; Cowan, 1997a).

In the next two parts of this chapter, we set out the parameters of homelessness law. Our analysis begins with a brief consideration of the key concepts of the homelessness legislation. In the second section, we argue that judicial decisions have fairly consistently undermined the original intentions behind the Act. This needs to be emphasised, even though it is well known (Loveland, 1996; Cowan, 1997b; Hunter and Miles, 1997), because of the recent belief espoused in the media of the 'radical' or 'liberal' judiciary (see, for example, Lightfoot and Prescott, 1995). It is argued that precisely the opposite is true (Griffiths, 1991; Cowan, 1997a, pp 156-60) and that the law is a legitimating process for decision-making practices which can be seen through a brief analysis of a recent case concerning a paedophile.

In the third part, however, we take a very different perspective. We look at some of the contexts which guide the decision-making practices in relation to paedophiles, locating the role of housing as one part of a broader matrix of criminal justice agencies. We draw upon the recent discourse around the management of 'risk' and society's apparently increasing need to know. These illustrate the different approaches to decision making which concentrate on surveillance techniques and tactics. We argue that the need to know impels the move towards interagency decision making, and that risk assessments and housing assessments often have a symbiotic relationship. At the same time, however, we argue that there is a language of homelessness, bound up with the legislation, which provides a filter for discussions and decisions. This filter also structures extraneous factors such as broader structural prejudices and biases. The homelessness decision-making process provides a broad reflection of societal pressures, casting local authority officers in the role of 'urban gatekeepers'. The relevance of law, from this perspective, is that it provides a legitimation for decision-making practices. Bias and prejudice are thus filtered and communicated through the language of the homelessness legislation.

Our research attempts to use the literature to reconfigure our understanding of this complex social process and through that to refine the literature itself. This is done in four ways. First, we contextualise decision-making practices by reference to debates concerning peripheral organisations, such as probation and the police, around the issue of risk and argue that these different discipline-based debates have an integral effect on housing decision making. Second, the resultant interagency working is potentially fraught with problems because each agency is working according to their own predefined boundaries or languages which structure the way each agency enters into discussions. Homelessness discussion is based upon homelessness decision-making criteria or upon what others believe those criteria to be. Third, paradoxically, these criteria hide the fact that decision making in the case of the paedophile can be shown to adopt its own risk assessment of future housing problems which an allocation might cause. The question does not concern a person's housing need but whether our systems are sufficient to enable surveillance and control of the paedophile so as to minimise housing management problems. Housing assessors have, from this perspective, become the mediators of the new criminal justice. Fourth, the law has a negative influence because it is used to reduce access to housing to the required minimum as well as to legitimate exclusion from housing. It supplies the filtration mechanism through which various structural prejudices and biases can be motivated. These 'true' motivating factors are extraneous, but hidden by the shroud of the law.

1996 Housing Act, Part VII: definitions and ideologies

In order to be entitled to accommodation, an applicant must successfully negotiate a number of different obstacles (Watchman and Robson, 1981) – within the terms of the legislation, the authority must find the applicant 'homeless', 'eligible', in 'priority need', and 'not intentionally homeless'. Only then will the applicant be entitled to accommodation which must be 'suitable' and for a minimum period of two years. However, if the applicant has no 'local connection' with the authority to which an application is made, that authority may refer the applicant to an authority with which the applicant does have such a connection.

Contrary to popular expectation, the definition of homelessness refers not to rooflessness (cf DoE, 1994), but to the more flexible principle of having no "accommodation which it would be reasonable for [the applicant] to continue to occupy" (Section 175(3))[1]. This phrase was always regarded as broader than rooflessness, although its limits were unclear. After an unfortunate decision by the House of Lords (*R v Hillingdon LBC ex parte Puhlhofer* [1986] AC 484), the definition was clarified so that a person could be regarded as homeless when they were occupying accommodation which it would not be "reasonable to continue to occupy".

At the same time as reasonableness was inserted into the definition, local authorities were also given a discretion to take into account the "general circumstances prevailing in relation to housing" in their area (now, Section 177(2)). Thus, a local authority might deny that a person is homeless because of the lack of appropriate housing (see Carlen, 1994). In short, reasonableness is judged by way of comparison with other housed persons. Where no comparison is possible an absurd situation arises where obviously poor conditions may not be enough to give a person any entitlement under the Act. The converse – that definitions should be wider where supply is plentiful – also seems to be correct.

Under the 1996 Act, certain people are made "ineligible for assistance". These people are any person who is "subject to immigration control within the meaning of the Asylum and Immigration Act 1996" (Section

185(2)). Those asylum-seekers not caught by this provision nevertheless are not eligible "if [they have] any accommodation in the United Kingdom, however temporary, available for [their] occupation" (Section 186(1)).

The third criterion is that the applicant must have a priority need. Ironically, this concept says little about need and certainly does not give priority. It is simply a further obstacle which must be jumped. For those with dependant children, it is easily cleared. One of the original purposes of the 1977 Act was to keep children and families together and so it might be argued that this tallies with the notion of protecting the family against all external forces (such as the state taking children into care). Those without children, including two-person households, must fit within a category of 'vulnerability' for some reason and/or 'emergency'. This debilitating terminology underlines the fact that if the applicant does not fit within either, all that the authority has to do is to provide 'advice and assistance', not accommodation.

The original Bill was regarded as a 'charter for queue jumpers' because it was believed that people would (ab)use its provisions to jump to the top of the housing queue. These people were variously described in Parliament as the 'voluntary homeless' or the 'self-induced homeless' or the 'self-inflicted homeless' (see, for example, *House of Commons Debates*, vol 926, cols 921, 972-5, William Rees-Davies MP). An amendment was made to enable local authorities to reject those applicants who had made themselves intentionally homeless (see Loveland, 1991 for discussion). This concept asks the local authority to judge the morality of the applicant's actions surrounding leaving their last settled accommodation. A household becomes intentionally homeless if they deliberately do or fail to do anything in consequence of which they cease to occupy accommodation which is available for their occupation and which it would have been reasonable for them to continue to occupy (now Section 191). Reasonableness once again is specifically related to the housing in the area. The complexity of the provision is mirrored in the complexity of the case law. Indeed, in order to make it work, the Court of Appeal had to alter the tenses used in the section: *Dyson v Kerrier District Council* [1980] 1 WLR 1205.

This provision has caused considerable confusion in practice – for example, Binney et al found in an early study that significant numbers of women, who had been beaten, were found intentionally homeless (1981, pp 78-85). More recent studies have found similar practices as well as more sophisticated techniques for avoiding obligations (Malos and Hague, 1993; Cowan 1997a, Chapter 6).

Notwithstanding such decision-making practices, the 1996 Act strengthened the intentionality provision to cover cases of collusion. In the Consultation Paper, it was argued that those asked to leave accommodation by family or friends should not be eligible so as to "reduce the abuse" of the legislation (DoE, 1994, para 8.2). A watered down version now appears in the Act such that where applicants are known to have constructed a charade of having been told to leave their accommodation by friends or family they may be found intentionally homeless (Section 191(3)). This new provision clearly marks out the broader, more punitive, terrain in which the government were pursuing their reforms.

Successful applicants are entitled to be provided with suitable accommodation for a minimum period of two years (Section 193). Where there is other suitable accommodation available in the area, the local authority are only obliged to provide "such advice and assistance as the authority consider is reasonably required to enable [the applicant] to secure such accommodation" (Section 197(2)). In other words, the authority is required to divert successful applicants into accommodation in other sectors. While there are doubts as to the use of the private sector, particularly in relation to its spatial distribution (Rhodes and Bevan, 1997), one might ask what would be the point in making a homelessness application if the authority is simply to act as a conduit to the private-rented sector. If this were the result, it would surely result in further deterring people from applying as homeless (see Carlen, 1994).

The judicial approach

Despite the inclusion of the intentional homelessness provision, judicial opinions have, with monotonous regularity, proceeded on the basis that the legislation does, in fact, enable certain persons to jump the housing queue. From this base, the House of Lords have argued that the homelessness legislation is "a lifeline of last resort; not to enable [applicants] to make inroads into the local authority's waiting list ...": *R v Hillingdon LBC ex parte Puhlhofer* [1986] AC 484, 517; regarded as "true and perceptive" by the House of Lords in *R v Brent LBC ex parte Awua* [1996] 1 AC 55. On the other hand, it appears that this was precisely what the Act was intended to do (see Loveland, 1996, pp 101-2). This frustration of legislative purpose, or intention, continually comes across in the case law. Judges start, it seems, from the position that homelessness applicants are seeking, in some way, to abuse the system and should be stopped; not from the position that applicants are trying to enforce legitimate expectations.

This comes across most clearly in a recent case concerning a convicted paedophile who, on release from prison, approached the local authority under the homelessness legislation. He was found intentionally homeless on the basis that he had "committed offences which were deliberate acts on [his] part which did as a matter of fact lead to [his] arrest, [his] remand in custody, [his] trial and [his] eventual imprisonment" (*R v Hounslow LBC ex parte R* (1997) 29 HLR 939, 941). The question in the case was whether there was a causal nexus between his acts and his loss of accommodation. Applying earlier case law, the judge held that the relevant test was whether "the fair minded bystander could say to himself 'He asked for it'" (*Robinson v Torbay BC* [1982] 1 All ER 726, 730). In the Hounslow case, the judge put it thus:

> ... the fair-minded bystander must be taken to know the relevant facts of the case, namely that the applicant had a long history of sexual offences with repeated long periods in prison; that if he committed further similar offences, there was no sensible ground for concluding that the court would deal with him otherwise than by a lengthy custodial sentence; that the applicant was impecunious and unable to keep up payments of his rent without housing benefit; and that housing benefit would cease after he was sent to prison. On that basis the fair-minded bystander would unhesitatingly conclude that the loss of accommodation was the likely result of committing further offences. (at p 949)

This blurring of the boundaries between civil and criminal law to justify the exclusion of R provides an important example of the willingness of the judiciary to manufacture a solution to a perceived problem (for local authority approaches in respect of ex-offenders more generally, see Cowan and Fionda, 1994). As Fionda and Cowan put it:

> In short, so many external events influenced the surrender of [R's] tenancy that only tortuous reasoning could lead to the conclusion adopted by [the judge]. Furthermore, while the fair-minded bystander might be taken to have known of R's history, it would be an incredibly knowledgeable fair-minded bystander who would know about the relevant housing benefit rules. (Fionda and Cowan, 1998, p 323)

The case also provides further evidence of the limitations of binary legalism as well as the importance of judicial perceptions of morality. Rather than answering the more pertinent questions which local authority and other officers must pursue, the court proceeds on the basis of the "eliminative ideal", which, "put bluntly, strives to solve present and emerging problems by getting rid of troublesome and disagreeable people with methods which are lawful and widely supported" (Rutherford, 1997).

Making an example out of the paedophile

An examination of the housing issues arising out of the 'case of the paedophile' provides evidence of different context(s) within which the homelessness legislation is administered. This context involves making a link between developments/confluence in homelessness and criminal justice policy (see Cowan, 1997a), as well as the discourse of risk and housing (Ericson and Haggerty, 1997; 6, 1998). Indeed, conceptualising this example in terms of risk enables a reconfiguring of the notion of allocating social housing according to need. Here we must think of need on the basis of a variety of different permutations as well as *potential* permutations. Risk requires not only an assessment of need but also an assessment of management roles and responsibilities: "Risk is an invention based on imagined fears and on imaginative technologies for dealing with them" (Ericson and Haggerty, 1997, p 39).

Risk, panopticism and transcarceration

While a number of chapters in this book consider the risk to individuals, this represents only one dimension of the contemporary concern with risk. Equally important is the growing concern with the identification and management of the risk which particular individuals are perceived to pose to society. The shift from need to risk is important because it is a move from positive to negative and, in this terminological change, we can detect the eliminative ideal: "... the concept of risk is now only associated with negative outcomes. Definitions of risk are now only associated with notions of hazard, danger, exposure, harm and loss." (Parton, 1996, p 105). Risk has also become the universal language of social control, defining inclusion and exclusion; and, tellingly perhaps, suggests that the assertion of Michael Howard (the former Home Secretary) that "Prison works" is misplaced within what Ericson calls the "risk society" (1994). In defining the risk that one individual may re-offend, there can be no absolutes because the question requires us to anticipate an individual's future actions on the basis of an imperfect appreciation of why people commit crimes (and/or re-offend) in the first place. Furthermore, while the ubiquity and terminology of risk suggests that it is an exact science, or nearly so, it is clear that there are only possible permutations; and each permutation is calculated according to the calculator's value system (see, for example, Kemshall, 1996). Any risk assessment can only draw upon the inadequate data which this previous research has produced (see Beckett, 1994, esp pp 56-7), thus compounding the original inadequacy (see the debate between Soothill et al, 1998 and Colledge, 1998).

The shift towards 'risk assessment' enables and requires us to increase our use of surveillance techniques (Cohen, 1985, pp 220-2; Ericson, 1994, pp 169-70), for only then can we begin to perfect our risk management systems (Ericson and Haggerty, 1997, p 52). The risk society then is a panoptic society best exemplified by the constant surveillance of some paedophiles after their release from prison (Tendler, 1998; see also Fielding, 1997). Risk, therefore, drives a wedge through the rehabilitative ideal and challenges the credibility of the criminal justice model based upon prison. Release from prison simply leads to *transcarceration* in the same way as release from hospitals are said to lead, occasionally, to transinstitutionalisation. In this sense, risk plays on our fears for our security. We can never know whether rehabilitation has been effective (cognitive behavioural therapy for sex offenders, the most widely used treatment, has an uncertain success rate) and it is this which provides our justification for subsequent, consistent surveillance.

Transcarceration and surveillance are the implicit and explicit motives behind the supervision register created under the 1997 Sex Offenders Act. They are also apparent in the Crime and Disorder Act's promotion of the sex offender order (Sections 2 and 3), which might operate to exclude sex offenders from certain areas such as nursery schools or playgrounds. The purpose of the register and the order are to "protect the public". So, for example, the Home Office consultation paper argued that "more must be done to protect society from sex offenders, who pose a *continuing risk*" (Home Office, 1997, para 2). But do they? If the question is whether, in respect of a known paedophile, they are likely to re-offend, different studies provide different answers (West, 1997). So Bedarf argues as follows:

> Advocates of sex offender registration laws continue to fuel this public misperception by touting high recidivism rates as the reason why registration laws are necessary.... [R]ecidivism is not as significant a problem as these advocates claim. Indeed, if actual recidivism rates motivated registration laws, drug dealers and burglars would be the prime targets of registration laws, rather than sex offenders. (Bedarf, 1995, p 898; see also Fisher, 1994)

The problem with both these orders and registers is that they form knee-jerk reactions to public debate which present unthought-out solutions to unthought-out problems. As such, their use is unclear. What is the purpose of a register? What are the limits to the sex offender order? The only answer given is 'the protection of the public'. Simply setting up a register is unlikely to protect the public – it depends what *use* is to be made of it (see Cobley, 1997), but "there has been very little consideration of the ethical limits to community-based management strategies" (Hebenton and Thomas, 1996a, p 109).

Simply applying for a sex offender order is unlikely to protect the public unless it is continually supervised (see Barron, 1990, for the effect of non-molestation orders and injunctions on those who batter their partners). It is here, also, that we have confusion, in the same way as the 'community' is never defined, what we mean by 'the public' is left hanging in the air (see Crawford, 1995).

Even the belief that the existence of registers and orders provide 'protection' can be challenged because, however we try, we cannot protect *completely*. They can minimise risk, or make risks acceptable, but risk itself can never be nullified: "The best one can do is seek security through calibrations of danger that will, one hopes, reduce the imagined losses or harms" (Ericson and Haggerty, 1997, p 88). As regards sex offenders, our assessment of risk is related to extraneous circumstances, such as media reports which heighten our sense of moral outrage and create fear for our security (see Kemshall, 1996; Hilpern, 1997). Statistics reporting low rates of re-offending do not give comfort because they are interpreted as a failure to detect and convict (Utting, 1997, paras 9.1-9.3). Anxiety is further fuelled by the belief that few offenders are ever caught so we can never *know* how many there are (Colledge, 1998). Even when we do know, our systems are unable to operate either because of a belief in 'due process' (so that new systems do not affect those who are released from prison, or who are not prosecuted, before the systems came into operation) or because the systems are unable to cope (Patton, 1997). It is from these different angles that, at one and the same time, we need to know but our knowledge is always incomplete.

Knowing

This thirst for knowledge, and inability to identify levels of risk with accuracy, has a number of consequential overlapping effects, two of which are considered here. First, the need to know must, in the liturgy of the law, be balanced against the rights of the (ex-)offender. Systems must be devised to enable the public, or certain members of the public, to be told of the existence of the sex offender in their community (the police defining public and community). Why they should be told is never explored, other than for their own protection, and the effect on the offender, from this perspective, must be balanced against the risk to the public. Second, the need to know (present) must be balanced against the need to manage (future), which in turn requires cross-disciplinary approaches:

> **Risk society is fragmented. Fragmentation results from the fact that risk as danger subverts institutional boundaries. Risks blur the boundaries of professional knowledges, raise complex ethical issues that require interdisciplinary approaches, force the adoption of more stringent institutional responsibility and accountability, and forge new interinstitutional alliances. (Ericson and Haggerty, 1997, p 118)**

Interdisciplinary working has come about through a belated discovery that single aspect solutions cannot solve complex problems. However, this approach raises problems of its own, particularly around the issue of knowledge: when should other organisations be told? how much should they be told? what can they do?

Community notification

A Home Office Circular provides guidance on when community notification should be based upon a risk assessment (Home Office, 1997, para 13), taking account of the following factors:

a the nature and pattern of previous offending;
b compliance with previous sentences or Court Orders;
c the probability that a further offence will be committed;

d   the harm such behaviour would cause;

e   any predatory behaviour which may indicate a likelihood that he will re-offend;

f   the potential objects of the harm (and whether they are children or otherwise especially vulnerable);

g   the potential consequences of disclosure to the offender and their family;

h   the potential consequences of disclosure in the wider context of law and order.

In *R v Chief Constable of North Wales Police ex parte Thorpe* [1998] 3 All ER 310, the North Wales police disclosed to the owner of a caravan site that certain paedophiles were living on the site. Disclosure had been felt to be particularly important because of the risk that Thorpe and others were there "during the Easter holidays when a large number of young children would be there". Furthermore, the police had asked Thorpe and the others to move but they had not done so. Lord Woolf MR said that "disclosure should only be made when there was a pressing need for that disclosure" (see also Hayes, 1992, in the context of disclosure of an alleged paedophile to current live-in partners by social workers). The police's decision to notify the owner was upheld even though they had not given the ex-offender the opportunity to correct certain inaccuracies because, even if they had been given the opportunity, it would not have altered the outcome. Yet, speaking extra-judicially before a Parliamentary Select Committee, Lord Bingham, the Chief Justice, who decided the case at first instance, made the following point:

> **One was left with a great concern. These people had not shown any propensity to re-offend at all. They were not hanging around schools, they were not doing anything they should not have done but one can well understand the concern of the police that *they should have been in that place at that time*. There has to be some public understanding unless people are just going to be treated as lepers for ever after a conviction of this kind. (emphasis added)**

This risk assessment therefore seems to have been based upon the ex-offenders being in the wrong *place* at the wrong *time*. The point Bingham is making (presumably) is that, in spite of our professed desire for tolerance, our anticipatory concern is whetted by fear of the location and time.

Our knowledge of their whereabouts causes this fear to exist in the first place, and this is exacerbated by other factors. It is this knowledge, however, which means that *any* place is the *wrong* place, and *any* time is the *wrong* time. At the same time, the role of witchfinder general now belongs to the guardians of the law and order consensus.

Disclosure also plays a key role in the labelling process – '(sexual) deviant' – within the confines of the community. Here, the community is defined by the persons to whom the police disclose the information, as well as the level of disclosure from (un)officially sanctioned leaks to local media through to selective disclosure to local primary school headteachers to non-disclosure. The paedophile has then become the most undeserving recipient of welfare – indeed, the present-day recipient of the Poor Law ethos.

Disclosure also involves non-legal processes encouraged by the need to know. Under the guise of 'protection of the public', local media insist on outing paedophiles living locally (see Younge, 1997). Pressure groups of parents are set up, such as SPEAK (Stop Paedophiles Exploiting and Abusing Kids), which seek to out and promise to watch suspected paedophiles – paedophile hunts have thus become the modern version of witch hunts. 'Protection of the public' is then the reason why "child sex-killer Sidney Cooke" was literally transcarcerated (from prison to police cell) and, while condemning the almost inevitable rioting outside the prison (Harding et al, 1998), ministers took a populist stance by proposing indefinite imprisonment for "dangerous child molesters" (Wood, 1998). Cooke is now 70 years old, yet the photograph used of him throughout the media is of a younger man in an evil pose (cf Myra Hindley). As Hebenton and Thomas put it:

> ... **public discussion (discursivity) of the sexual offender threat is related to everyday life, drenched with experience and plays with cultural symbols. It is also highly media-dependent and manipulable. It is 'at odds' with the criminal justice system's 'calculated knowledge' of risk assessment and management. (Hebenton and Thomas, 1996b, p 441)**

Interdisciplinarity

A further characteristic of the 'risk assessment' is its cross-disciplinary nature. By its very nature, a risk assessment implies that no single organisation, discipline, or individual has the requisite knowledge/power to provide the necessary comprehensiveness. This is a well-known phenomenon in child protection, and various forms of needs assessments. In this sense, the risk assessment is about the disempowering of individual professions as no one agency is "the sole possessor of necessary expertise in the area" (Langan, 1993). This process of disempowerment is occurring at the same time as lay people have begun to appreciate the problem of such assessments and so call into question the professionalism on the basis of different criteria:

> **The faith that supports trust in expert systems involves a blocking off of the ignorance of the lay person when faced with the claims of expertise; but realisation of the areas of ignorance which confront the experts themselves, as individual practitioners and in terms of overall fields of knowledge, may weaken or undermine that faith on the part of lay individuals. (Giddens, 1990, p 130)**

Interdisciplinarity also *creates* problems. The point often made is that our own disciplines dictate the way we receive information and knowledge (Fish, 1994, p 239). Each discipline has its own set of logics, its own culture and understanding, and brings all of this within the umbrella of the interorganisational network. It is in the nature of disciplines that they are "normatively closed, but cognitively open" (Teubner, 1984). The important question (for our purposes) relates to the understanding of housing need within these organisations and its importance in their processes. And the answer seems to be that housing need often forms a crucial part of a risk assessment, for in this context risk and need have a symbiotic, self-referential relationship. Risks are related to needs, and needs to risks. We are required to assess a person's housing need as an integral part of a risk assessment, and risk assessment also influences the assessment of housing need. But the relationship is not symmetrical. For example, it is *non*-housing agencies who determine when housing need assessments are required for the purpose of a risk assessment. Any risk assessment is important in determining housing need but housing professionals are likely to be denied this knowledge.

Regarding the relationship between assessments as self-referential is also problematic. As we have seen, the homelessness legislation has a fairly specific method of filtering societal prejudice into assessments of housing need. The language of homelessness, from this perspective, dictates the way homelessness agencies receive and impart information. This language differs from that used in other interpretative systems involving, for example, risk assessments. The language of homelessness is about judging past behaviour against its own set of criteria. These criteria require the homelessness agency to develop their own barriers which inhibit their ability to work with other agencies, for it is the homelessness officers, and they alone, who are responsible for making the housing decision(s). Rather than talk about housing (or any other sort of) need, they must talk about reasonableness or priority need or intentionality because that is required by the system. It is housing officers who are required to make these assessments because that is their professional preserve.

Homelessness assessments: the salience of housing need

So far we have examined how the law has been interpreted to reinforce societal views on the deserving and the undeserving groups in society. We then moved on to explore 'risk'. In this section we bring these ideas together to determine how decisions by homelessness officers may be informed by their own bias, their own assessment of the risk presented by paedophiles and their organisation's ability to manage that risk. The process can be unpicked to reveal a number of issues being factored in and weighed against each other.

There is the concern that the identity of the paedophile will become known in the area. The consequences are unpredictable but may include both verbal and physical harassment as well as attacks upon the paedophile's home (and therefore damage to the landlord's property). In some cases the paedophile may well have to flee, which may lead to that person 'going underground' in the private rented sector (English, 1997). In other cases a landlord who has seen the warning signs may relocate the paedophile but with the renewed possibility of community confrontation. Or knowledge of a paedophile in the neighbourhood may prompt existing tenants to make transfer requests. How are these requests to be treated? Does the presence of a paedophile constitute a *risk* to any and every child? If one transfer is allowed does it encourage others? How many transfer requests have to happen before an estate becomes difficult to let?

This issue of outing raises a number of other issues. The outing process cannot be controlled by housing officers. Outing may be carried out by the police, social services, other agencies and/or the media for, in their view, the purposes of public protection. Outing may equally come from within the housing authority itself as happened in Birmingham in 1996 when a housing officer informed the community of a decision to rehouse a paedophile (Murray, 1997). This raises the further issue of who has the right to know a paedophile's history. Should the community be informed so that they may manage the risk to their children? Should the community be informed as part of their rights as tenants? Should the concept of the tenant as a partner, who is consulted on substantive policy changes and to whom officers and members are accountable, be suspended in these instances?

Earlier in the chapter we discussed concepts of the deserving and undeserving. Many groups of people have claims to be rehoused. Undoubtedly a factor for officers to consider is who will make the best use of the housing. In the case of a paedophile, the officer may judge that this person will re-offend because such behaviour is uncurable. As a result of that re-offending, that person may well be evicted and subsequently found intentionally homeless. This line of thinking may lead to the conclusion that there is no point allocating housing to a person who will subsequently be evicted (colloquially expressed as being 'set up to fail'). Yet, allocation of a property is seen by many as a necessary part of the package of measures intended to prevent re-offending. The point to be emphasised is that allocation is just *one* part of that package. The housing concern is that appropriate systems need to be in place to provide surveillance and control of the paedophile. These systems need to monitor that person's behaviour. But who should carry out the monitoring? Should this be carried out by occasional visits by a probation or police officer, or by housing officers monitoring CCTV video tapes in tower blocks?

Finally, there is the uncertain impact of political feeling from elected members. The role of politicians in the homelessness decision-making process is less than clear, though part of our current research has revealed that in some authorities elected members have predetermined a quota of applicants who may be 'successful' in the homelessness process. However, in the particular context of the paedophile, it appears that pressure has been brought to bear by councillors in Rhonda Cynon Taff and Middlesbrough to exclude them from the housing register (Ford, 1997; Tendler, 1997). Councillor Michael Carr, chair of Middlesbrough Council's housing committee, argued in a letter to *The Guardian* (1997) that a council tenancy was not a requirement for rehabilitation and, additionally, that "council tenants should [not] accept conditions which no other sector of housing would tolerate". This may be local politicians fearful of the backlash on the street and at the ballot box if 'outing' occurs or it is known that members have agreed to local protocols which link housing policies with broader objectives of criminal justice organisations. Equally, such a response could be seen as a fight back by the local authority sector which is unwilling to sink into a welfare role.

We have highlighted how homelessness assessments require facts relating to a person's housing to be filtered through a particular language. Those assessments may use similar detail to that used for the purpose of risk assessments; but, within the detail, the emphasis will be different. All of the information about past housing histories will be affected by the emphasis given to questions by the housing officer when interviewing an applicant. The interview provides the filtration site for the interviewer will ask questions based upon their own appreciation (or lack of it) of the law and the local authority's policy. The information given by the applicant will be filtered into this matrix; and the subsequent decision will refer to it. Empirical research reveals that the tone of the interview often relates to the interviewer's belief about the morality of the applicant's actions and a 'gut feeling' as to the truth about the applicant's story – leaving a partner because of that person's violence (Malos and Hague, 1993), or a belief that young people should stay at home until they are old enough to cope (Cowan, 1997a). All the time, the interviewer is weighing up the applicant's story against their own value system. The search, then, is not for truth but *the interviewer's truth* – "it is here that the direct relationship between discretion and power lies. This is the heart of the unavoidable power imbalance between applicant and decision-maker" (Halliday, 1998a). As well as this, though, the housing decision maker makes a risk assessment concerning the applicant's predicted pathway in the local authority stock. Broadly, any assessment of housing need within the language of homelessness will be influenced by views on how any housing allocation will be managed (risk management).

Assessments of housing need require, therefore, not only a consideration of past housing histories, but also future housing management issues. As important as the reason why a person becomes homeless is the (ab)use they will make of any accommodation. The argument is that if you place a paedophile in secure housing, they can be better supervised and controlled because we *know* where they are (council housing is the panopticon). This argument is one favoured by, among others, Lord Woolf MR in the *Thorpe* case. It makes sense as well, because a person who is required to move around from one short-term let to another is bound to be more difficult to track.

It could, however, be argued that placing a person in secure accommodation will make them *less* likely to register for fear that knowledge of their past will infiltrate the local community. Disclosure of the Thorpes' presence has meant that "they had 'gone to ground' to escape further hounding" (Gentleman, 1998). But secure housing is not, in any event, what is often given to successful applicants because they are entitled simply to two years accommodation either in council or private rented accommodation. The Labour government has added that successful homelessness applicants are guaranteed a reasonable preference on the waiting list. Even so, such a tenant might, with other waiting list applicants, be offered an introductory tenancy with limited security. In any event authorities have a duty first to consider whether they are able to divert successful applicants into other tenures (the "suitable alternative accommodation" provision: Section 197) and so any successful paedophile applicant could be diverted into the private rented sector anyway (although cf Section 197(4)(a) – duty to take into account "the characteristics and personal circumstances of the applicant" in the decision whether or not to use the diversion procedure). Thus, broader housing processes and legislation mean that security simply does not exist any more (although policy makers commonly assume that it does).

Conclusion

Housing officers have become crucial mediators in the new brand of punitive criminal justice, as well as having an important voice in cross-disciplinary risk assessments. Such cross-disciplinary bodies are regarded as good practice in the context of allocation of housing to paedophiles by the Chartered Institute of Housing (CIH), for they enable information sharing and a cross-agency response (CIH, 1997, p 5). What housing officers can bring to the discussion is local knowledge (particularly true of decentralised housing officers), potential reactions within the local community, and knowledge of peripheral issues such as child density levels (although the first two are, to a certain extent, based on subjective perceptions). They may not come to the table with offers of accommodation. There must be some doubt as to what housing officers can add to such bodies for, as the CIH itself posits, "*[Risk assessment] is not the role of housing professionals*" (1997, p 6, original emphasis). We have argued, however, that risk assessment is precisely what housing professionals do, albeit from their own perspective.

Indeed, risk assessment is bound to be taken into account by housing officers in their housing assessment. Assessment of housing need within the language of homelessness will equally relate to, and take account of, how any housing allocation will be managed. When all of this is added to two other factors – the residualisation of housing and the exposure of housing officers to the societal imagery of the paedophile as folk-devil – the relevance of law within the administrative process can only be limited. Administrative decision making here may well adopt what jurisprudents term 'result-oriented' approaches – cloaking instant moral judgements with the legitimacy of legality. Referring to a paedophile as 'intentionally' homeless might be described as a classic example of this, for it simply does not fit within the original intention behind the provision. That the judge in the Hounslow case was able to fit intentionality to that scenario says more about the result-oriented thesis operated by judges than anything else.

Note

[1] Certain persons are deemed homeless, the most important being those subjected to violence from an 'associated person' (see Malos and Hague, 1993, 1998).

References

6, Perri (1998) 'Housing policy in the risk archipelago: towards anticipatory and holistic government', *Housing Studies*, vol 13, no 3, pp 347-76.

Arden, A. and Hunter, C. (1997) *Homelessness and allocations*, London: Legal Action Group.

Barron, J. (1990) *Not worth the paper...?*, Women's Aid Federation, England.

Beckett, R. (1994) 'Assessment of sex offenders', in T. Morrison, M. Erooga and R. Beckett (eds) *Sexual offending against children*, London: Routledge.

Bedarf, A. (1995) 'Examining sex offender community notification laws', *California Law Review*, vol 83, pp 885-939.

Benn, T. (1990) *Conflicts of interest – Diaries 1977-1980*, London: Arrow.

Binney, V., Harkell, G. and Nixon, J. (1981) *Leaving violent men*, Women's Aid Federation, England.

Black, J. (1996) 'Constitutionalising self-regulation', *Modern Law Review*, vol 59, pp 24-59.

Bramley, G. (1993) 'Explaining the incidence of statutory homelessness in England', *Housing Studies*, vol 8, pp 128-47.

Carlen, P. (1994) 'The governance of homelessness: legality, lore and lexicon in the agency-maintenance of youth homelessness', *Critical Social Policy*, vol 41, pp 18-35.

CIH (Chartered Institute of Housing) (1997) *Rehousing sex offenders – A summary of the legal and operational issues*, Coventry: CIH.

Cobley, C. (1997) 'Keeping track of sex offenders – Part I of the Sex Offenders Act 1997', *Modern Law Review*, vol 60, pp 690-7.

Cohen, S. (1985) *Visions of social control*, Cambridge: Polity Press.

Colledge, P. (1998) 'The true scale of the problem', *New Law Journal*, vol 148, pp 955-6 (1), pp 990-1 (2).

Cotterell, R. (1992) *The sociology of law*, London: Butterworths.

Cowan, D. (1997a) *Homelessness: The (in)appropriate applicant*, Aldershot: Dartmouth.

Cowan, D. (1997b) 'Doing the government's work', *Modern Law Review*, vol 60, pp 276-86.

Cowan, D. (1998) 'Reforming the homelessness legislation', *Critical Social Policy*, vol 57, pp 435-54.

Cowan, D. and Fionda, J. (1994) 'Meeting the need: the response of local housing authorities to the housing of ex-offenders', *British Journal of Criminology*, vol 34, no 4, pp 444-59.

Cranston, R. (1985) *Legal foundations of the welfare state*, London: Weidenfeld & Nicolson.

Crawford, A. (1995) *The local governance of crime*, Oxford: Clarendon.

Dicey, A. (1902) *The law of the constitution*, London: Macmillan.

DoE (Department of the Environment) (1989) *The government's review of the homelessness legislation*, London: DoE.

DoE (1994) *Access to local authority and housing association tenancies*, London: HMSO.

DSS (Department of Social Security) (1998) *Beating fraud is everyone's business*, Cm 4012, London: The Stationery Office.

English, S. (1997) 'Jeering mothers drive paedophile off council estate', *The Times*, 11 January.

Ericson, R. (1994) 'The division of expert knowledge in policing and security', *British Journal of Sociology*, vol 45, pp 149-75.

Ericson, R. and Haggerty, K. (1997) *Policing the risk society*, Oxford: Oxford University Press.

Fielding, N. (1997) 'Helpless to stop child pervert', *The Mail on Sunday*, 8 June.

Fionda, J. and Cowan, D. (1998) '"He asked for it": paedophiles and the homelessness legislation', *Child and Family Law Quarterly*, vol 10, pp 321-9.

Fish, S. (1994) 'Being interdisciplinary is so very hard to do', in S. Fish (ed) *There's no such thing as free speech ... and it's a good thing too*, Oxford: Oxford University Press.

Fisher, D. (1994) 'Adult sex offenders – who are they? Why and how do they do it?', in T. Morrison, M. Erooga, and R. Beckett (eds) *Sexual offending against children*, London: Routledge.

Ford, R. (1997) 'Council considers ban on housing paedophiles', *The Times*, 9 January.

Franklin, B. and Clapham, D. (1997) 'The social construction of housing management', *Housing Studies*, vol 12, p 7.

Gentleman, A. (1998) 'House paedophiles, demand top judges', *The Guardian*, 19 March.

Giddens, A. (1990) *The consequences of modernity*, Cambridge: Polity Press.

Golding, P. and Middleton, S. (1982) *Images of welfare*, Oxford: Basil Blackwell.

Griffiths, J. (1991) *The politics of the judiciary*, London: Penguin.

Halliday, S. (1998a) 'Administrative justice, administrative process and the social construction of knowledge', Paper given at the Socio-Legal Studies Association Conference, Manchester Metropolitan University, April.

Halliday, S. (1998b) 'Researching the "impact" of judicial review on routine decision-making', in D. Cowan (ed) *Housing: Participation and exclusion*, Aldershot: Dartmouth.

Harding, J. et al (1998) 'Hijacked by the mob', *Bristol Evening Post*, 24 April.

Hayes, M. (1992) 'Bad practice, bad law and a breach of human rights?', *Family Law*, pp 245-51.

Hebenton, B. and Thomas, T. (1996a) '"Tracking" sex offenders', *Howard Journal of Criminal Justice*, vol 35, pp 97-112.

Hebenton, B. and Thomas, T. (1996b) 'Sexual offenders in the community: reflections on problems of law, community and risk management in the USA, England and Wales', *International Journal of the Sociology of Law*, vol 24, pp 27-43.

Hilpern, K. (1997) 'Law and the lynch mob', *The Guardian*, 19 February.

Home Office (1997) *Community Protection Order: A consultation paper*, London: Home Office.

Hunter, C. and Miles, J. (1997) 'The unsettling of settled law on "settled accommodation": the House of Lords and the homelessness legislation old and new', *Journal of Social Welfare and Family Law*, vol 19, pp 267-87.

Kemshall, H. (1996) *Reviewing risk: A review of research on the assessment and management of risk and dangerousness*, London: Home Office.

Langan, M. (1993) 'New directions in social work', in J. Clarke (ed) *A crisis in care? Challenges to social work*, London: Sage Publications.

Lightfoot, L. and Prescott, M. (1995) 'Too big for their wigs', *Sunday Times*, 5 November.

Loveland, I. (1991) 'Legal rights and political realities: governmental responses to homelessness in Britain and the USA', *Law and Social Inquiry*, vol 16, pp 249-319.

Loveland, I. (1992) 'Administrative law, administrative processes, and the housing of homeless persons: a view from the sharp end', *Journal of Social Welfare Law*, vol 13, pp 4-26.

Loveland, I. (1995) *Housing homeless persons*, Oxford: Oxford University Press.

Loveland, I. (1996) 'The status of children as applicants under the homelessness legislation – judicial subversion of legislative intent', *Child and Family Law Quarterly*, vol 8, pp 89-106.

Malos, E. and Hague, G. (1993) *Domestic violence and homelessness*, Bristol: SAUS Publications.

Malos, E. and Hague, G. (1998) 'Facing both ways at once?', in D. Cowan (ed) *Housing: Participation and exclusion*, Aldershot: Dartmouth.

Mashaw, J. (1983) *Bureaucratic Justice*, New Haven, CT: Yale University Press.

Murray, I. (1997) 'Tenants back official accused of tip-off about sex offender', *The Times*, 9 January.

Niner, P. (1989) *Homelessness in nine local authorities*, London: HMSO.

Parton, N. (1996) 'Social work, risk and the "blaming system"', in N. Parton (ed) *Social theory, social change and social work*, London: Routledge.

Patton, L. (1997) 'Most sex offenders dodge list', *The Guardian*, 15 September.

Rhodes, D. and Bevan, M. (1997) *Can the private rented sector house the homeless?*, York: Centre for Housing Policy, University of York.

Rutherford, A. (1997) 'Criminal policy and the eliminative ideal', *Social Policy and Administration*, vol 31, pp 116-35.

Sainsbury, R. (1992) 'Administrative justice: discretion and procedure in social security decision-making', in K. Hawkins (ed) *The uses of discretion*, Oxford: Oxford University Press.

Soothill, K., Francis, B. and Ackerley, E. (1998) 'Paedophilia and paedophiles', *New Law Journal*, vol 148, pp 882-3.

Tendler, S. (1997) 'Council refuses to house sex offenders', *The Times*, 6 March.

Tendler, S. (1998) '30 police will keep watch on freed paedophile', *The Times*, 27 March.

Teubner, G. (1984) 'Autopoiesis in law and society: a rejoinder to Blankenburg', *Law and Society Review*, vol 18, pp 291-8.

Teubner, G. (1987) 'Juridification: concepts, aspects, limits, solutions', in G. Teubner (ed) *Juridification of the social spheres*, Berlin: Walter de Gruyter.

Utting, W. (1997) *People like us*, London: The Stationery Office.

Waddington, M. (1998) 'Too poor to stay here: "illegal immigrants" and housing officers', in D. Cowan (ed) *Housing: participation and exclusion*, Aldershot: Dartmouth.

Watchman, P. and Robson, P. (1981) 'The homeless persons obstacle race', *Journal of Social Welfare Law*, 1 (Pt I), 65 (Pt II).

West, D. (1997) 'Sexual molesters', in N. Walker (ed) *Dangerous people*, London: Blackstone.

Wood, N. (1998) 'Indefinite jail sentences for child molesters', *The Times*, 6 April.

Younge, G. (1997) 'Exposing the guilty is a public service', *The Guardian*, 10 June.

NINE

Old and homeless: a double jeopardy

Derek Hawes

Introduction

By the spring of 1992, the local authority homelessness crisis had reached its peak; in the 12 months to 31 March of that year, 145,000 families had claimed to be statutorily homeless, had been assessed as being unintentionally so and in priority need, thus becoming eligible for eventual rehousing by councils.

Ever since April 1975 when, in response to a joint Department of Environment and Department of Health circular, local council housing departments had first begun to take on the responsibility from their social services colleagues, numbers of homeless families had begun to increase relentlessly. For the next 17 years, each annual set of returns showed increases substantially larger than the previous one.

Inevitably the numbers of families resorting to Bed & Breakfast hotels, hostels and women's refuges also expanded and local authorities were constrained to find ever more ingenious temporary solutions as the tensions between waiting list applicants and those on the fast-track homeless route to permanent tenancies, became palpable.

However, despite the peak of the crisis having been reached by March 1992 and the very substantial annual reductions each year since, the emerging picture reveals a number of anomalies and problems for researchers and practitioners alike. The tide, as it were, in receding, has left contradictions and exposed a number of issues which mean that the official statistics must be treated with caution: the end of the crisis is only one way of describing the position which now faces both practitioners and policy makers.

Not the least of the confusions remaining concerns terminology. 'Statutory' homelessness is of little value in understanding the extent of housing shortage. It refers to those families and individuals who are covered by the 1977 Housing (Homeless Persons) Act and the successor legislation, currently the 1996 Housing Act. The statutes severely limit those who are eligible for assistance; not only must the applicant have no home, but must demonstrate that their loss of home is 'unintentional'; also that they are in priority need. Normally this means having children or some medical or other vulnerability which places them at risk.

Even on the basis of official figures garnered from local authority returns, in a typical year, for every hundred families rehoused under these rules, a further 108 were turned away after having been given advice. Not counted at all are those who, for reasons discussed in detail in this chapter, do not come within the ambit of council homeless departments. So 'statutory homelessness' has little relation to the total of those without a secure roof over their head.

But perhaps the most fascinating question to emerge from the apparently receding tide of the homelessness crisis relates to older people. By 1995, three years after the peak, housing practitioners were, at an anecdotal level, beginning to remark that although numbers were decreasing, the proportion of older people claiming to be homeless and vulnerable due to age, was, if anything, on the increase (Hawes, 1997). Given that this group had always represented a small percentage (no more than 4 or 5%) of the total numbers, the issue appeared to be significant. Why were the numbers of older people not reducing at the same rate as other categories of household? And what were the implications, not only for housing departments and their specialist stock, but also for the support services?

This chapter examines the phenomenon, seeking not only to establish the validity of practitioners' perceptions, but to expose the consequent issues for policy makers and underlying causes for the picture which is revealed. It is based on surveys, interviews and focus group discussions conducted among English local authorities, homeless charities and key actors, as well as the construction of a series of case histories of older people who have been homeless (Hawes, 1997). Some comparisons are made with the position of older homeless people in Scotland and Wales, and with lessons learned from the research on similar trends in the United States.

A slippery concept

The phenomenon of older homelessness is a difficult one to research for a number of practical and technical reasons discussed below. Characterised by an earlier writer (Crane, 1994) as "elusive and slippery" – an epithet for both the concepts and the subjects of enquiry – the task is made more problematic by the lack of agreement about who should be encompassed in the term 'older' and by the growing number of vagrant or 'street' homeless who rarely fall within the statutory local authority procedures for dealing with those who are both homeless and 'vulnerable due to old age'.

It is therefore clear that the statistics utilised from official sources present only a partial picture of the scale of homelessness among older people. The issue is more complex than these would suggest, not least because they do not include those who fall through the welfare net and who, because of physical or psychological problems or through discharge from prison or other institutions, find themselves homeless in later life. These people are not caught by the legislation. Many of them are between 50 and 60 and the simple lack of a secure home is part of a far more intricate pattern of deprivation; they are what one researcher has termed the "chronically homeless" (Crane, 1994).

Separate constituencies of need

We can detect then, two distinct kinds of response to those who find themselves without a settled home in later life. First there are those who are assessed and assisted by local authority housing departments under the 1996 Act. Their experience and the housing outcome that emerges is markedly different from that of the second category. Generally the process is sympathetic, swift and results in appropriate secure rehousing. Less formal, haphazard and varied responses are made to those older people who do not approach local authorities and who, in addition to having no settled home, may lack any family, financial or social resources. For this group, the chances of a settled and secure rehousing with the appropriate level of support are more remote; it will certainly take longer and will, in many cases not end in a long-term satisfactory outcome for the client (Hawes, 1997).

Many of the latter category may have been abandoned to the streets and might be dependent upon drugs or alcohol. These are the chronically homeless. Such people may use hostels, night shelters or other informal networks of vagrancy, or have been accommodated from the streets by informal or voluntary projects designed for the purpose.

By the summer of 1995 many of the local authority homelessness managers who were reporting informally a noticeable increase in the numbers of people presenting as homeless who were being accepted for rehousing on grounds of vulnerability due to age were at a loss to explain the trend. It seemed at odds with the claims by government ministers that statutory homelessness was falling sharply after 1992.

At the same time concern was being expressed by professionals in the housing and care fields that despite the introduction of community care policies and the recognition that housing was an important ingredient in effective strategies for care in the community, many older people were falling through the net of provision (Arblaster et al, 1996).

The purpose of this chapter, therefore, is to examine just how far the official statistics support the anecdotal and impressionistic perceptions of practitioners and project workers and to establish whether there has been a significant growth in older homelessness. If significant growth has occurred then we need to examine the scale and spatial distribution of older homelessness and to consider whether it is a temporary phenomenon.

Secondly, the chapter considers the causes of loss of accommodation among older people and thirdly, it examines the kinds of responses made by local authorities who accept these applicants as priority cases for rehousing.

A fourth strand to the discussion considers to what extent there is scope for a convergence of policy: is there a possibility that strategies for dealing with older homelessness can be assisted by strategies for dealing with increasing numbers of sheltered housing units which are proving difficult to let or are becoming redundant or unpopular; a problem facing both councils and other registered social landlords across the country (Tinker et al, 1996).

How far have local authority strategies for housing and community care recognised the potential which redundant sheltered stock offers for imaginative new investment in supported housing as part of an assessed care package for older people?

As to the size of the missing cohort – the street homeless who do not feature in government statistics and who so often fail to be captured in the networks of community care – some realistic estimate has to be made of the volume and nature of this population, as a preliminary to understanding their needs and abilities.

The 1996 Housing Act

New regulations and guidance were issued under Parts VI and VII of the 1996 Housing Act – in particular Statutory Instrument 1996 No 2754

The Homeless – which significantly alter the local authority response to older homeless people. They took effect in January 1997. Further regulations covering detailed aspects of waiting lists and allocations procedures were published some months later. By common consent the new Act had the effect of reducing the priority to be given to the homeless by local councils and reducing councils' responsibilities to applicants.

Part VII modifies the duties owed by a local authority towards homeless people. A person who is statutorily homeless and in priority need will be housed for a period of up to two years (renewable) and cannot be offered security of tenure.

The Act uses the framework of the 1985 Act as a starting point for redefining authorities' duties in this field. The most important changes to the regime are a new duty to provide advice and information about homelessness and its prevention and a closer definition of intentional homelessness. A new emphasis and potential penalties are placed on collusion and on failure to take advice or assistance offered.

Duties towards asylum seekers and refugees are defined more sharply and Section 193 contains a new provision that an authority's duty will be for up to two years. An authority has no duty, under Section 197, if it is satisfied that alternative accommodation is available locally.

The guidance issued makes clear that permanent housing can be offered only to people on a housing register which authorities must establish under Section 162 of the Act, but that there should be ample scope within an allocation scheme to allow for discretion to meet a person's care and support needs. New procedures are promised to ensure that assessment and referral by another agency can be dealt with within the allocation rules. However, indications from the Labour government installed in May 1997 that the provisions of the 1996 Act may, in due course, be relaxed and that homelessness will regain the priority which it enjoyed in the 1985 Act, are still awaited by practitioners.

Meanings and understandings

Any discussion of homelessness in older age must face additional problems of terminology utilised by those who seek to interpret and understand its implications. For example, the most important of these is the lack of agreement as to what constitutes 'old age' in relation to responding to need. The 1996 Act requires that those who are vulnerable due to old age are given priority but does not specify a particular age; instead, the Code of Guidance suggests that all applications from people over 60 should be considered carefully (para 6.10). In practice, local authorities operate a wide range of approaches.

In contrast, professionals working with the street homeless often argue that living a vagrant life can cause earlier ageing and will consider anyone of 50 and over for assistance (Rich et al, 1995).

Some disagreement also exists as to what constitutes 'homelessness'. The Code of Guidance includes not only those without a roof at all, but people under threat of losing their home, those with homes who, for specific reasons such as a threat of violence, cannot utilise it and those whose homes are inadequate or unsuitable for other than temporary use, or are too expensive.

Some of the people who might qualify to be called chronically homeless have existed in night shelters, hostels and friends' homes for years and have chosen these transitional locations as their permanent mode of living. We are therefore also faced with differing perceptions – shades of homelessness – which include a range of people whom Rossi (1989) defines as "precariously housed", in which about the only common factor is an extreme manifestation of poverty and residential instability (Bassuck and Buckner, 1992). Not all such people, however, would define themselves as homeless. Such a diverse and ambivalent landscape of understandings needs to be contextualised.

Setting the context

Perhaps the first principle in the study of ageing and the problems associated with it is that of heterogeneity: there is no such phenomenon as the aged (Sheppard, 1995). The population of older people contains widely differing subgroups and, indeed, sub-age groups. Just as clearly, the category of older homelessness is demonstrably made up of a number of groups and causes. Economists of ageing have found that income distribution of the 60+ population reveals one of the largest indexes of inequality: a fact that reliance on median scales of income can obscure, hiding the vast difference between the highest and lowest (Rich et al, 1995).

It is also evident that in examining the causes and growth in older homelessness we must look beyond the immediate factors such as mental health problems or physical impairment, family dysfunction or alcohol abuse, to exogenous factors such as inadequate housing policy, constrained benefits regimes and employment circumstances, over which the individual is often powerless to exert influence. As has been explored in earlier chapters of this book. Larger, overarching factors, related to the economic cycle, structural changes in the housing markets and demographic trends, clearly also influence the housing outcomes for the most vulnerable segments of the population.

Earlier research reviewed

Although in the 1960s and 1970s studies of homeless men in London and the USA showed that between 27% and 35% found in shelters and temporary hostels, or on the streets, were over 60, little was suggested by way of cause or remedy; at that time a British study also found that 18% of those sleeping rough were 60+ (Lodge Patch, 1971).

Even more recent research and academic commentary on homelessness in the UK has paid scant attention to the specific phenomenon of older people who lose their accommodation. Indeed, it is difficult to disagree with Crane's conclusion that our understanding of the issues is 'rudimentary', especially in regard to the relative importance of the personal and structural causes of this 'exceptional' behaviour (Crane, 1994).

However, in 1993 a study of single homelessness for the Department of the Environment by York University included 225 'over-60s' interviewees among its sample of 1,763 people. This work began to distinguish the volume and the causes of older homelessness; it found that, of the older respondents, 80% were in temporary shelter and 20% were sleeping rough. Sixteen per cent said their loss of home was due to the death of a spouse or close friend and a further 7% blamed relationship breakdown. Other main causes cited were eviction (7%), closure of property (8%) and rent or mortgage arrears (6%) (Anderson et al, 1993). The study by Anderson et al, however, had nothing to say about underlying influences or about the difference between those who were recently rendered homeless and those who had a longer and more persistent experience of chronic homelessness.

In 1993 Crane also studied street homelessness in inner London, targeting 50 of those aged 60 and over. Her study provided an in-depth profile which discussed their motivations, 'street history', behaviour, and health as well as their preferences with regard to accommodation (Crane, 1993). Crane makes specific recommendations concerning the need for further research, for more services and appropriate interventions, drawing heavily upon responses made in cities in the USA. More recent research, completed in 1996 by the London Research Centre (LRC), found that nine out of ten councils reported increases in applications from vulnerable people, many of whom were elderly and, it was claimed, were homeless as a result of failures in the community care system (LRC, 1996).

An earlier examination of the British experience in this field, by the Audit Commission, which concentrated on the local authority process for dealing with cases under the 1985 Housing Act, points out that despite the legislative duty on housing departments, many older people sleep on the streets each night (Audit Commission, 1989). However, the Commission, despite making 35 recommendations, had no advice to offer on dealing with such elderly people.

Most recently, Crane has returned to her earlier work in order to re-examine more closely the causes and scale of chronic homelessness and to highlight some of the developing examples of good practice which have emerged in British cities (Crane, 1997).

The study confirms the paucity of good data, the significant incidence of mental illness and the multiplicity of causes underlying the lack of a safe abode among those whom Crane typologises as 'lifetime' homeless, 'mid-life' homeless and 'late-life' homeless: she finds that "no policies and few homeless services are targeted specifically at older homeless people" (Crane, 1997).

Experience in the USA

In the United States, where many more studies of older homelessness have been undertaken, recent work echoes the view of British researchers that there is ambiguity and lack of consensus both about what constitutes homelessness and what is defined as old age. All have included people who have access to marginal or temporary shelter, and 'flophouses' (Douglass et al, 1988; Cohen and Sokolovsky, 1989; Rich et al, 1995).

Most American work includes people in their 50s. Indeed, Rich et al, whose sample included 72.5% of people between 50 and 60, argue that the generally accepted age in the literature is 50+ and that over-50s who experience a precarious street life may be considered old because stresses, nutritional problems and untreated health conditions contribute to premature ageing.

In the British context it might be difficult to apply this argument to those who present to local authorities immediately after losing a secure home, although the case should certainly be conceded in regard to those with longer-term accommodation, instability and vagrancy histories.

Douglass et al interviewed 68 men and 17 women aged 54+ in Detroit and noted such factors as lifelong difficulties in relating to other people as a major factor in homelessness, accompanied by a lack of family support, criminal behaviour and drug dependency. Discharge from an institutional context was the major immediate factor in lack of a home (Douglass et al, 1988).

In New York, Cohen and Sokolovsky (1989) were more concerned with understanding the coping mechanisms among chronic homeless men and the means they use to survive on 'skid row'. Their sample of over 280 were aged 50 and above, among whom they found psychological trauma as a result of breakdown in relationships, alcohol abuse and inability to hold a job, all combining to induce people to 'choose' homelessness in what an earlier reseacher has termed 'retreatist' behaviour (Merton, 1957).

Tampa Bay, Florida is, for reasons of climate and geography, something of a mecca for retired people and is thus a good site in which to examine the relationship between age-concentrated populations and older homeless people. Rich et al sampled 103 inhabitants who use such services as soup kitchens, temporary shelters and clothing replacement stores.

They construct a profile of the characteristics and needs of the sample and the service and policy implications for the authorities, with particular recommendations in regard to housing policy and the pertinence of social service relief programmes. They advocate targeting those at risk of homelessness and supporting the poorest with preventive measures.

The stereotyping of both ageing and homelessness, and the distorting effects on US policy, is examined in depth. Innovative interventions and empowerment strategies are discussed against a background in which the plight of younger families without a home has obscured a growth in the incidence of homelessness among the over-50s, similar in scale and cause to that of the British Isles (Rich et al, 1995).

The pertinence of the US experience in this field is that considerably more research has been done there than in the UK and that the pattern of US housing policy, which relies heavily on market forces and private provision, presages the direction in which UK policy is heading. The concept of low-cost social housing assumes a largely private sector basis of supply with reducing levels of centrally provided benefits to the individual. The fact that housing no longer features among the key spending priorities of the New Labour government suggests that there will be little change of direction from that of previous administrations.

What the statistics show

After March 1992 the annual flow of families into the homeless units of English town halls began to reduce substantially. Since then the annual figures show a steady decline in total acceptances of between 3% and 7.5% (See Table 9.1). In the four years to 1994/95 the cases in priority need drop from 139,630 to 116,340, a reduction of over 16% and the number of total acceptances had fallen from 145,080 to 120,440 (-17%). By 1997/98 the total was down to 103,480, a drop of 26% from the peak year.

Within these figures there were also reductions, for example, in the numbers in Bed & Breakfast hotels, in short-life accommodation and other temporary homes, including women's refuges. Substantial percentage reductions in these categories occur each quarter of each subsequent year.

However, in the period to 1994/95, as Table 9.1 demonstrates, the number of cases of those deemed to be vulnerable by reason of old age and accepted as in priority need grew slightly from 5,960 to 6,040, and actually grew as a percentage of all priority need, from 4.2% of the total in 1991/92 to 5.19% in 1994/95. The possibility that this increase was a temporary phenomenon is raised by the fact that by 1997/98 the percentage had returned to 4%, giving way to increased figures for those vulnerable to mental illness and physical disability – trends discussed in detail below (p 200) and suggesting that the care-in-the-community reforms are benefiting from imaginative new approaches to the use of earlier models of specialist housing.

However, the issue becomes more significant when examined at the local authority level. In a representative sample of 50 English councils, the numbers of elderly applicants in this category increased in at least three of the four years reviewed (see Table 9.2).

Table 9.1: People accepted by local authorities in England as unintentionally homeless (1991/92-1994/95)

	1991/92	1992/93	1993/94	1994/95
Total accepted	145,080	140,580	129,930	120,440
Priority need	139,630	136,190	125,360	116,340
Old age	5,960	6,060	6,060	6,040
Older cases (%)	4.2	4.4	4.8	5.19

Source: DoE forms P1(E) (Housing) 1992/98

Table 9.2: Incidence of acceptance of homelessness cases of people in priority need 'by reason of old age' (1992-95)

Authority	1992	1993	1994	1995
North Somerset	12	19	20	21
East Cambridgeshire	2	7	9	11
Peterborough	7	6	16	16
Halton	16	17	18	20
Carrick	14	16	18	29
Bath	10	13	17	17
Harlow	6	15	19	17
Plymouth	54	54	60	61
Hove	17	14	29	37
Maldon	7	10	12	14
Tewkesbury	2	8	6	9
Great Grimsby	5	11	14	15
Maidstone	7	8	10	18
Tonbridge Wells	12	20	16	27
Blackpool	3	8	8	9
Pendle	5	6	20	17
Ribble Valley	2	4	6	7
Leicester	47	51	48	64
Northern Kesteven	5	4	6	9
Broadland	14	16	11	21
Blyth Valley	10	11	14	16
Bridgnorth	5	6	7	9
South Somerset	13	23	25	33
Lichfield	8	8	11	12
St Edmundsbury	5	6	6	7
Arun	11	24	25	31
Crawley	10	15	17	18
Horsham	3	6	10	10
Worthing	7	10	13	14
Thamesdown	15	21	26	33
Trafford	50	56	77	66
Liverpool	37	38	47	43
Sefton	21	28	31	34
Newcastle	30	45	46	47
Sunderland	14	11	15	24
Birmingham	196	217	188	235
Coventry	11	5	9	12
Dudley	32	28	44	43
Sandwell	19	21	34	38
Calderdale	19	21	30	37
Ealing	32	43	76	76
Harrow	32	39	44	53
Havering	14	18	23	25
Lewisham	17	22	30	53
Tower Hamlets	12	27	28	35
Westminster	140	111	144	201

In many local housing departments the percentage increases were large, but given the very low starting point, the increase in numbers is less dramatic (see Table 9.2). For example, East Cambridgeshire had housed two cases by reason of old age in 1992 and this increased in each subsequent year to reach 11 in 1995. Trafford Metropolitan Borough Council dealt with 50 in 1992, growing to 77 in 1994 and reducing to 66 in 1995. Other examples, set out in Table 9.3 and taken from a range of differing kinds of authority, demonstrate the spatial similarity of the trend.

What this random selection of local authority returns demonstrates is that, starting from a very low base at the point when homelessness figures were at an all-time peak, those found to be homeless and vulnerable due to old age, by homelessness officers all over England, have increased in number steadily and unspectacularly ever since. The trend is similar in all geographic areas, in London and other big cities, county towns and small district councils.

It also becomes clear, in the process of looking at the administrative procedures, that many council figures are understated for reasons which relate to local practice and interpretation by officers.

For example, the Code of Guidance requires that, in addition to considering cases in which a person may be over 60 and vulnerable, an authority must evaluate vulnerability in cases of 'mental illness' or 'physical handicap'. The quarterly returns provided to the Department of the

Table 9.3: Increases in cases of older homelessness by regional distribution of authority (1992-95)

Authority	1992	1993	1994	1995
Carrick	14	16	18	29
Peterborough	7	6	16	16
Plymouth	54	54	60	61
Tewkesbury	2	8	6	9
South Somerset	13	23	25	33
Crawley	10	15	17	18
Newcastle	30	45	46	47
Birmingham	196	217	188	235
Sandwell	19	21	34	38
Ealing London Borough Council	32	43	76	76
Havering London Borough Council	14	18	23	25
Tower Hamlets London Borough Council	12	27	28	35
Westminster London Borough Council	140	111	144	201

Environment, Transport and the Regions (DETR) also make this distinction (DETR Form P1(E)[Housing]). Discussions with officers at local authority level reveal that some of the people in the latter two categories may also be elderly; practice varies as to the statistical category in which they are recorded. Nearly 10% of authorities indicated that some proportion of elderly people would be recorded in these other categories.

Survey data from 50 authorities utilised in this chapter suggests that over 70% of councils interpret the DETR Code of Guidance as requiring them to treat all over-60s applicants as elderly and therefore as vulnerable by reason of age. This was true throughout the South and South East although many Northern authorities differentiate between males and females, using 65 as the trigger for men. A minority tended to consider the actual circumstances involved and therefore to accept some applicants of 58 and others not until they were in their 70s. It is also clear that all authorities strenuously avoid responding to older applicants by offering temporary accommodation or Bed & Breakfast hotels. Permanent secure tenancies or nomination to a housing association tenancy are invariably the first response unless the circumstances are of an emergency nature.

In detailed discussions with groups of practitioners a number of common themes emerged: officers frequently make conscious efforts to avoid facing older people with the complex processes involved in being assessed as homeless, vulnerable and in need. This results 'more often than not' in cases not being recorded in official returns.

On the other hand, 80% of councils surveyed also said that they would accept elderly applicants in many cases who were not without a home or imminently so, if their current property was unsuitable. In many cases a home only becomes unsuitable as impairment, frailty, disability or other factors emerge slowly over time. For some authorities it is more convenient or quicker to treat such people as homeless rather than to offer a transfer through normal council procedures.

The reason why such cases are often not dealt with through waiting list and pointing procedures is that officers believe it is quicker and easier to use the homelessness procedures especially where such action assists in reducing the void-rate figures recorded by the authority. Although this distorts recorded statistics somewhat, some officers estimated that such cases amount, at most, to 10% of their annual figure for older applicants. However, one authority said that 50% of its older cases fell into this category.

How then do these trends impact upon the other social landlords who do not have a direct statutory role in meeting the needs of the homeless? Discussion with housing association officers, especially in London and the home counties, also reveals that significant numbers of older people who are about to lose their home apply and are accepted for associations' sheltered accommodation without seeking help from the council homelessness unit and are therefore not recorded as homeless. All the allocations officers for housing associations contributing to the research acknowledged some level of 'direct' applications and said they were frequently welcome as potential tenants for otherwise vacant sheltered housing units.

This phenomenon seems most likely to occur in areas where associations have surplus or void sheltered stock to fill and where the threat of homelessness is related to failure to maintain mortgage payments.

The DETR Code of Guidance makes clear that there are no simple tests of reasonableness in this situation and there is no doubt that a wide range of practice and interpretation operates in the field, much of it leading, for the reasons explained above, to an understatement of the true volume of older homelessness.

Updating the statistics

The nationwide growth in vacant sheltered housing would appear to have a more than accidental relationship to latest trends in the local authority homeless figures. The original data on which this chapter is based ended in 1994/95 and when subsequent figures are taken into account, a more complex explanation of trends emerges.

By 1998 the total numbers of homeless families accepted under the new homeless legislation was down by 25% on the peak year of 1991/92. The percentage of those accepted as vulnerable due to old age, having increased in the subsequent three years, steadied at around 4% of the annual total. This means that between 4,000 and 5,000 older people still lose their home each year, with similar trends in Wales. London figures continue, stubbornly, to remain higher than the other English regions.

But of greater interest to analysts is the fact that acceptances of other kinds of vulnerability – in particular people with mental illness and physical disability – now form a greater percentage of the annual totals, as do those in an ill-defined 'miscellaneous' category. In the seven years from 1991/92, when total homelessness peaked, to 1998, those with mental illness have risen as a percentage of acceptances from 3% to 7% and those with physical handicap from 3% to 5% (see Table 9.4). The interrelation between causes and responses to these trends is complex.

Town Hall allocations officers, on whose figures these analyses are based, acknowledge a number of factors accounting for the new trends. First, the problem of unpopular sheltered housing, originally researched by Tinker et al in 1996, and which is discussed later in this chapter, continues to escalate and is as much, if not more, of a problem for housing associations as councils (Hawes, 1997). This provides a ready resource, whether entirely appropriate or not, for dealing with vulnerable people, whether old or not.

One homelessness manager said: "Even if it is sometimes not ideal practice to utilise a vacant property in a community of sheltered tenants, it is almost always better than the alternative, especially if we can offer additional support tailored to the person's needs".

Second, the demands on social landlords made by other professional colleagues under the care-in-the-community accords, often include younger clients or patients with handicaps and mean that the range of housing for special needs has constantly to be expanded. In the absence of sufficient capital finance for new-build, the imaginative utilisation of redundant sheltered schemes is, more and more, a feature of annual refurbishment programmes. "The Housing Corporation is switching its emphasis to regeneration and refurbishment for just such reasons", reports a Corporation strategy officer. "Many such clients are presented to us urgently and we will use the homelessness procedures if that achieves a quicker result", confirms a council allocations manager.

Table 9.4: Categories of vulnerable people accepted by local authorities in England as unintentionally homeless (1992/93-1997/98) (%)

Year	Physical handicap	Mental illness	Domestic violence	Miscellaneous
1992/93	3.5	3	3	3
1993/94	4	4	4	3
1994/95	5	5	5	4
1995/96	5	6	6	4
1996/97	6	6	7	4
1997/98*	6	7	7	5

Notes: * provisional.

Source: DETR April 1999

Third, if such clients also come with the promise of support and assistance or funding for aids and adaptations, there is little further incentive needed by landlords to get redundant or unpopular stock back into use. This new flexibility in the re-use of difficult-to-let stock is evident in many areas and is one of a number of responses to an otherwise embarrassing and financially crippling situation for landlords. It also represents a challenge to local authorities as the community care legislation makes ever more sophisticated calls on housing resources of councils and associations.

These issues are at the heart of the interorganisational collaboration between key agencies, and as the volume of family homelessness falls and the housing needs of the elderly ease, it would appear that those with other kinds of vulnerability are beginning to come to the fore. The optimistic interpretation of these figures, from the evidence of practitioners and local strategists, is that the greater prominence of vulnerabilities other than age in the homeless statistics represents more solutions being achieved at the local level rather than an increase in need.

The chronically homeless: the missing dimension

The discussion so far has been concerned with those who come to the attention of local authorities and are counted statutorily homeless. But what of those older households who are not counted at all? Because official statistics fail to include the street homeless it is necessary to make some attempt to quantify the number of older people who exist in the eclectic range of voluntary hostels, group homes and 'rough sleeper' initiatives to which many older homeless people resort, either temporarily or serially. The question is, just how strong is the argument that by failing to capture this aspect of older homelessness in the statistics, the picture is substantially understated.

It will be seen from Crane's review discussed above that such investigations that have been carried out among hostel dwellers and street homeless people reveal that anything from 18% to 35% are over 60 (Crane, 1994). Typically, people in these circumstances are said to exhibit 'lifelong difficulties with other people' or to have suffered trauma such as bereavement or a disruptive childhood. Low skills and poor education are often evident. Drugs or alcohol figure frequently in their histories. The evidence suggests too that among the prime triggers of older street homelessness, mental ill-health, disrupted family life, ejection from the cocooning effect of institutional life are constant factors (Crane, 1997).

Over half of those who achieve resettlement become homeless again and, oddly, include people who, despite having a place to live, resort back to street life (Hawes, 1997).

This suggests strongly that unless a carefully designed degree of support is offered as part of the rehousing package, resettlement is likely not to be a success in the long term; a point which many front-line workers have been making to social workers from the inception of care-in-the-community. Work needs to be done to identify those at risk, utilising out-reach techniques to contact those who have become isolated. We need to be clear too, that group hostels and direct access units should always be seen as only an interim step to permanent resettlement however long the process takes. These issues are explored in a European context in Chapter Twelve.

It is evident too, from Table 9.9 on page 209, that the housing histories of many who utilise hostels or sleep rough only rarely result in their utilising the formal processes of assessment under the 1996 Housing Act; they represent only 1% of those assessed in Town Hall homeless departments. Moreover, it would appear that, under present constraints, it is just as rare for them to access the more appropriate process of assessment under the 1990 National Health Service and Community Care Act.

This is not to suggest that the two cohorts of 'official' and 'informal' homeless are mutually exclusive and rigidly compartmentalised. Case histories constructed for this chapter illustrate that it is possible that rough sleepers and others can be brought within the formal networks and benefit from supported social housing: equally, those who lose a stable home can, and do, sometimes fall through the net and slide into an existence on the streets or into a transient half-life of flop houses, night shelters or vagrancy.

It is also evident that external factors such as the impact of economic recession on unskilled labour, the restrictive approach to social welfare and the failure of community care programmes, result in many of those who rely on institutions or tied housing, losing such security as these traditionally offered.

Little seems to have changed in the decade or so since the earlier research conclusions outlined above but, in order to get a glimpse of the current picture, in this chapter we attempt to assess the current scale of older homelessness on the street and the frequency with which elderly people appear among the wider population of people for whom the lack of a home is only one of a range of problems in coping with everyday living. It has been possible to utilise statistics from several voluntary projects and from research material collected by national bodies such as Crisis and Shelter to piece together what is, at best, a partial snapshot.

Snapshots in time: the specialist hostel populations

In a voluntary project in Cardiff set up in 1992 to attempt the rehabilitation of older people, the 42 residents had been referred by other agencies or come directly from the street. Thrity-six of the residents were over 50. In this case rehabilitation means for many a move on to secure tenancies and the project has now become part of a registered housing association in order to facilitate this process.

In North West London a similar but larger specialist housing association provided, in 1995/96, residential services to over 500 older homeless people over 50. It also delivered daycare services to over 800, more than 30% of whom were women without homes. It also provided specifically targeted accommodation, support and specialist help to 1,300 such clients.

In fact, this body manages 1,200 units of housing throughout London and the South East, and of the 3,511 lettings made in 1995/96, 44% of tenants had slept on the street the previous night and 38% were over 50 years of age. In another 400-bed London hostel for the homeless, 64% of residents were reported to be over 50.

What these projects seem to confirm is that in any temporary community of homeless people, there is indeed a significant number of people over 50 who, in terms of need, ability and state of health, should be included in the term 'older'.

Users of Crisis shelters

Perhaps the sharpest focus of any snapshot in this field can be obtained by looking at emergency schemes, Crisis shelters and projects of the kind highlighted at Christmas and through the government's rough sleepers initiative (RSI). It is in these projects, aimed at all vagrant people, that some judgement can be made about the numbers of older people within the whole group.

Table 9.5 analyses the age and sex of those who were assisted in winter Crisis shelters during the winter of 1994/95, in five central London schemes. It demonstrates the significantly larger male clientele and the consequently larger percentage of older men than women to be found on the streets. It also illustrates too, the heavy concentration of older people in the 50/60 age group, tailing off sharply after 60.

Table 9.6 is derived from counts undertaken by the Homeless Network on 23 May 1996 among those living on the street in the London RSI zones of Central, Whitechapel and City (West and Central Zone [WACZO]) areas. In undertaking the count, researchers estimated that in the central area the majority had been on the street for more than five years including 10 out of 29 over-60s. Sixty-eight out of the 227 sheltering in the central area of the city were over 50 (30%).

Table 9.5: Numbers of people using five London Crisis shelters, by age and gender (Winter 1994/95) (%)

	Leighton Road (London Borough of Camden)		Neville House (St Mungo's Association)		Southwark Street (Crisis)		Turnstile House (English Churches Housing)		Victoria House (Salvation Army Housing)	
	F	M	F	M	F	M	F	M	F	M
	91	n/a	55	268	29	45	63	293	n/a	53
Under 18	2		0	0	6	0	1	0.3		0
18-25	29		24	15	24	14	38	24		11
26-35	30		35	28	35	31	18	30		23
36-49	29		30	37	28	31	27	30		40
50-59	9		4	13	7	13	14	10		18
Over 60	1		7	7	0	11	2	6		8
Average age (years)	33		36	40	25	35	33	36		40

Source:'Crash' (1995)

Table 9.6: Rough sleepers in London RSI zones, by age (23 May 1996)

	Central		WACZO	
Age range	Number	%	Number	%
Under 18	6	3	-	-
18-25	53	23	3	9
26-49	100	44	15	45.5
50-59	40	18	14	42.5
Over 60	28	12	1	3
Total	227	100	33	100

Source: Homeless Network

The Winterwatch programme is a series of shelters outside the zones targeted for the RSI. It is organised by the housing charities Crisis and Shelter. In a snapshot survey of 26 projects nationwide, during the winter of 1995/96, 299 users completed questionnaires (see Table 9.7). 252 were male and 47 female. Ninety-six per cent described themselves as white, 1% as black and 3% of mixed race. Compilers of these figures state that in the age group 40/59, approximately a third were over 50.

These three statistical snapshots, taken in differing locations at differing times, at least confirm the volume and consistency with which older people appear in the peripheral and precarious shelters and hostels of our cities. They do not pretend to scientific accuracy but they confirm the proposition that until older people appear in more formal, official databases, they will inevitably form a 'hidden' aspect of the overall picture of homeless older people in Britain.

But the possibility that some new light – some more coordinated, coherent national policy initiatives – may emerge to deal with this aspect of homelessness is offered with the creation, in 1997, by government of the Social Exclusion Unit situated in the Cabinet Office. An early focus of the Unit's work was single homelessness and rough sleeping.

In July 1998 the Unit reported to Parliament on the result of its public consultation exercise and the possibility of reducing the volume of rough sleeping to 'near zero' by 2002 (Social Exclusion Unit, 1998).

The report confirms much of the picture reported in this chapter and is equally hampered by the lack of a systematic, thorough and comprehensive process of counting those who sleep rough. Utilising single night counts and other ad hoc surveys the unit estimates that about 6% of rough sleepers are over 60 but, among a series of proposals for coordinated responses and more second-stage support networks, it has little to say specifically about the particular needs of the older people on the streets. Nevertheless the initiative will facilitate the drawing of fruitful new associations between the analysis of single homelessness and emerging academic work on the nature of social exclusion.

Some comparisons with Wales and Scotland

While this chapter has concentrated on the position in English authorities it is pertinent to look briefly at the Welsh and Scottish experience, utilising Welsh Office figures and some recent research among Scottish councils.

Statistics for Wales indicate a very similar trend to that in England, in which the total of families accepted as in priority need has been falling

Table 9.7: Occupants of winter shelters not in RSI zones, by age and location (Winter 1995/96)

Agency location	Under 18	18-25	26-39	40-59	Over 60	Total
Alfreton	2	4				6
Birmingham		1	4	1		6
Bristol		3	17	7		27
Canterbury		4	2			6
Chester			1	4	2	7
Croydon		2	4			6
Dundee		3	6	2	1	12
Edinburgh	1	5	3	10	5	24
Glasgow – Blue Triangle		2	1			3
Glasgow – Wayside Club			3	2		5
Godalming		2	2	1		5
Leamington		1	2			3
Lincoln – Nomad Trust	1	5	2	3		11
Manchester	1	8	8	6	2	25
Newham	1	2	5	6		14
North Hertfordshire		1	3	1		5
Norwich		5	9	7		21
Reading		5	7	2	1	15
Southampton		3	5	4		12
Stoke-on-Trent	1	5	2	2		10
Swansea		5	6	5		16
Wallasey		3	9			12
Watford	1	1	3	4		9
Wearside	6	9		6		21
Winchester			3	3		6
Woking	2	2	2			6
Total	16	81	109	76	11	

Source: Crisis (1996)

consistently since 1992, but the proportion of those vulnerable by reason of age has increased. Table 9.8 suggests the same type of small but inexorable percentage increase as witnessed in England. Once again the statistics after 1995 suggest a continuation of the trend, although less pronounced.

Recent research into homelessness among older people in Scotland by Wilson (1995) makes a series of recommendations essentially related to the Scottish context of housing policy, but at the same time provides some interesting parallels with the situation in England.

The way in which Scottish Office statistics are analysed, Wilson argues, makes it difficult, if not impossible, to get an accurate picture of trends. The only figures for older people refer to 'single elders: retirement age and above', which are set out in Table Four of the Scottish Office bulletin (HAG, 1993/94). This therefore omits couples entirely. Wilson is able to demonstrate, from council records, that between 9% and 34% of older people presenting as homeless were, in fact, couples!

Moreover, the Scottish Office's own central research unit has demonstrated that older people represent about 7% of councils' total homeless applicants (Evans, 1994). Similar issues of interpretation at local authority level and the treatment of age 60 or 65 as the official definition of 'old' occur in Scotland as in England, which further blurs the position, but Wilson believes that, at a conservative estimate, between 1,400 and 1,500 older households annually become homeless and are dealt with by local councils. He does not report the official figures but suggests they are substantially less than his research reveals.

Why older people lost their home

What are the key factors which lead to the kind of cataclysm represented by losing one's home in later life? Two prime groups of linked causes offered by applicants for rehousing indicate that most are grounded either in various kinds of relationship breakdown within families or between partners, or some serious financial crisis resulting in either rent arrears or

Table 9.8: Homeless households accepted for rehousing by local authorities, Wales (1992-95)

	1992	1993	1994	1995
Total accepted in priority need	7,332	7,757	6,875	5,923
Vulnerable through old age	359	335	348	308
% of total	4.89	4.31	5.00	5.20

Note: The figures are derived from 37 Welsh councils prior to local government review in 1996.

Source: Welsh Office Housing Statistics Bulletin (1992/95)

the failure to maintain a mortgage. Table 9.9 demonstrates that 65% in fact were related to the former and 32% to the latter group of causes.

Marriage breakdown and intergenerational conflict

A remarkable outcome of discussions with those who work daily with older people in housing distress is the scale and complexity of circumstance in which personal relations break down to the point where homelessness results. The scale of conflict – and even of violence – within older marriage and the breakdown of relations between the generations within a family raise important questions for late 20th century understanding of family dynamics.

If marriage break-up, so long thought to be a phenomenon of younger partners and transient alliances, is rife among the over-60s, is there perhaps a need, as Johnson (1995, p 253) argues, to "recognise that significant changes in family formations and in the life expectations of all who survive into mid-life, represent two of the most fundamental changes in social structure".

The evidence in this chapter would support such a view since homelessness can be seen as an extreme outcome of family conflict. In short, to paraphrase Johnson (1995), old age and the family encompass the centre ground of a major policy and political discourse, in which the forces which conspire to render one homeless in later life are as important to understand as they are to combat.

Retirement from active work is a time of particular strain in long-standing marriages. Husbands or partners, so long absorbed in work for most hours of the day, are quite suddenly a permanent and largely unoccupied resident. "Under my feet all day..." was a much used phrase

Table 9.9: Main causes of home loss (1992-95) (%)

Partnership breakdown	39
Family dispute	25.5
Private mortgage failure	15
Mortgage failure (Right to Buy)	10
Landlord action	7
Emergency (fire etc)	2
Street homelessness	1
Other	0.5

by women with whom this issue was discussed, and whose daily life had been thrown into disarray by a partner recently retired, especially where the employment had been demanding and all-absorbing; the ability of couples to realign or renew an earlier joint way of life may be impaired in later life. Certainly these factors were too regularly cited by contributors to this research to be dismissed or underestimated.

Another explanation of partnership breakdown offered by many practitioners is that older people in unsatisfactory relationships, who might otherwise put up with less than a perfect marriage, can be influenced by the greater readiness of their married children to sever and start again. "When I saw how much better my daughter was after her divorce, I thought 'why not me...?'" commented one such applicant.

Many homelessness officers comment upon what is termed 'Autumn relationships' in which people in later middle years who have been widowed or divorced after many years, marry again, perhaps relinquishing a tenancy to move into a new partner's home, only to find that they are incompatible and split up: "Winter often comes all to soon...".

Recent research has established that a wide range of factors are involved in the creation of tensions between the generations of families (Clarke et al, 1993). The notion that portrays the family as a place of either peace, harmony and refuge, or as a place of abuse, anger and violence, fails to understand the subtleties and changes over time, of kinship, loyalty and friction which most extended families experience (Bengtson et al, 1996). As these researchers comment, "families are typically the source of our greatest pleasure and our greatest pain through life" (1996, p 26).

Finance and friction

Sociologists working in this field identify causes of quarrels in families such as child-rearing, ideology, work habits and household management, but in the context of this discussion of older homelessness, it is the economic and money issues which seem to be at the heart of those conflicts which, in the extreme, result in older people becoming homeless.

During the 1980s many middle-aged people were encouraged to take up the Right to Buy their council home (RTB), with inducements rising to as much as 70% discount off the market valuation. In an environment of rising property values, the possibility of a capital asset which could be passed on to the next generation was tempting to many thousands of people on low incomes and nearing retirement who would otherwise have been content to remain in the public sector tenure for the rest of their lives.

The idea that the asset could be passed on was equally attractive to both purchasers and their offspring, many of whom encouraged and contributed to RTB acquisitions (Forrest and Murie, 1990).

However, the evidence suggests (see Table 9.9) that the dream of home ownership has gone sour for many. The long depression in housing markets after 1989, the approach of early retirement, sometimes enforced, and reduced income for large sections of the labour market, has exposed the fragility of the economic judgements made by thousands who were enticed into house purchase, and the insubstantial nature of subsidised markets such as RTB.

Survey evidence from those areas in which the volume of RTB was highest reveals a consequentially high incidence of homelessness caused by the ultimate failure of such transactions among older purchasers (Hawes, 1997).

A number of examples of intergenerational pacts based upon unsecured financial arrangements, followed by subsequent breakdown due to failure in health or need for care, unforeseen monetary problems or simply disputes and quarrels, feature in the records as reasons for loss of one's home. Failing health of a family elder who has perhaps spent much of an active middle life living with married children and assisting with rearing a third generation, leads, in a number of instances to a disinclination on the part of householders, to continue the live-in arrangements, sometimes after a spell in hospital, although officers assessing such cases report strong suspicions of collusion in such applications.

Violence: a many-faceted phenomenon

This chapter is based in part on detailed discussions with groups of homelessness officers as well as on conversations with those who have experienced becoming homeless in later life. They reveal that violence, in many forms, is the motivation for an increasing number of older people seeking to establish homelessness. In compiling case histories examples were found of women being violent to older husbands, of men beating their partners and of elderly couples being abused by the children with whom they lived. In one example a grandchild was systematically and secretly abusing her grandmother to the point where resort to a refuge was enforced.

While elder abuse is a well-researched phenomenon in sociological literature (McCreadie, 1991), it is more than a little alarming to find so consistent a thread of violence in all areas and perpetrated by all generations, so extreme as to lead to the loss of a home. This indicates that the problem is by no means limited to relations between carers and those they care for, the main concern of modern research (Phillipson and Biggs, 1992; Penhale and Kingston, 1995). Cases related in discussions for this chapter refer not only to physical abuse but to the application of psychological and material pressures and, while Penhale and Kingston refer to the 'appalling' record in the UK in institutional settings, one is led to feel that it is not only a problem for community care or for the poor and those on the fringes of society, it is a housing problem too.

Responding to older homelessness: a role for surplus sheltered stock

Research by Tinker et al (1996) has established that 92% of councils and 79% of housing associations have difficult-to-let sheltered housing within their stocks.

In discussing approaches to meeting the needs of the homeless many housing officers were able to confirm this finding and indeed it would appear that even very recently built specialist dwellings and 'frail elderly' schemes produced by associations as part of a council-led strategy, are proving exceptionally difficult to attract tenants. Practitioners argue that this is not only to do with location or quality, or even size of unit, and that even traditionally popular schemes now face the same dilemma. The evidence suggests that these problems are faced in all regions of the country, and by both rural and metropolitan authorities.

However, the emergence of a continuing surplus of sheltered stock occurring at the same time as the trend in older homelessness has allowed authorities to offer quick solutions to applicants who might otherwise be faced with temporary habitations of a less congenial kind. Most authorities indicate that they are able, in many cases, to look first to the possibility of a sheltered tenancy when faced with an old and vulnerable applicant. Indeed, one senior housing manager was able to say that, although there was an undoubted increase in older applicants, "there is not a consequent housing problem". Virtually all of the 50 authorities who contributed to this discussion said that they saw their sheltered stock as an important resource in dealing with older homeless people, although eight said it was never their first response.

The increasing evidence of a substantial pool of vacant sheltered stock, of varied age, form and location, suggests that it would be appropriate to re-evaluate on a comprehensive basis the earlier approach and purpose of this kind of housing. It would be important to include even the most modern forms of very sheltered homes in any such review. From the up-dated statistical trends in homelessness discussed above (p 200) and the responses of practitioners it is clear that already, more flexibility in the use of sheltered housing is being introduced and a more entrepreneurial approach to policy is emerging.

Some councils have sought to adapt and upgrade earlier models and one major housing association which specialises in this field, and who found that up to 11,000 of its bedsits were, in effect, redundant, have taken a lead within the association sector. Others are providing a wider range of care services and linking them to the demands of care-in-the-community strategies, offering a joint approach with social services staff to assessment and allocations in meeting the needs of older clients.

Tinker's study for the Department of the Environment (Tinker et al, 1996) and her earlier work on very sheltered housing stress the sensitivities which need to be recognised in any attempt to re-adapt this stock for new uses. Mixing younger with older tenants or those with heavy support needs and those still relatively able can cause severe management problems. It is crucial to see these schemes as living communities but nevertheless, with care and consultation, and by maintaining through new lets, a balance of ability, they can be enabled to thrive and regenerate, with an internal life of their own.

It remains true, however, that any approach to large-scale refurbishment and upgrading must be a long-term strategy in which long lead-in times are a necessary ingredient. Successful solutions to these problems are likely to be small in scale, accurately targeted in regard to the kinds of support offered and sharply differentiated in terms of the kinds of need addressed.

It is important that in devising their proposals for housing and community care, local authorities approach the issue of redundant sheltered housing in a strategic way, and that capital funds for the regeneration of this stock begin to flow as part of a unified plan for housing and support embracing all social housing providers. Provided that older people with support needs are also recognised as a specific client group within community care plans, the opportunities for policy synergy are obvious.

Inevitably the role of wardens in sheltered housing will change too, with the need for retraining and new relationships which identify both housing management roles and those associated with care management.

As Tinker points out, despite exhortations from government that approaches to the reprovisioning of services must be localised and involve close interorganisational planning between the key agencies, the 'seamless service' referred to in Department of the Environment/Department of Health circulars is stubbornly slow to emerge.

So that, while it may be coincidentally convenient that surpluses of this stock are available at a time of increased homelessness among older people – and are convenient as a solution – it is, in policy terms, important to consider the possibilities of a more structured and coherent strategy. A strategy which seeks, on the one hand, to quantify the needs arising for supported housing, demands for adaptations, for more intensive care and for a 'lifetime homes' approach to accommodating those with support needs, and on the other, the possibilities for redesign, adaptation and imaginative reuse of such stock.

These questions do suggest the need to do further research, in the context of the interface between social services and housing agencies, followed by some authoritative guidance to social landlords of all kinds. Local authority practice suggests that where sheltered housing is not available, ground floor or bungalow units are offered in many cases, to homeless elders. Since all authorities operate a 'one offer only' policy to applicants there are no records of refusals in any category of offer, even where difficult-to-let studio flats are utilised.

It is pertinent to point out that authorities which indicated that they never offer sheltered housing to older homeless applicants were situated in the North, North East and North West regions, reflecting the lower percentages of sheltered housing in all categories, in those regions (McCafferty, 1995).

Conclusion

This chapter has been largely concerned with the practical and policy-oriented issues which surround the phenomenon of older homelessness. However, beyond issues of process, form-filling and terminology, beyond questions of resourcing community care or of the reuse of redundant sheltered housing, lies another terrain. This has to do with wider theoretical discussions on social polarisation, wealth inheritance and differential accumulation.

As explored in more detail in Chapter Three, the notion of social exclusion allows the re-conceptualisation of single homelessness and rough sleeping, characterised by the inability of this section of the community to get access to the labour market, to health and welfare services and suitably supported social housing. This is especially crucial to those over 50, as is the need to re-establish links with family, with social networks and the structures of community interaction.

It is evident too, that the chaotic medley of factors which bear down on those at risk of losing a safe abode in later life are little different in origin from those detected in other facets of society discussed in this book. While it might have been thought that after 50 years of the British welfare state, they were largely immune, we can see the emergence of a 'new precariousness' for older people: the same proneness to risk.

Risks associated with structural change in the labour market, the shrinking of social provision in the face of determined privatisation and the degradation of family ties and traditional networks of support are all present in the story of homelessness among older age groups. The issues discussed here also link inexorably with the burgeoning debate about social exclusion which is examined in the contributions of other authors in this book.

References

Anderson, I., Kemp, P. and Quilgars, D. (1993) *Single homeless people*, London: HMSO.

Arblaster, L., Conway, J., Foreman, A. and Hawtin, M. (1996) *Asking the impossible? A study of inter-agency working to address the housing, health and social care needs of people in general needs housing*, Bristol: The Policy Press.

Audit Commission (1989) *Housing the homeless: The local authority role*, London: HMSO.

Bassuck, E.L. and Buckner, C. (1992) 'Out of mind, out of sight', *American Journal of Orthopsychiatry*, vol 62, no 3, pp 330-1.

Bengtson, V., Biblarz, T., Clarke, E., Giarrusso, R., Roberts, R., Kichlin-Klonsky, J. and Silverstein, M. (1996) 'Intergenerational relationships and ageing', Paper presented to the Annual Conference of the British Society of Gerontology, Keele University, August.

Clarke, E., Preston, M., Raskin, J. and Bengston, V. (1993) 'Family conflict in older parent–adult child relationships', Paper read to the AGM of Gerontological Society of America, New Orleans, November.

Cohen, C.I. and Sokolovsky, J. (1989) *Old men of the bowery: Strategies for survival among the homeless*, New York, NY: The Guildford Press.

Crane, M. (1993) *Elderly homeless people sleeping on the streets of inner London: An exploratory study*, London: Age Concern Institute of Gerontology.

Crane, M. (1994) 'Elderly homeless people: elusive subjects and slippery concepts', *Ageing and Society*, vol 14, Part 4, December, pp 631-40.

Crane, M. (1997) *Homeless truths: Challenging the myths about older homeless people*, London: Help the Aged/Crisis.

Douglass, R. et al (1988) *Aged, adrift and alone: Detroit's elderly homeless*, Ypsilanti, MI: Eastern Michigan University Press.

Evans, R. (1994) *The Code of Guidance on homelessness in Scotland*, Edinburgh: Scottish Office.

Forrest, R. and Murie, A. (1990) *Selling the welfare state*, London: Routledge.

Hawes, D. (1997) *Older people and homelessness: A study of greed, violence, conflict and ruin*, Bristol: The Policy Press.

Johnson, M.I. (1995) 'Interdependency and the generational compact', *Ageing and Society*, vol 15, pp 243-65.

Lodge Patch, I. (1971) 'Homeless men in London: demographic findings in a lodging house sample', *British Journal of Psychiatry*, vol 118, pp 313-17.

LRC (London Research Centre) (1996) *Trends in homelessness in London in the 1990s*, London: LRC.

McCafferty, P. (1995) *Living independently*, London: HMSO.

McCreadie, C. (1991) *Elder abuse: An exploratory study*, London: Age Concern Institute of Gerontology.

Merton, R. (1957) *Social theory and social structure*, Glencoe, IL: Free Press.

Penhale, B. and Kingston, P. (1995) 'Elder abuse: an overview', *Health & Social Care in the Community*, vol 3, pp 311-20.

Phillipson, C. and Biggs, S. (1992) *Understanding elder abuse*, London: Longman.

Rich, D., Rich, T. and Mullins, L. (eds) (1995) *Old and homeless – Double jeopardy: An overview of current practice and policies*, Westport: Auburn House.

Rossi, P. (1989) *Down and out in America*, Chicago, IL: University of Chicago Press.

Sheppard, H.L. (1995) 'Foreword', in D. Rich, T. Rich and L. Mullins (eds) *Old and homeless – Double jeopardy*, Westport: Auburn House.

Social Exclusion Unit (1998) *Rough sleeping*, London: Cabinet Office.

Tinker, A. (1989) *An evaluation of very sheltered housing*, London: HMSO.

Tinker, A., Wright, F. and Zeilig, H. (1996) *Difficult-to-let sheltered housing*, London: Age Concern Institute of Gerontology/HMSO.

Wilson, D. (1995) *We will need to take you in ...*, Edinburgh: The Scottish Council for Single Homeless.

TEN

Homelessness in Russia: the scope of the problem and the remedies in place

Yana Beigulenko

Introduction

In recent years, Russians have been observing increasing levels of homelessness, especially in the big cities. Of course, homelessness was bound to be more readily identified, once people were allowed to recognise social and economic problems that had previously been studiously ignored. But there seemed also to be more to notice. Changes in the economy seemed to be taking their toll, especially on pensioners and others with fixed incomes, on the young and disabled people, and on those at the margins of society. At the same time the Russian population was becoming more mobile as restraints on travel were lifted and people moved in search of economic opportunity. Simultaneously, the country was absorbing waves of refugees from conflict-torn parts of the former Soviet Union. Not all these new arrivals had places to live, especially in cities where, even before privatisation, housing supply was insufficient to meet demand.

The end of the nuclear confrontation, the collapse of the Soviet Union, Russia's first faltering steps towards democracy. These are all events of the not too distant past. It is not surprising that for a country which has no tradition of democracy, such a large territory, and a persistent memory of imperial glory, Russia is finding it hard to make the transition to what Mikhail Gorbachev called the civilised world. In the 13 years since Perestroyka began and the seven years since communism and the Soviet Union disappeared, the Russian government has so far failed to complete the path of political evolution which took the countries of Western Europe several centuries to traverse. Outsiders – and many Russians – notice the ragged economic reform, the corruption and high levels of crime, and the suffering of the people inflicted by the collapse of the primitive, but reliable, social security network which the Communists provided. On the other hand, few weigh the other side of the scale: the seven democratic elections conducted in difficult circumstances with a minimum of fraud; the emergence of a whole new generation of young, energetic and highly qualified professionals; the openness of the country to new ideas, freedom to travel, the rapid growth of the social work industry. All the aforementioned form the basis of the creation of the civil society. In a country whose autocratic traditions go back a thousand years, these are remarkable achievements.

Nevertheless, over the past several years, it has appeared that many ordinary people have become losers in the transition brought about by the rapid move to a market economy. They have witnessed a severe drop in living standards. It is obvious that the welfare of children and families has slipped down the ladder of the Russian government's priorities. Widening income disparities have left more women, children and old people in poverty, and have undermined the security of public sector workers such as doctors and teachers. Pressure on social services has escalated at the same time as inflation and tax evasion have reduced the resources available to them, and administrative and legal capacities have shrunk.

The state is also unable to attend to the needs of thousands of refugees and forced migrants from the former republics of the Soviet Union. It is important to note that when the Soviet Union collapsed in 1991 there were 25.3 million ethnic Russians resident in these republics. By the end of 1995, 2.2 million Russians had returned to Russia and over 1 million incomers had been registered with the Federal Migration Service as refugees or forced migrants (Pilkington, 1997). Most of these people lost their homes, savings, employment, extended family and friends, all of which are so central to the survival strategies of families in post-Soviet Russia.

The failure by the state to resolve their housing problems satisfactorily was, and still is, the most distressing aspect of life for the majority of returning Russians. This is true especially for women with children, some of whom have lost hope for a better future and have little real prospect of satisfying a basic human need – having a place of their own (Beigulenko, 1994). Many families spend months or years in insecure and uncomfortable housing, for example, in rooms in hostels, rented rooms, living quarters constructed in empty buildings, even cow sheds, in the hope that employers, local authorities or the state will be able to rehouse them on a permanent basis (Pilkington, 1997).

The purpose of this chapter is to investigate the current definitions of homelessness and existing management of the problem using particular examples of the housing experience of women and children in Russia in order to present a picture of their plight in a period of uncertainty and transition. It reviews the assistance now available to them, investigates the issue of concealed homelessness among women, and touches on legal, administrative, political and social conditions that may serve as obstacles to needed improvements. The chapter draws on a number of qualitative interviews carried out by the author in 1997 with young families in housing need.

Defining and managing homelessness

Defining the homeless

In Russia, the semi-official name for the homeless is 'BOMZH', an acronym formed from the initial letters of the Russian words 'having no place of permanent residence' (the term is used in various state documents but not in any legislative acts). Generally, BOMZHes are understood to have neither permanent nor temporary accommodation, nor means of subsistence. As a rule, they are without relatives or guardians, guaranteed pensions, unemployment benefits and such social rights as the right to education and medical care. The term 'BOMZH', as used by law-enforcement agencies, has always implied censure. Comparable terms in English might include 'vagrant' and 'tramp'.

Homelessness as a social phenomenon exists in many societies, but it is only within the territory of the Russian Federation that it is formalised: the homeless in Russia do not possess residency permits (*propiskas*). The propiska is a unique Soviet legal institution which has survived the collapse of the Soviet Union in parts of Russia. Propiskas can still be used to control the mobility of the population (Alden et al, 1998). The absence of a propiska ensures that BOMZHes do not have any legal right to housing, medical care, work and so on.

Statistical data provided by state institutions gives a sense of the magnitude of the problem of homelessness in Russia. Altogether, no less than four million homeless people exist in a country with a population of 148 million, according to unofficial statistics supplied to the mass media by unofficial researchers (*Komsomolskaya Pravda*, 1998). This is unlikely to be an overestimate, although accurate figures are notoriously difficult to ascertain. For example, official statistics collected by the Russian

Ministry of the Interior are an order of magnitude higher than those of the Moscow Police Department, owing to differences in the methods used to define the homeless (see Table 10.1). Alex Nikiforov, who works with the homeless in Moscow, believes that no one has accurately assessed the number of homeless people in Moscow (population 8.7 million), but it is highly probable that the number is increasing every day.

The difference in figures for Moscow, provided by the Ministry of the Interior and the Moscow Police Department, could partially be explained by the fact that nearly half of all homeless people in Moscow, while having no permanent residence in the city, do have housing outside Moscow, sometimes many kilometers distant. These people are not categorised as BOMZHes and are not counted in the official statistics (*Na Dne*, 1996a). There are several explanations for migration to the city. Chronic levels of unemployment in the former republics of the Soviet Union, such as Ukraine, Moldova, Belorussia and parts of Russia, have driven people to seek a job in the city. Many ethnic Russians in the new states found themselves no longer welcome, and were forced to seek social justice in Moscow, as economic or forced migrants, following a trend established when the city was the capital of the Soviet empire. Such migrants were, and still are, frequently mugged on the train, or upon arriving at the railway station in Moscow, and the loss of documents and money may result in a temporary state of homelessness (*Na Dne*, 1996c).

Table 10.1: Official numbers of homeless in Russia and Moscow

	Ministry of the Interior of the Russian Federation	Moscow Police Department
1990		
Russia	40,000	–
Moscow	10,000	1,660
1991		
Russia	67,000	–
Moscow	11,500	no data
1992		
Russia	93,000	–

Source: Bodungen (1994)

Refugees from the former Soviet Union also contribute to the number of homeless. Moscow, with its wide spectrum of job opportunities, is perceived to be an attractive place to settle. In the past few years this perception has changed since Russia no longer welcomes forced migrants and refugees. Two laws – the Refugees Act (affecting those compelled to leave their native land to avoid persecution) and the Forced Migrants Act (pertaining to refugees who are citizens of Russia) have attempted to clarify the situation (Bodungen, 1994). On their arrival, refugees and migrants were issued with special certificates, entitling holders to medical and social services, including the use of public childcare services and so on. This initially liberal immigration legislation was amended in 1995 to minimise the number of incomers eligible for state institutional and financial support in the course of their resettlement (Pilkington, 1997). The Federal Migration Service has been unable to house all of the refugees and migrants. Families who resettle in urban areas frequently have to share a single hostel room. Four family members were sharing a single small room in one hostel where I interviewed women refugees, most of whom admitted their state of homelessness (Beigulenko, 1994). Some single women of pensionable age take up live-in employment as, for example, hostel caretakers, in order to secure a roof over their heads (Pilkington, 1997).

Current housing legislation does not define anyone who officially has a roof over his/her head to be homeless. However, such people may be deeply dissatisfied with accommodation that is perceived to be inadequate and overcrowded. Concealed homelessness has been largely ignored by policy makers and housing scholars in Russia. There has been no attempt made to adopt a broad and non-specific definition of homelessness, whereby living with friends or relatives in overcrowded conditions, in reception centres, hostels, refuges, in poorly maintained housing and so on would be defined as homelessness. Concealed homelessness may be defined as the state that ensues when a person considers their present accommodation to be inadequate, according to the forementioned criteria. Sociologists, representatives of the other social sciences and the mass media in Russia persist in using the old-fashioned definition of homelessness, which is usually applied to people sleeping rough on the streets.

According to Nikiforov (*Na Dne*, 1996b), 55% of Moscow's homeless are categorised as BOMZH. One third of these are former citizens of Moscow who have been released from prison (convicts sentenced to prison terms of more than six months lose their permanent residence permits under Article 60 of the Housing Code of the Russian Federation;

see below). The remainder are either people expelled from their homes by relatives, or people who have sold their flats for low prices and are unable to afford new homes. Often, people lose their housing following divorce, or when they attempt to extricate themselves from a violent relationship. Others may lose housing provided by employers when they lose their jobs. Other routes into homelessness in Russia include children who run away from their parents or from orphanages, and foreigners who choose to remain in Russia after the cessation of a period of work or study. The smallest group of BOMZH comprises those who choose to live on the streets. Although only 5% of Moscow's homeless consciously choose such a life-style, they still represent the stereotypical image of the homeless, whose degree of degradation is beyond measure (*Na Dne*, 1996b). Eighty-five per cent of all homeless people in Moscow are men, and 75% of homeless in the city are between 20 and 50 years of age. As Nikiforov points out, while there are those among the homeless who have given up hope, the majority aspire to live with dignity, contributing to the society in which they live.

In St Petersburg, Russia's second largest city (population 4.4 million in 1996; Alden et al, 1998), the number of homeless is probably 30-50 thousand (equivalent to 580-990 per hundred thousand population) (Sokolov, 1994). Approximately 63% of this figure comprises former residents of St Petersburg proper (Sokolov, 1994). In 1994, 3,515 BOMZHes died in St Petersburg, principally owing to cold weather during winter and lack of food; although some committed suicide (*Na Dne*, 1996a).

Legal and administrative approaches to homelessness

Until recently, the state denied the existence of homelessness, referring to the homeless as criminals and parasites on society who refused to work. Such people were disgraced by the Soviet state and were condemned to be reformed in corrective labour institutions (Bodungen, 1994). Article 209 of the Criminal Code of the Russian Federation embodied the concept of vagrants as criminals worthy of punishment, rather than people in need of a helping hand. This Article, later amended by a decree of the Presidium of the Supreme Soviet of the Russian Federation of October 11, 1982, provided for imprisonment or confinement of vagrants in corrective labour camps for a term of one to two years (Bodungen, 1994).

Until December 1991, BOMZHes could be given prison sentences of 10 or more years for repeated violations of passport registration rules.

Citizens who could not be identified on detention, because they possessed no papers (including under-age children, disabled and elderly people) were sent to the Interior Ministry's 'filtering centres', where vagrants and the homeless were identified. These people were detained for two weeks to a month, while law-enforcement agencies tried to identify them and examine police records (Bodungen, 1994). It was, and still is, easy for ex-convicts to become BOMZHes. As noted above, under Article 60 of the Russian Federation, those sentenced to prison terms of more than six months automatically lose their residence permits the moment the sentence takes effect. If their permanent residence permits are cancelled while they are serving their sentences, as if often the case, they often do not have a place to live when released. They also lose their social guarantees and the opportunity to secure a job.

At the end of 1990, when the USSR accepted certain international legal standards, including the Universal Declaration of Human Rights, changes were introduced to the criminal code of the Russian Federation. In particular, Article 209 was revoked. On 18 April 1991, the Supreme Soviet of the Russian Federation adopted a resolution that removed the filtering stations for the homeless from the Interior Ministry's control ('Independent report on the state of homelessness in Russia and its meeting the international pact on civil and political rights', 1995). On 17 September 1992, the Government of the Russian Federation adopted Resolution 723, which created the social security agencies responsible for converting the filtering stations into a network of social welfare institutions (Bodungen, 1994). As a result, vagrancy is now looked upon – in principle, at least – as a social security issue, rather than a crime. The Resolution changed the social status of the homeless from criminals into persons entitled to social protection.

Not only does the state now recognise that the homeless have social rights potentially equal to those of all other citizens, it also gives the homeless the opportunity to exercise these rights. All homeless persons can now, after an identity check, receive passports and other identification documents on the condition that they must re-register every 120 days (Babushkin and Volodarski, 1995). This fact demonstrates that there is an attempt on behalf of the government to guarantee social rights for all. Still with the fiscal crisis facing the state it is unable to commit itself to meeting housing requirements of all its citizens. For the time being keeping the definition of homelessness to its minimum (treating homelessness as rooflessness only) helps to hold the scale of the official problem as manageable as possible.

Disease and medical treatment

One of the most serious problems confronting the homeless, especially in the past as a result of being denied legal status, was the absence of medical treatment available to them. Life on the street during severe winter weather conditions, exacerbated by excessive drinking and related behaviours, may combine to cause many serious diseases which require urgent medical treatment.

According to the aid agency Médecins sans Frontières, tuberculosis, cardiovascular disorders, skin, venereal and gastrointestinal diseases and lice infestation are common among the homeless (*Kuranty*, 1993b). At filtering stations, BOMZHes were only treated for lice infestation, and reinfestation was bound to occur, since superficial disinfection of places where the homeless sleep was inadequately financed in the budget. The homeless often die because they are denied medical treatment in clinics, owing to the absence of a propiska. A number of cases of death by alimentary dystrophy have been reported in the past. Ninety-nine vagrants died at Moscow railway stations in 1990, and in 1991, the figure rose to 108 (Bodungen, 1994). The situation may improve if the government and the voluntary sector develop a joint strategy aiming to improve medical provision for homeless people in as many parts of the country as possible.

What kind of help is available to the homeless in Russia?

According to Sokolov (1994), Federal agencies in Russia appear to be confused by the problem of homelessness, and seem interested in shifting responsibility for solutions onto other organisations. Local authorities, for their part, are unwilling to locate hostels or refugee camps in their territories for fear that such facilities will require extra financial support and organisational effort. Meanwhile, voluntary organisations addressing problems of homelessness mainly concentrate their efforts in large cities such as Moscow and St Petersburg which have to cope with a constant lack of funds and unsympathetic responses from the local authorities and the business sector, which need to adopt more cooperative, interagency initiatives.

According to some estimates, there are now more than 30 organisations in Moscow alone that deal in one way or another with the problems of the homeless (Bodungen, 1994). These include: Médecins sans Frontières (MSF); Samaritan Philanthropic Society (Switzerland); Charity and Social Protection Order; Christianskoye Miloserdie (Christian Charity); Rossiya

Charity Centre (RCC); Russian Charity Foundation; Overnight Hostel; Special Department of the Ministry of Labour and Social Protection.

Médicins Sans Frontières' office in Moscow, established in 1990, for example, brings together physicians and social workers. Because BOMZHes are denied access to Russia's public health system, MSF set up a scheme to provide medical services to Moscow's homeless. In Spring 1992, MSF workers, in cooperation with the Independent Physicians' Association, launched a programme of first-aid to homeless people in their most common living places such as the Paveletsky Railway Station (Bodungen, 1994). Two doctors there received patients three times a week. They worked night shifts serving on average 40 people. Later that year, MSF established a travelling outpatient service for vagrants and has negotiated an agreement with a number of Moscow's hospitals, whereby the hospitals took an official obligation to treat homeless patients sent to them by MSF staff. MSF are also working on enabling homeless children to be placed in orphanages.

The Samaritans in Russia have been involved in working with the homeless since 1991. They distribute free hot meals and second-hand clothes and also supply food to children's homes.

BOMZHes who apply to the Charity and Social Protection Order, registered in Russia since 1989, are entitled to receive a free supply of food and some clothes, as well as a sum of money. The Order's strategy is to give the homeless an opportunity to earn some money rather than to create a dependency culture among them. As a rule, the Order helps BOMZHes to find odd jobs that do not require much effort or concentration. Despite the temporary nature of these jobs, they constitute an important step towards social adaptation of BOMZHes. The Order is also actively involved in programmes that provide educational opportunities for Russian orphans with special talents.

The Christian Charity, established in 1992, is responsible for running several programmes, such as, for example, taking homeless children off the streets of large cities, such as Moscow and St Petersburg, and accommodating them in special hostels. They also run charity canteens for the homeless.

The Russian Charity Foundation, established in 1992, dedicates a large amount of its effort to running an orphanage-cum-shelter for children who leave home trying to escape violent abuse from their alcoholic or drug-addicted parents. The children can enjoy total freedom of movement, that is, they can come and go from the shelter whenever they want to. As well as receiving food, clothing and shelter, those who wish to study can attend classes. Children can also receive psychological counselling (Bodungen, 1994).

Thus, while a range of activities are occurring in the voluntary sector, the coverage of the homeless population is partial and there is clearly a lack of a comprehensive strategy to deal with the full range of problems that exist.

Homelessness among women

For many women, the gradual transition to a market economy in Russia has proved very painful. Many highly educated women lost their jobs and migrated to the low-paid, unskilled sector (Statistical Bulletin, 1995). Despite a very high level of education among women, there is a striking gender segregation within the workforce. Women earn on average 30% less than men in almost all sectors of the economy (Rzhanina, 1996). Moreover, according to the Federal Employment Service, women constitute 47.1% of the workforce in Russia, but make up 70-75% of the registered unemployed.

Women have never been considered attractive labour force by potential employers because many of them required and still do various social benefits, such as maternity leave, child benefit and so on, which must either be met by the employer, or by the state. For example, 76% of unemployed women in Russia have children, and 40% of these have children of pre-school age. For most women in Russia, becoming a housewife and mother, especially in the post-communist era, entails total economic dependency on their husbands, once they lose their jobs (Baskakova, 1994). Traditionally employed in lower-paying jobs in state enterprises, particularly in such fields as education, health and the light industry, women have seen their salaries dwindle as the state enterprises run out of money to pay them. In Soviet times, the average woman made 70% of the average man's salary, according to the Centre for Gender Studies. Now as men stream into the private sector or are chosen for a few lucrative jobs in the state enterprises, that figure has plummeted to 40% (Centre for Gender Studies cited in the *Moscow Times*, 1995). Still, according to the Centre for Gender Studies, around half (about 48%) of women work mainly in state enterprises, while only 25% of women work in the more competitive and better-paying private sector.

Many women have had their hours reduced or have been sent on forced leave, deprived both of their full salaries and the unemployment benefits they would have received had they been fired. And with the collapse of the state system, other benefits, such as child support and day care, have vanished as well.

Women have also suffered from other consequences of the break up of the Soviet System. The government has no system to enforce child support payments by divorced fathers, who under the Soviet system had the money automatically deducted from their wages. And state subsidies for single mothers, 55% of whom are living on the poverty line (Centre for Gender Studies cited in the *Moscow Times*, 1995) are only for mothers who were never married. Divorced mothers as a result have the hardest time (*Moscow Times*, 1995).

Changes in the economic fortunes of women in Russia have combined with a decrease in the affordability of housing to increase the difficulties faced by women, relative to their male counterparts. One of the commonest routes into homelessness among women in Russia results from trying to escape a violent relationship. Domestic violence has only recently been subject to scrutiny in Russian society. According to unofficial statistics provided by the Moscow Crisis Centre for Women, 14,000 women in Russia were killed in 1993 and 57,000 wounded as a result of domestic violence (Beigulenko, 1997b). Traditionally in Russia, domestic problems have been considered to be a private matter (Pisklakova, 1994). Even after divorce, 70% of victims of domestic violence admit that the police are unwilling to intervene. As a result, women sometimes have to leave their homes in the middle of the night in order to seek shelter, either with friends or relatives, or in a refuge centre. There is currently only one refuge for women in St Petersburg, which has been operating since May 1996. It can accommodate up to only 30 women with children, and is inadequate to meet the needs of a city with a population of 4.4 million. Moscow with the population double that of St Petersburg still does not have its own women's refuge.

At the present time, there exists only one night shelter for homeless roofless women in Moscow, and this is on the verge of being closed owing to lack of funding. This fact illustrates how little attention is being paid to the problem of homelessness among women. Yet the homelessness problem among women is clearly as significant as it is among men and differs from that among men. For example, in the five years from 1985 to 1989, 6,894 people passed through the Moscow filtering stations: 3,791 men, of whom 90% were ex-prisoners and 32% natives of Moscow, and 3,103 women, of whom only 45% were ex-prisoners and 26% were natives of Moscow (Bodungen, 1994). The problem faced by women is exacerbated by the fact that the current housing situation in Moscow makes it particularly difficult for women to enter the housing market: housing tends to be the most expensive asset to acquire and, as was noted above, women tend to have considerably smaller financial resources to draw on than men.

Women and the issue of concealed homelessness

Now, when unemployment is increasingly becoming a women's issue, the prospect of losing financial support from a husband seems to be catastrophic for a lot of women. Very often, young Russian women are forced to keep their marriages, despite continuous physical and psychological abuse.

Serious housing problems often prevent women from leaving violent partners. According to the data produced by the Moscow Longitudinal Household Survey (1992-95), in 1992 almost half of all households within the lowest income group were overcrowded; in 1995, one third of the poorest income group was overcrowded. Households in the highest income group had a much lower incidence of overcrowding in 1995 (at least 10% less) than any other income group.

If the incidence of actual homelessness is difficult to ascertain accurately, the incidence of concealed homelessness is still more elusive. Given the particular problems facing homeless women in Russia, it is likely that concealed homelessness, too, is particularly problematic for women. Moreover, failure to recognise the phenomenon of concealed homelessness – both on the part of the women involved and on the part of the authorities – could encourage women to blame themselves for (and therefore remain trapped in) their inadequate housing situation. Watson and Austerberry (1986) have argued that the less women in difficult housing situations recognise the tragedy of their housing situation, the less actively they will act to change it.

In Russia, according to various estimates it would take at least 25 years for a family to buy a house or a flat, spending no money on anything else. Such poor prospects of acquiring new housing undoubtedly makes a lot of people feel very unhappy and insecure. This is especially true of young families. At the moment, there are about 6.5 million young families living in Russia, a total of about 20 million people. The incomes of young families are usually 1.5 times lower than the incomes of other groups of the population (Russia in Figures, 1995). Young families experience the most serious financial difficulties, since they have an added responsibility of looking after children. This usually means that only one member of the family can work full-time, usually the father. Only 9% of young families consider themselves to be high earners; 41% medium earners and 50% have a low income (Antonov, 1995). Thus, 91% of young families in Russia experience to a varying extent a feeling of dissatisfaction with their standards of living. Only 9% of young families estimate the chances of income increase as very good, whereas 43% think of these chances as quite small and 24% consider the chances as non-existent (Antonov, 1995). It is not surprising therefore that 81% of young families in Russia rely on the financial help of parents.

But the most serious problem for the majority of young families in Russia is the absence of separate housing; in other words, housing which does not have to be shared with other relatives. A survey conducted by Goskomstat of the Russian Federation in December 1995 revealed that 49% of young families consisting of both partners under 25 lived together with their parents. These young families were unable to purchase their own home despite a strong desire to create an independent household. The results of the survey also revealed that 50% of young families have only five square metres of living space per member of the family. As a result, only 15% of families interviewed considered their housing conditions to be satisfactory. According to the same survey, only 19% of young families in Russia contemplate the idea of buying or building their own flat or house (data cited at the National Conference 'Youth, society and state: realities and perspectives', April 1996). Housing policy makers are currently trying to focus the new stage of housing reform on creating a system of housing benefits for young and single parent families with Western models of housing loans. But the current reality is that commercial banks are unwilling to grant every citizen a loan for 20-30 years (*Finansoviye Izvestia*, 1995). The loans currently available are not accessible to ordinary people, particularly the aforementioned categories of families, who tend to experience very severe financial difficulties. For example, the income at which a Sberbank loan for individual housing construction was affordable exceeded the average family income 14-fold (Kosareva et al, 1995).

Evidence suggests that sharing a flat or a house with parents usually has a negative impact on young families. The following statistics provide a very good illustration of this point. Among the young families who have never lived with their parents in the same flat or house, 91.5% are satisfied with their marriage. Among those families who did not have a chance to live independently, only 60.6% believe they have a satisfactory marriage (Youth in Russia: social development, 1992). According to the same source, only 6% of young families have the opportunity of living in their own apartment independent of their parents. This situation puts a lot of young families in Russia and women in particular, into a situation of permanent crisis making them feel increasingly insecure, vulnerable and even homeless.

A recent study conducted in Moscow among women under 30 years of age, representing young families (Beigulenko, 1997a), reveals that it is not unusual for women, both tenants and homeowners living in overcrowded conditions, to experience concealed homelessness. Here are some of the thoughts women have found the courage to share with the researcher (Beigulenko, 1997a):

> ... I often have a feeling that this place is just a temporary abode, despite the fact it's my parental home.... [Lana, a muscovite, currently living with her five-year-old son and husband in a three-room privatised apartment with her parents and grandmother]

> ... I don't feel this place is temporary for me and my family since I don't have any hope to improving my present housing conditions ... and I do feel homeless ... I am even prepared to leave this place and go back to the Chernobyl area, which I left 11 years ago. I left my home behind then.... [Katya, a forced migrant from the Chernobyl zone, currently renting a room in a hostel for construction workers with her husband and a six-year-old son]

> ... I don't have a feeling of home ... It just does not exist.... [Sveta, a Muscovite, currently living with her husband and a six-year-old son in a three-room apartment of a privatised flat with her parents and sister]

> ... I do long to come home, but then when you see neighbours walking around you get very depressed and become very reserved ... sometimes I don't even want to live.... [Galina, came to Moscow nine years ago with her husband who found employment there. She, her husband and an eight-year-old son are currently renting a tiny room of a communal flat with another family occupying the second room. Kitchen and bathroom facilities are shared]

Homelessness among children

Alexei Severnii, the president of the Independent Association of Children's Psychiatrists and Psychologists, told Interfax on 21 October that there are at least 1 million homeless children in Russia. Severnii estimated that Moscow and St Petersburg each have some 60,000 homeless children, not including the offsprings of refugees and immigrants. (The BEARR Trust, 1997a)

These figures reveal that children have been particularly vulnerable to the political, economic and social upheavals in the country. The process of achieving higher standards of living for Russian children is developing very slowly, owing to the present political and economic situation. In 1993, 60,982 children were received by the filtering stations in Russia. Youngsters sent to the filtering stations represent only a small proportion of those detained for vagrancy. According to official statistics, 6,495 youngsters were detained for vagrancy at railway stations in Moscow alone in 1992 and only 2,528 were sent to the filtering centres (Bodungen, 1994). From the filtering centres, children normally proceed to orphanages or special nursing homes, depending on their physical condition and mental state. However, many children remain on the streets.

There are several reasons why children become homeless. One of these is that children run away from home. They may be acting on an urge to be independent of their parents, on an impulse to make the parents suffer for an injustice they have done to the child, or even to search for romantic adventure. The police normally return such children home, and the incident ends at that (Bodungen, 1994).

There are, however, much more serious cases of child homelessness – 50,000 such cases in Moscow alone (Bodungen, 1994). Many children find themselves out in the street due to their parents' greed and because Russia's laws do not guarantee the housing rights of children under 16 in privatised apartments (Bodungen, 1994). There are quite a few private, apartment-hunting businesses who persuade parents to sell their apartments. At the end of the deal, children are frequently left behind without a roof over their heads. Often the parents do not come back.

Although the Public Prosecutor's Office of Russia has on numerous occasions pointed to the fact that housing privatisation laws do not take account of under-age youngsters and their rights (children's names are not entered on apartment sale contracts),

> the situation remains unchanged and children continue to be
> victims of the present-day privatisation boom. Constituting over
> a half of all homeless children, these 'disinherited' kids
> involuntarily become vagrants exposed to the hard life on the
> streets. (Bodungen, 1994, p 12)

Another reason for homelessness among children is parental cruelty and outright child abuse. Russia's only Child Abuse Protection Foundation studied the problem of child abuse in Russia. According to unofficial statistics presented by the Foundation, 102,682 children were left without parental care in 1994 – a 26% increase on the previous year. Alcoholism, drug abuse, psychological disorders suffered by parents and socio-economic factors contributed to the increase in known cases of child abuse. The research confirmed that this problem is widespread in Russia, but is still largely unrecognised, despite the fact that the country is a signatory to the United Nations Convention on the Rights of Children (*The BEARR Trust*, 1997b). Children often run away out of an instinct to survive. Their tragic experiences teach them not to trust adults. They are preoccupied only with their own survival. Nearly 2,000 of them even commit suicide annually, most driven to despair by their parents' cruelty (Bodungen, 1994).

Many teenage vagrants turn to crime as a means of survival, which later becomes a way of life. About 80% of all children who find themselves in the filtering centres have a police record. Homeless teenagers committed 200,000 crimes in Russia in 1992 alone (*Rossiiskaya Gazeta*, in Bodungen, 1994). To treat these children as criminals is not the ideal way. More than anything they need professional help from social workers and psychotherapists, which may not be readily available.

Finding housing is one of the greatest problems for those leaving orphanages at the age of 18. In theory, as stipulated by law, the provision of housing is the responsibility of the state, but in fact orphanage leavers have themselves to deal with the problem of looking for a vacant room, talking officials into making out the necessary papers and so on. Between 1990 and 1994 452 children left orphanages. Only a half of those in need of accommodation found a vacant room. Despite the ordinance issued by the Moscow government from time to time (such as 'On measures to improve the provision of housing to orphanage school leavers'), 214 youngsters leaving orphanages received no accommodation from 1989 to 1992, and another 250 were put on a waiting list in 1993. As a result many new young homeless people can be expected to appear on the streets of Moscow. Those who do manage to find a place to live usually end up sharing it with a friend from the orphanage, thus turning their room into a small orphans' home (*Na Dne*, 1996b).

Conclusion: is there a way forward?

Housing plays a central part in how we live our lives. The dwelling place is the site of intense human activities and interpersonal relationships. People spend a lot of time at home, and invest both financial and emotional energy in their homes. Indeed, homes may be described as "among the most central physical settings of human life" (Altman, 1993, p 29).

The absence of a home may have a devastating effect on a person, destroying his or her life dreams, aspirations and feelings of comfort and security. In Russia, negative public attitudes towards the homeless are in large part influenced by a long-established official tradition, which responds to the problems of socially disadvantaged groups by isolating them from the rest of society. Russian society has been slow to stop treating homeless people as criminals and to recognise them as an unprotected population group. Until quite recently, vagrancy was a criminal offence in Russia.

The problems of the homeless in Russia are aggravated by poor legislative and administrative measures, and by lack of enforcement, together with a lack of relevant inter-state agreements within the Commonwealth of Independent States (Bodungen, 1994). The shortage of reliable data – on how many people in Russia are homeless, and what kind of assistance they require – means that those in authority do not have a clear idea about the kinds and levels of service Russia needs if it wishes to tackle homelessness effectively. This lack of information has led to virtual neglect of the homeless in recent social welfare budgets (Sokolov, 1994). For example, there is no system in place to help the homeless find temporary, low-skilled employment, which would assist them in social adaptation by giving them the dignity of earning a wage rather than having to beg for money.

If the homeless are to have more than merely an abode and food for a day, special social adaptation centres must be created alongside night shelters, to serve as centre points where social security agencies, employment and training agencies and medical practitioners could be gathered together under the same roof. It has further been suggested that the problem of homelessness among refugees can be resolved by recruiting them to revive abandoned Russian villages for their own use, forming so-called 'new' or 'young' towns (*Komsomolskaya Pravda*, 1998). One problem with this solution is that refugees are often former city residents, and feel reluctant to settle in rural parts of the country (Beigulenko, 1994).

It is now obvious that the social consequences of the housing and more general economic reforms in Russia in facilitating the growth of concealed homelessness have hitherto been neglected. Like the situation in the UK (Lidstone, 1994) of scarcity of financial resources allocated for public spending rationing becomes a typical response of local authorities to homelessness.

It is evident that an integrated approach needs to be adopted in Russia to enable the voluntary agencies, official state agencies, the police and commercial organisations to cooperate more fully in trying to tackle the growing problem of homelessness. A broad definition of homelessness must also be adopted, in order to address the problem of concealed homelessness, which is particularly common among women. Special attention must be paid to the ever-increasing problem of homelessness among children. A fresh approach to social policies would achieve more than merely saving the children most at risk of becoming homeless: it would represent an investment for the future of all children in Russia. The need for an integrated approach to the problem of homelessness has been emphasised by the European Observatory on Homelessness:

> **Homelessness must be regarded as a condition rather than as an event. It is tempting to treat it simply as the loss of a roof or shelter but homelessness is more than this. It occurs usually within a broader process of marginalisation which involves not just housing or financial inadequacy but an inability to participate in the quality of life and opportunities enjoyed by the rest of the society. (European Observatory on Homelessness, 1992 cited in Lund, 1996, p 100)**

To conclude, homelessness should be paid special attention to by the policy makers particularly during the times of uncertainty and transition, since home is one of those unique places where an individual can find a true sense of security and hope for the future.

References

Alden, J., Beigulenko, Y. and Crow, S. (1998) 'Moscow. Planning for a world capital city towards 2000', *Journal of Urban Policy and Planning (CITIES)*, vol 15, no 5, pp 361-74.

Altman, I., (1993) 'Foreword', in E. Arias (ed) *The meaning and use of housing: International perspectives, approaches and their applications*, Aldershot: Avebury.

Antonov, A. (1995) *Depopulation and family crisis in post-Soviet Russia: Who is to blame and what to do?*, Bulletin of the Moscow State University, Serial 18: Sociology and politology, no 2, pp 79-86.

Babushkin, A. and Volodarski, P. (1995) *A short note to a homeless person on how to defend his rights and where to turn for help, if you have become homeless*, Moscow: Intellect.

Baskakova, M. (1994) *Social conditions of the unemployed (familiy aspect): Personality and family in the period of social transition*, vol 11, Moscow: Institute for Socioeconomic Studies of Population, Russian Academy of Sciences.

BEARR *Trust, The* (1997a) 'Are children the main losers in transition?', no 20, November.

BEARR *Trust, The* (1997b) 'The OZON Centre: research and action to protect children', no 17, March.

Beigulenko, Y. (1994) 'Women in difficult housing conditions: their opinion on home and homelessness', Unpublished paper.

Beigulenko, Y. (1997a) 'The international perspective on gender, housing and homelessness: The case study of Moscow', Paper presented at the ENHR/YHR Seminar 'European housing in transition', Budapest.

Beigulenko, Y. (1997b) 'Domestic violence: will the new law help?', *The BEARR Trust Newsletter*, no 17, March, pp 1-2.

Bodungen, A. (1994) *Homelessness in Russia*, London: Charities Aid Foundation.

Finansoviye Izvestia (1995) 'It is getting easier to obtain a loan for purchase of a unit', 22 August.

'Independent report on the state of homelessness in Russia and its meeting the international pact on civil rights' (1995) St Petersburg: Charity Foundation (*Nochlezhka*).

Komsomolskaya Pravda (1998) 'We will show you where the BOMZHes spend their winter!', 5 January.

Kosareva, N., Puzanov, A. and Tichomirova, M. (1995) *Russia: Fast starter. Housing sector reform 1991-1995*, Moscow: Urban Institute.

Kuranty (1993a) 'Migration update', 14 August.

Kuranty (1993b) 'The health of the homeless', 6 August.

Lidstone, P. (1994) 'Rationing housing to the homeless applicant', *Housing Studies*, vol 9, no 4, pp 459-71.

Lund, B. (1996) *Housing problems and housing policy*, London: Longman.

Moscow Times (1995) 'Market freer, but not fairer', 6 March.

Na Dne (1996a) 'A simple story', no 14, March.

Na Dne (1996b) 'Who is he – the Moscow vagrant?', no 15, April.

Na Dne (1996c) 'What do I think about homelessness?', no 16, May.

National Conference 'Youth, society and state: realities and perspectives', *Report*, April 1996, Moscow.

Pilkington, H. (1997) 'The "other" Russians. Migration, displacement and identity in post-Soviet Russia', *British East–West Journal*, no 107, September.

Pisklakova, M. (1994) 'Cry for help – the experience of work of crisis centre for women', *Personality and Family in the Period of Social Transition*, vol 11, Moscow: Russian Academy of Sciences, Institute for Socioeconomic Studies of Population.

Rzhanina, L. (1996) 'Labour mobility of women', *Women in the Russian Society*, no 1, January, pp 9-12.

Sokolov, V. (1994) 'Without a right on ... (homelessness in St Petersburg)', in *Petersburg in the early 90's: Crazy, cold, cruel*, St Petersburg: Charitable Foundation (*Nochlezhka*).

Statistical Bulletin (1995) *Women of Russia*, Moscow: Goskomstat of Russia.

Watson, S. and Austerberry, H. (1986) *Housing and homelessness: A feminist perspective*, London: Routledge and Kegan Paul.

ELEVEN

Implementing 'joined-up thinking': multiagency services for single homeless people in Bristol

Jenny Pannell and Siân Parry

Introduction

The HUB advice centre in Bristol has achieved a national and international reputation for multiagency working in the field of services for single homeless people. By uniting staff from voluntary and statutory, and local and national organisations, The HUB has broken new ground in bringing together a wide range of agencies to work holistically to meet the complex needs of single homeless people. It has won awards and has received a constant stream of visitors seeking an explanation for how Bristol has managed to achieve such a combination of expertise under one roof. The Hub is only one of a number of linked multiagency activities directed at homeless people in the city.

This chapter explores the 'new terrain' of Bristol's policy response to single homeless people. It has been widely acknowledged that there is a need for an integrated policy approach and coordinated service planning between both statutory and voluntary not-for-profit agencies. This has become known in recent policy debates as the need for 'joined-up thinking' (Social Exclusion Unit, 1998; Cabinet Office, 1999).

Multiagency working has been widely discussed in the literature over the past few years (Goss and Kent, 1995; Arblaster et al, 1996; Hambleton et al, 1996; Oldman, 1997), yet examples of successful multiagency working remain limited, particularly where housing and employment services are involved alongside health and social services and there is full participation by the voluntary as well as the statutory sector. Private sector involvement also played a limited but key role in the Bristol experience, and this too appears to be unusual. There is widespread interest in whether services developed in one locality are replicable elsewhere.

After considering the potential and difficulties involved in multiagency working, the chapter considers the growth and effectiveness of Bristol's multiagency services in meeting the needs of single homeless people, drawing on a research study carried out during 1997. The research focused on how local multiagency projects had come about and on issues which had arisen during their development and management, as well as considering how effective the services were in meeting the needs of single homeless people.

The study focused at service delivery level on six projects:

- The HUB, a multiagency housing advice centre;
- a primary healthcare team working with single homeless people;
- a voluntary day centre;
- a voluntary outreach team;
- a winter shelter;
- specialist staff working with homeless people within a multiagency mental health service.

It examined the networks between both statutory and voluntary agencies associated with the multiagency advice centre The HUB. Methodology included observation, analysis of records, and interviews with 30 service users and with many senior and front-line staff in a number of voluntary and statutory agencies.

The need for multiagency working

During the last decade there has been extensive research on the causes and effects of single homelessness, on the complexity of the problems faced by single homeless people, and on the advantages of multiagency working to tackle such problems (Caton, 1990; Cohen and Thompson, 1992; Anderson et al, 1993; Bines, 1994; Connelly and Crown, 1994; Knight, 1994; Mental Health Foundation, 1994; Allen, 1995; Burrows et al, 1997). As understanding of the complexity of the causes and problems has grown, so has the sophistication of the recommended policy responses. Yet the extent to which such understanding at policy level is translated into services 'on the ground' is still surprisingly limited, which is what makes Bristol's experience so interesting to both policy makers and practitioners.

Single homeless people are frequently experiencing a range of social and health problems which require an holistic response if they are to be effectively remedied. Yet, research suggests that many single homeless people are unable to access appropriate services. Much of the available accommodation for single homeless people fails to meet their multiple needs. For example:

- Over half those refused admission to direct access hostel provision were rejected because of drug or alcohol related reasons; barriers are created by a lack of knowledge of the needs of single homeless people with physical disabilities or other specific needs (Ham, 1996).
- Nearly two thirds of hostel residents had wanted some help with a range of problems but, with the exception of health difficulties, only a minority had received the help they wanted (Randall and Brown, 1996).

The complexity of problems faced by many single homeless people requires solutions to address a broad range of issues. It is beyond the capability of a single agency to deliver a 'complete' service to all single homeless people. This highlights the need to develop models of interagency working which will deliver holistic solutions (Oldman, 1997).

The increase in multiagency working has been driven by different interests and reflects wider changes following the Conservative government's marginalisation of local government and its encouragement of greater private and voluntary sector involvement in service planning and provision (Pierson, 1994). Some of the key changes include:

- the changing role of local authorities from providers to purchasers and enablers;
- the strategic role of social services departments in relation to community care planning and provision and their responsibilities under the 1989 Children Act;
- the increasing role of voluntary sector providers in both strategic planning and service provision;
- and the interest of the private and business sector in social welfare issues.

Interagency provision for single homeless people has been growing since the early 1980s. Multiagency working was a feature of Phase 2 of the Rough Sleepers Initiative (RSI) in London. Consortia were set up to coordinate work in geographical zones, which was intended to lead to better liaison across agencies, notably the police, local authorities and mental health services (Randall and Brown, 1996).

The government may have changed in May 1997, but interest in multiagency working continues, albeit from a different policy perspective. Welfare to Work, Best Value and measures to combat social exclusion have all highlighted the importance of agencies in these fields working together more effectively (Lee, 1998). The Labour government has made social care one of its key policy platforms. Tackling the interaction between different aspects of deprivation and improving interagency working to prevent problems arising in the first place are essential (Hirst, 1998). The recent Social Exclusion Unit report on rough sleeping concludes that a 'joined-up solution' is needed, starting with Whitehall, including training, employment and health as well as housing and social services, and engaging with both business and the voluntary sector (Social Exclusion Unit, 1998; Cabinet Office, 1999). Mullins (1998) points out that social housing interventions can only be effective when undertaken in conjunction with other policies such as employment, education and health care to tackle patterns of institutionalised discrimination (Mullins, 1998, p 258).

The policy focus is also on strategies to meet the needs of specific groups within society such as young people, older people, or those with specific needs such as people involved in substance abuse. Such strategies cut across traditional professional and agency boundaries: multiagency approaches have to be devised and supported by agencies across the board and in both voluntary and statutory sectors. Because this type of approach is thought to be more productive and effective, the government argues that it can be done without necessarily levering in additional resources. However, both the Bristol study and other studies on multiagency working (Goss and Kent, 1995; Arblaster et al, 1996) show that additional resources do need to be drawn in to pump-prime new initiatives.

The nature of multiagency working: problems and opportunities

Multiagency working is acknowledged to be a difficult process. Challenges to effective joint working include:
*   different approaches to needs assessment by housing, social care and health organisations;
*   different definitions and understanding of what constitutes effective care;
*   varying priorities of different agencies with differing planning structures involved;

- the organisational impact of restructuring and reorganisation;
- problems related to confidentiality and information-sharing.

The relative 'newness' of multiagency working has also impeded its effectiveness – partners are all on a steep learning curve (Goss and Kent, 1995). There are substantial barriers to effective collaboration, including vested interests, short-term thinking, the sheer complexity of some tasks and divergent professional and organisational cultures. Successful collaboration needs to balance effective service delivery with adequate arrangements for accountability, yet there can often be a tension between these two requirements.

Multiagency working also has to be seen as more than an 'add-on' to ongoing activities. Hambleton et al (1996) suggest that requires participants to:

- identify shared objectives;
- question established approaches and welcome innovation;
- commit time, energy and resources;
- establish clear reporting mechanisms;
- create mechanisms for regular review of the whole approach to collaboration.

Arblaster et al (1996) undertook research on multiagency working between health, housing and social services and identified a number of characteristics which are of more general relevance. In particular, in many cases:

- there were very few three-way links;
- multiagency working often took place at only one level (senior staff or front-line staff);
- initiatives lacked key players at the right level and with access to resources, yet these factors were crucial;
- it was necessary, but extremely difficult, to agree common goals;
- there was very limited knowledge and understanding of the role and professional culture of other agencies.

Finally, despite widespread interest in user involvement in most areas of social policy, commentators note that this is rare in multiagency working. The exception has been in services where users and parents/carers were already active and pressing for more involvement, such as services for certain groups of disabled people. For example, the Community Care, Housing and Homelessness Project found "little evidence of user or carer involvement in strategic planning, or of strategic thinking about how housing, social services and health agencies might find ways of working in partnership with users" (Means and Smith, 1996, p x). A number of reasons are given for this weakness, including the complexity of multiagency working arrangements and the dominance of professional agendas.

Bristol's experience: problems and solutions

Bristol is a large, relatively prosperous regional centre with a progressive city council and a well-developed voluntary not-for-profit sector providing a range of services for single homeless people. The extent of single homelessness and the development of multiagency services in the city was recognised by the government when Bristol became the first city outside London to receive grant aid under the Rough Sleepers Initiative (RSI).

The research study on which this chapter is based focused on six projects, examining the 'new terrain' of multiagency working at The HUB advice centre and a number of projects linked to it (see Figure 11.1).

Figure 11.1: Multiagency projects surveyed in Bristol

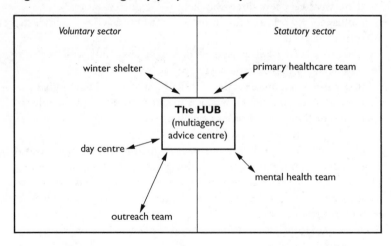

A multiagency project committee runs The HUB with members from all the participating agencies. Funding is complex: staff are employed by their 'parent' agencies, with the voluntary organisations receiving statutory funding for this, while initial costs were met from Partnership Fund capital resources. The following agencies (in alphabetical order) are involved and provide staff and services as follows:

- *Avon Health Authority:* health link workers, accessing primary healthcare for HUB users, referrals and liaison with health services.
- *The Benefits Agency:* benefits staff, offering benefits advice and processing benefits claims.
- *Bristol City Council Housing:* HUB manager, managing the centre and coordinating its work; homelessness staff, assessing the entitlement of single people and childless couples under the homelessness legislation and placing those deemed to be vulnerable; staff administering Housing Benefits and the Deposit Bond Scheme (to enable single homeless people to access private rented housing).
- *Bristol City Council Social Services:* social workers, providing support, advice and assistance, especially to homeless young people and those with mental health needs.
- *Bristol Cyrenians:* 'front of house' staff, including initial assessment, referrals and finding accommodation.
- *Employment Service:* employment staff (part-time) – training opportunities, job interviews and employment for over-18s.
- *Learning Partnership West:* careers staff (part-time) – further education, training and jobs for 16- to 17-year-olds.
- *Shelter:* advice staff, offering specialist advice and advocacy on housing and welfare benefits.

The HUB is unique in having voluntary sector staff (Cyrenians and Shelter) working alongside statutory sector staff, and in the involvement of such a wide range of agencies, in particular the Benefits Agency, with a staff member on site with access to the Benefits Agency computer system. Thus clients have access to a 'one-stop shop' with a full range of services under one roof. Information is shared between all the agency staff, subject to the agreement of the client and the centre's confidentiality policy.

All the other projects in the study had a wide range of links with each other and with The HUB, including:

- joint outreach work (outreach team, primary healthcare team);
- health surgeries (primary healthcare team at day centre);
- housing advice surgery (HUB staff at winter shelter).

The HUB was developed as a result of increasing concern in the city about the extent of homelessness among single people, including rough sleepers, from the 1980s onwards. Local research in the city echoed the national picture. In the 1991 Census, the Bristol area had recorded over a hundred rough sleepers (although care needs to be taken with such snapshot statistics: see, for example, Kemp, 1997). Local voluntary groups became aware of the need to back up demands for funding with statistical evidence, and this was used by the City Council in its Housing Strategy Statements: for example, by the early 1990s, voluntary groups estimated that at least 600 people were sleeping rough in the course of each year (Bristol City Council, 1993). A 1993 survey by a local voluntary forum on homelessness and mental health showed that a third of all residents in two direct access hostels in the city had mental health problems, and 36% of residents had used psychiatric services in the past (Avon Voluntary Housing Forum, 1993). The largest voluntary sector provider of services for single homeless people reported that over half its service users had been hospital inpatients, 27% within the previous six months (Bristol Cyrenians, 1993).

In 1994, the Bristol Cyrenians *Under one roof* study, sponsored by the Employment Service, proposed a multiagency advice centre for single homeless people. This was followed by the creation of a steering group with representatives from six statutory agencies, the voluntary sector and the private sector. The HUB opened in June 1995.

How Bristol did it: the role of key players

The importance of "enthusiastic key players" (Hambleton et al, 1996) came out strongly in an examination of the development of The HUB. Of crucial importance was "a core group of people ... who actively promote and support joint working [with] sufficient status or authority within their own organisations to influence strategy" (Goss and Kent, 1995, p x). Status is important because although front-line workers can establish informal links, it needs senior staff to develop new services. It seems likely that in areas which have not succeeded in developing joint working, this is at least partly because of a lack of will at a senior enough level: Goss and Kent found little evidence of interagency work between health and housing organisations, and although there were "pockets of understanding and collaboration among front-line staff ... [this] does not necessarily flow up" (1995, p x).

One of the features which helped Bristol to succeed was undoubtedly the commitment of senior managers. This was confirmed in interviews with agency staff:

> **"It takes key individuals, or the idea would have been killed off before it got off the ground."** **[Statutory agency]**

> **"You need key individuals who are willing to take a risk ... at a level with authority and power."** **[Voluntary organisation]**

The importance of a small group of key players is not, however, without its own risks: some concern was expressed during interviews with senior staff about what would happen when the present generation of senior staff move on or delegate their roles to staff below them in their organisational hierarchies. However, some 'new blood' coming on to the scene was also identified and it was hoped that they would continue with the multiagency focus.

Individuals can make or break successful interagency working: "personalities can be critical" (Hambleton et al, 1996). Certain names were mentioned in a number of interviews as charismatic leaders who could bring people together and who held on to a vision. These were not just in housing organisations: homelessness needed 'champions', especially in non-housing agencies such as the health authority, or Employment Services where it could otherwise be sidelined. Working together on other interagency projects for homeless people, such as outreach services, had helped to identify such 'champions' in the non-housing agencies and developed the necessary understanding and liaison.

Voluntary sector respondents also commented on the knowledge of, and commitment to, rough sleeping issues among senior staff in the city council housing department, which they found "very unusual for someone in a council housing department". This reaction reflects the traditional lack of interest in single homelessness and rough sleeping on the part of local authorities. These issues have generally been left to the voluntary sector to pick up.

Much of the literature talks about the problem of developing working relationships over time, which in many areas has been frustrated by organisational change (for example, of local government and the NHS), the lack of coterminous boundaries, and senior staff changes. The city has been fortunate in the number of key players who have remained in the city over a long period, with some making career moves within the city, between services or across the voluntary/statutory divide. The lack of such staff continuity elsewhere could be another reason why Bristol's experience has not been replicated.

Fora can be important in establishing better coordination, though one study found that they varied in their effectiveness. The weakest were "loose coalitions of purchasers and providers", and were dismissed by participants as mere talking-shops; the strongest were involved in "genuine co-ordinating activity: assessing local need, reviewing existing provision and developing plans for future service provision" (Oldman, 1997). From the early 1980s onwards agency staff in Bristol were starting to work together and meeting at a number of interagency homelessness fora. As the fora developed, they were able to tackle real issues and have retained the commitment of staff at a senior enough level to deliver.

The Bristol research identified a chain of events which facilitated the development of close working relationships over a long period. A vital integrating link throughout the different stages was the stability of senior staff in key positions referred to above.

By the early 1980s the government was planning a closure programme of all resettlement units and the closure of the local resettlement unit for single people was the first event in the chain. Funding was made available for replacement with small-scale, specialist hostels and move-on housing, provided by the voluntary sector. A consultative body of statutory and voluntary agencies was created to plan the replacement provision, necessitating close working between senior staff in both statutory and voluntary agencies. The process was facilitated by the appointment of a designated staff member whose responsibilities included the promotion of multiagency working. The availability of ring-fenced finance from the Department of Social Security provided a further incentive to develop creative partnerships: real money was a prize worth cooperating for, even if some of the participants at that stage were somewhat suspicious of each other.

The next link in the chain was Bristol's winter shelter group, which has provided a shelter every winter since 1991-92. Key professionals in both statutory and voluntary sectors came together following a conference held by one of the voluntary sector fora, which highlighted the lack of such provision in the city. A multiagency steering group has run the project each year with members from a wide range of both statutory and voluntary agencies.

Studies have noted that where multiagency working has succeeded "professionals have been the main change drivers in the case studies, not elected members" (Hambleton et al, 1996). This has certainly been the case in Bristol. However, effective professionals need to take their elected members with them into new policy areas. In the city, councillors and 'quasi-politicians', such as health authority members, were aware of homelessness issues over a number of years, partly from the success of some of the other projects linked to The HUB. Social services councillors were concerned about young people leaving care, the health authority were committed to the primary healthcare team, and both authorities were already working together in developing the mental health team.

The role of the private sector

Key professionals also enlisted support from Bristol's private sector and business community to add their influence to the call for central and local government action. As Cochrane argues, private sector involvement in social policy at the local level is a feature of the post-Fordist restructuring of the welfare state, where in extreme cases, welfare "is justified largely by the way it makes places more or less attractive to business" (1994, p x). Publicity about the number of rough sleepers in the city was causing concern about both the extent of street homelessness and its effect on the image of the city centre. The Board of the city centre shopping centre was also concerned about its image in the face of competition from a regional shopping centre on a new site just north of Bristol.

By 1993 the city's chamber of commerce, quoting a local business survey, pointed out that "the issues of homelessness are a top concern for local business leaders. The private sector is ready to stand shoulder to shoulder with the public and voluntary sector to effect real change" (Bristol Cyrenians, 1993). Visits were organised to homeless hostels under the auspices of Business in the Community and Common Purpose. The Bristol Chamber of Commerce and Initiative was a member of the steering group which planned The HUB. The Chamber has also formed a Housing the Homeless Group to assist the public and voluntary sectors.

What is perhaps unusual about Bristol is the way in which people who would have had little reason even to meet a decade earlier were able to find enough common ground to work together. This is despite the fact that differences of opinion remain on how best to tackle certain sensitive issues such as begging in the shopping centre. One voluntary sector respondent summed up the situation in Bristol in surprisingly glowing terms, given the differences which undoubtedly still exist:

> "This city is unique – the voluntary sector, statutory agencies, the police, the business community – they have the same agenda and street homelessness is high on it."

The need to establish clear principles and shared values

All the literature stresses the importance in multiagency working of reaching agreement at the outset on aims, objectives and principles, and if possible on shared values as well. "At the local level, the first step is to develop clarity about shared goals and desired outcomes between organisations" (Goss and Kent, 1995, p x). Failure to agree these is identified as an important barrier to effective working between agencies, and is no doubt another reason why there are not more examples like The HUB. Yet lack of agreement on these fundamental issues is much more difficult to achieve than merely expressing policy platitudes about the need for joint working (Malpass and Murie, 1994).

The HUB advice centre contained the widest variety of both professional and organisational cultures. Despite the development of working relationships over a number of years, as discussed above, there was still what was described as a 'legacy of mistrust' which had to be overcome between certain agencies. Members of the project committee worked hard to establish core values and aims and objectives for the project which they could all commit to; they then had to take these back to their parent agencies to commit as well (hence the importance of having people at a high enough level to be able to do this). The committee set out clear aims and objectives, based on the core values of access, choice and confidentiality.

Participants talked about a 'can-do attitude', a determination to make things work, and a willingness to discuss problems so that they could be overcome: "It was very energising to be involved, though there were wrinkles – you don't get totally addicted by the magic!" Interest in the project has helped to maintain 'the magic' because both the individuals and their parent agencies have benefited from their association with a flagship award-winning project.

The impact of different professional backgrounds and organisational cultures

A major obstacle to agreeing the shared values referred to above is the impact of professional and organisational cultures. Key issues are:

- the different approaches of medical/nursing and social care professions;
- traditional hostility between professionals (eg, housing and social workers);
- statutory agency professionals not valuing the role of support workers or voluntary agency staff;
- perceived status differences within or between professions and roles (eg, nurses and doctors).

There are a number of measures which can be taken to overcome these problems:
- new styles of management;
- key post holders authorised to network;
- joint training;
- other staffing arrangements such as shadowing, placements and secondments.

These issues were significant in all the projects surveyed for the research, especially at The HUB. They had been (largely) overcome by a variety of means within the projects themselves.

At The HUB, the voluntary sector had been involved right from the start and a decision taken that they should provide the front-of-house team and housing advisers. There were initial tensions between voluntary and statutory agency staff. Frank discussion, clear leadership and awaydays (including a residential two days, sponsored by the private sector) appear to have largely overcome this tension. Staff were very positive about working together across both professional and voluntary–statutory divides:

> **"Working together broke down a lot of barriers – for example people found that ... [agency staff] didn't have two heads."**

> **"They [ie, staff from other agencies] didn't realise how far we could go, what we could do for people."**

> **"It's much easier here to confront other agencies if you don't feel they're fulfilling their obligations."**

> **"Barriers between agencies are at ankle level here – elsewhere they're at neck level."**

A manager in one of the agencies involved echoed many comments when he spoke of the high quality of staff attracted to work at The HUB:

> **"They were top of the range people with a specialist interest in homelessness – there was the kudos of being involved at the beginning in something new and different and dynamic there, working with others to make it work and also in a high quality environment."**

However, problems relating to organisational cultures and professional hostilities remained a significant issue in 'outside' relationships with mainstream services. Such problems were reported to arise infrequently between staff from different backgrounds within specialist projects such as The HUB and the primary healthcare team. For example, GPs and nurses worked well together at the primary healthcare team, and one GP commented on how impressed he was by the cooperation between voluntary and statutory agencies. Problems were also rare in the context of the frequent liaison between staff from the different specialist homelessness projects. Most problems were reported to arise when specialist staff had to deal with mainstream services, even when the specialist staff member came from the same professional background. Thus it appears that although multiagency working helped in lowering boundaries between and within specialist services, new barriers arose between specialist and mainstream services for a number of reasons.

Such problems affected all professions, but status seemed to be a particular problem for health staff and voluntary sector staff. Health staff in a number of the projects had wide experience and nursing backgrounds, but feared that they were not taken seriously, particularly when referring clients on within the health service. Some voluntary agency staff also felt looked down on by statutory agency staff, not by colleagues with whom they worked closely, but, again, by staff from mainstream statutory services. Staff in voluntary sector projects such as the day centre and the outreach team had devised various methods to help with this problem, especially using colleagues from statutory agencies in projects like The HUB and the primary healthcare team as 'go-betweens'.

There were issues concerning loyalty to the specialist team versus loyalty to the parent organisation or profession, and the perceived conflicting demands of professional advancement versus multiagency working. Staff at parent statutory agencies were reported to refer to colleagues based in the multiagency services as having 'gone native' or as 'swanning around' with a lighter case load and an easier time than those in the mainstream services; there appeared to be little understanding or appreciation that the 'lighter' workload (when measured by numerical throughput) was because of the complexity of the cases being dealt with.

Staff in the specialist services enjoyed the scope of multiagency working and the strength of the team, but feared a de-skilling in relation to their own professional background and, sometimes, weaker links and loss of career advancement in their mainstream organisation. Focusing on single homeless people narrowed the range of clients in terms of professional experience, but was compensated by learning much more about the role of other agencies.

The importance of developing a real project delivering services is key to overcoming such problems. Although there were tensions at all the projects, working together for the good of clients enabled staff to find solutions. Staff commented on how developing formal procedures, and sometimes communicating with close colleagues in writing about a case, helped to de-personalise the problem. They acknowledged that it was a difficult line to tread between being too 'cosy' and too confrontational (especially for staff from the voluntary sector who were accustomed to a role where they needed to challenge decisions made by the statutory sector), but felt it was usually about right.

The impact of resource issues

Resource issues are central in encouraging (or discouraging) multiagency working. Goss and Kent (1995, p x) point to the need for "flexible and imaginative use of resources ... not only finances but also information, staff and 'political' support". Hudson suggests that

> ... a higher collaborative threshold could be pursued in several ways, including achieving coterminous services, rewarding enterprising localities with additional funds and making collaboration an integral part of NHS performance indicators. (Hudson, 1997, p x)

Funding issues were certainly crucial in establishing multiagency projects in Bristol. There are a number of funding models for the projects included in the study:

• some services work in a multiagency way but are mainly funded by one parent statutory agency (eg, the primary healthcare team);

- some have originated from Joint Finance, which offered 'pump-priming' funding for innovative new projects;
- some have been funded by two parent statutory agencies, such as the mental health team, funded originally by health and social services, though later with RSI funding;
- some are funded from a number of statutory sources, such as The HUB, where both statutory and voluntary agency staff are funded from statutory sources;
- some voluntary sector projects receive funding from both statutory and charitable sources: for example, the winter shelter group and the day centre and outreach organisation receive funding mainly from grants from the statutory sector, but also fundraise from the general public, from the private sector and from charitable trusts.

The variety of funding mechanisms is historic and also depends on the agency/agencies involved. What is clear is that the availability of funding can encourage new initiatives and can also encourage agencies to work together. Examples include the Department of Social Security funding for replacement accommodation following closure of the resettlement unit, and more recently the development of the RSI Consortium to plan services and housing funded by the RSI programme.

Pump-priming funding is clearly important; however, many respondents expressed concern about what would happen to new initiatives when their initial funding (such as from Joint Finance or the RSI) expired and the tab was left to be picked up by hard-pressed statutory agencies. This concern was voiced as often by front-line staff as by senior managers: all were anxious about the future of their projects in an uncertain funding regime. There is a real problem in planning and maintaining such services for the future. Participants in voluntary sector settings delivering housing advice services to older people (Parry and Means, 1999) voiced similar concerns.

Costs and benefits

Both the literature and the research fieldwork emphasised the importance of the cost-benefit equation of multiagency working. In Bristol, a key factor in successfully establishing The HUB was undoubtedly a lucky coincidence of shared priorities between agencies which enabled them to come together and put resources into such a joint project. Respondents suggested that such a congruence was extremely fortunate because it enabled senior staff in all the agencies involved to 'sell' the idea of The HUB to their own organisations as a means of achieving their organisations' goals.

Yet multiagency working becomes threatened when this convergence disappears because of changes in priorities, so that the multiagency project is no longer 'flavour of the month' and is competing for scarce resources within each of the parent agencies. There can be extra costs involved in a specialist, multiagency project like The HUB: staff may not achieve the same throughput figures as their colleagues in the mainstream services. In an age of performance monitoring, this can make them particularly vulnerable to cuts. Although this problem affects all agencies, those operating nationally (for example, the Employment Service, the Benefits Agency) are particularly at risk of such changes in national organisational priorities, whereas local authorities and local voluntary organisations are at least more likely to have some influence over their local priorities. For example, if throughput measures are rated more highly than reaching the 'hard-to-reach' through outreach work, specialist staff may be sacrificed at the altar of performance monitoring.

All the staff interviewed, at both senior and front-line levels, agreed that it took time to network and build relationships, and that it was especially important that all parties involved saw some benefit to themselves in working with others. It was suggested that networking should be a performance target to encourage staff to give time to it.

The importance of power relationships between agencies

Although power relationships between all agencies can be problematic, it is acknowledged that voluntary organisations face particular difficulties when working with statutory agencies, with the voluntary organisations quoted as feeling subject to "tokenism and power games ... the poor relation ... under-valued" (Arblaster et al, 1996). This led to the argument that:

> ... for the voluntary sector to survive collaboration with the statutory sector it needs to be an 'irresistible force' and to have a very strong management structure capable of withstanding great pressures. (Arblaster et al, 1996, p 26)

A study of single homelessness projects in six areas found voluntary sector organisations "because they were often in receipt of grant aid or were in a service agreement, felt that there was an imbalance of power which affected joint working" (Oldman, 1997, p x).

It would appear that the close working relationships developed in Bristol have gone a long way to overcome these problems, although it would of course be naive to suggest that no tensions remain. The local authority was beginning to work more closely with the voluntary sector from the early 1990s onwards, no doubt encouraged by the Conservative government's emphasis on partnership working if local authorities wanted to attract additional finance for new initiatives. For example, the Housing Strategy Statement 1993-97 referred to one of the voluntary sector fora as "a major new partner in the process of identifying housing needs", and commended the forum's "new initiatives like the cold weather strategy" (Bristol City Council, 1993), although this itself could be seen as part of the 'rhetoric of partnership' and should not be taken uncritically (Marsh, 1998, p 23).

The voluntary sector itself has changed over recent years: as one senior staff member reflected:

> "We, the voluntary sector, have grown up, it's a mature approach now ... Some of our idealism had to be tempered, we had to be more pragmatic.... We used to be heroic, taking on everything, but now it's different.... It's part of the professionalisation of the voluntary sector and taking ourselves more seriously ... there's less eccentricity now, and we focus on the product, on service delivery ... health and safety, employment practice, aims, objectives, mission statements, business plans, performance indicators ... and all this may have helped [multiagency working] because there's less difference now between us and the statutory agencies."

However, there was still the feeling in some quarters that the voluntary sector were used as a 'dumping ground' by statutory agencies for the people they couldn't cope with.

There was also some suggestion that there were issues over power relationships within the voluntary sector itself, with some voluntary organisations having a virtual monopoly of access to funding and others being outside a perceived 'inner circle'. This may reflect a different ethos and the effects of the growing professionalisation in some parts of the voluntary sector, which in Bristol as elsewhere consists of a wide variety of organisations. For example, most voluntary organisations working with single homeless people in the city employ staff, but a few rely only on volunteers. Some respondents, while acknowledging that some organisations may feel excluded, commented that this is because they may not network through the various fora and liaison groups.

Some organisational animosities remain, whether historic or based on personalities: as one respondent commented: "some old hatchets still need to be buried".

A voluntary sector staff member regretted the effect of competition for funds that had affected the degree of cooperation within the voluntary sector: "It's changed since certain agencies got the money, and we've drifted apart a bit recently". There was a feeling that some church groups may be feeling left out as they didn't fit the RSI criteria, and in some cases were also relying on untrained volunteers.

In terms of power relationships between statutory agencies, the literature reveals how various agencies have felt peripheral or excluded from joint working, particularly housing from health–social services liaison on community care, and health from housing issues (Arblaster et al, 1996; Oldman, 1997). In the specific services surveyed for this research, these problems had been overcome, but they are still significant in broader terms. For example, health works closely on the specific initiatives such as the primary healthcare and mental health teams and the advice centre. However, both voluntary agencies and statutory organisations explained it was difficult to progress on wider issues such as hospital discharge, access to out-of-hours medical attention, and social work input from mainstream services for certain categories of clients such as homeless 16- to 17-year-olds.

How effective are the Bristol services in assisting single homeless people?

Measuring 'effectiveness' is fraught with difficulty, especially in services for people with complex needs, many of who do not stay in contact with services for very long. As a related study shows (Parry and Means, 1999), there are complexities in measuring organisational performance in delivering services such as housing advice due to the nature of the service, the differing levels of advice work and the adequacy of monitoring systems. This study therefore focused on the strengths and weaknesses of the multiagency approach in service delivery, drawing primarily on interviews with service users and staff; rather than attempting a full-scale evaluation of the six projects themselves. Attempts to compare quantitative data from the six projects were of limited use as the information was kept in very different formats and varied in its reliability; it is hoped that monitoring for the city's RSI programme will produce more robust data.

The study used criteria derived from literature on performance management (Sanderson, 1992), and on the known difficulties of multiagency working (as discussed above), together with the projects' own principles and objectives.

Accessibility and referral systems

All the projects aimed to make a wide range of services accessible to single homeless people by a variety of means, particularly by using multidisciplinary staff teams, siting services in convenient and pleasant environments, publicising their services, and providing effective referral systems between agencies.

Some projects were based in one location; others provided outreach services. Even though services based in one location (such as The HUB advice centre) were physically accessible, provided a pleasant environment and a high standard of comfort, they were not always psychologically accessible to those on the streets. Staff acknowledged this:

> **"Rough sleepers are too alienated – they need outreach services to reach them."**

> **"You have to build relationships quickly, but this can be difficult ... you can't do it all in one go and set everything up at once, you need more time ... but getting people to come back can be a problem."**

Outreach staff agreed that their role was to try to build relationships and be able to intervene at the right time, as their clients were often living chaotic life-styles. This was borne out by the statistics. Only 15% of The HUB's clients were sleeping rough, and most of their work was preventative with the newly homeless, whereas between 30% and 40% of the other services' users were rough sleepers.

Information about services was effectively disseminated among many users, who were familiar with the network of services in the city through word of mouth, and posters and leaflets in places they used (such as *The*

Big Issue office). Not surprisingly, newcomers to the city, or residents who had recently become homeless, found it more difficult to access services; this was sometimes the case even when they had contacted statutory services that should have referred them on to specialist agencies.

There appeared to be good referral systems in place between the agencies surveyed in the research study, and both formal and informal links between staff. In some cases this was facilitated by informal networking between front-line staff, many of whom had worked at different projects over time, often starting as a volunteer and then progressing to relief work and a permanent post. A day centre staff member was typical: she had previously been a volunteer at the winter shelter, and also worked on a relief basis at the women's direct access hostel.

Referrals worked well between specialist services, but less well into mainstream services, as discussed above. Staff were concerned that their clients were disadvantaged when accessing mainstream statutory services, and that the very existence of the specialist services could encourage mainstream staff to sideline the needs of single homeless people or 'dump' clients inappropriately on the specialist service:

> **"If they don't know what else to do with someone then they'll send them to us. One person came in in pyjamas, with a hospital bracelet still on!"**

This applied particularly to difficulties in accessing care in the community services.

This was reflected in user comments:

> **"There's been a lot of contradictions this time round – you get told one thing by one place and then something different somewhere else – it would be better if everyone told you the same thing." [Day centre user helped by outreach staff after being given wrong information by statutory service]**

> **"People work together here [in the winter shelter], but other staff aren't the same." [Winter shelter user talking about mainstream services]**

User choice and confidentiality

All the services emphasised the importance of user choice and confidentiality in their objectives: the ethos was of empowering users to take their own decisions, and for staff to respect user choices. Some services stressed the importance of offering users a choice of staff members (or sometimes volunteers) with whom to build a relationship, and to have the opportunity to use different staff for specific purposes for example, housing advice or counselling for women.

Users spoke highly of the respect with which they were treated by staff in the specialist projects, and this was confirmed by research observation. No one criticised staff attitudes, even though in some cases staff had been unable to resolve specific issues for them:

> "The staff are very good and it's better now with more of them because if you don't get on with one, then there's others you can talk to – you can't get on with everyone." [Day centre user]

> "The lady doctor's damn good, listening to what you're saying ... if they can help, they do." [Primary healthcare user]

> "They were really friendly like and because I was still using, they didn't judge me on my drug use or anything which I was frightened they might, being professionals, but they were really helpful ... and I've come off drugs and that...." [HUB user]

They also contrasted staff attitudes in the specialist agencies with those in mainstream services:

> "They treat you as a person, not a number – other places like the Social they tend to be a 9 to 5 job, it's not personal – but here it's a relaxed, very calm atmosphere and they do help you – it's like talking to a friend." [HUB user]

> "[Other services] are all right, but they don't offer as much support as this place – it's the staff that make the difference." [Winter shelter user]

Conclusions: the strengths and limitations of multiagency working

The Bristol research study showed that multiagency projects can deliver a more effective and appropriate service to single homeless people. Users themselves commented on this, and staff found that they can more easily achieve satisfactory outcomes, especially for people with complex or multiple problems.

In Bristol, multiagency working in specific areas of service delivery has encouraged agencies from both voluntary and statutory sectors to develop an understanding of each others' roles and to work together to overcome professional barriers, even on sensitive and difficult issues such as confidentiality. Certain agencies and fora within the voluntary sector have been recognised as playing a key role and have sometimes been equal partners in service development alongside specialist services from the statutory sector. Strategic planning and coordination has been improved by multiagency working through a variety of fora, and collaboration has enabled the city to lever in extra funding from central government through the RSI.

However, before getting too carried away by what one staff member described as the 'chocolate box' image of multiagency working being perfect, it must be remembered that limitations remain. Multiagency working cannot overcome problems caused by lack of resources, even if it can help make the best use of the resources that are available. Gaps in services remain, and there is still poor coordination in some areas.

Staff were particularly concerned that for all the achievements of multiagency working, many of the structural problems remain, as discussed in earlier chapters of this book. At the most fundamental level, the difficulty of implementing an initiative in a context where supply is limited in relation to needs is well established (see, for example, Mullins and Niner, 1998). There was some cynicism about resources being channelled into advice and outreach services when they were not available to provide more housing. One experienced staff member described much of the current work as 'a sticking plaster approach' and commented that it was primarily the benefit changes which had forced young people onto the streets, so that unless such underlying policy issues were tackled, multiagency working would remain of limited use.

Staff in specialist services can be isolated from their mainstream agencies in a 'bubble'. Professional cultures remain a barrier, both within and between different organisations and professions and ways need to be found to resolve these problems.

Although Bristol has been fortunate in the existence of key players who have acted as 'champions' to spearhead multiagency working, the process may be overdependent on a few individuals and unless multiagency working becomes embedded in the cultures of the organisations themselves, it could decline when the key players move on.

Is the city's experience replicable? Multiagency working in services for single homeless people came together in the city over a number of years, growing organically. It happened because of a combination of factors, particularly the existence of key players, the development of a number of practical projects that have built confidence in working together, and access to resources to enable projects to become established.

In other localities, the possibility of replication will depend on the local history, personalities and networks already established. The study suggests that multiagency working needs to grow organically. It cannot be imposed from above. Although it can be either encouraged or discouraged by policy and funding initiatives, it cannot be created without the prior existence of networks and a degree of mutual trust between agencies and individuals. The possibility of replication appears to be strongest where agencies can take a 'small steps' approach to working together on practical projects, building up confidence and trust over time.

Note

This chapter is based on research commissioned and funded by Bristol City Council and Avon Health Authority through the Bristol Joint Consultative Committee. The authors are grateful for their permission to use material from the research; the views expressed are the responsibility of the authors.

References

Allen, C. (1995) 'Caught in between the acts', *Roof*, vol 20, no 1, Jan-Feb.

Anderson, I., Kemp, P. and Quilgars, D. (1993) *Single homeless people*, London: DoE.

Arblaster, L., Conway, J., Foreman, A. and Hawtin, M. (1996) *Asking the impossible? Inter-agency working to address the housing, health and social care needs of people in ordinary housing*, Bristol: The Policy Press.

Avon Voluntary Housing Forum (1993) *Homelessness and mental health in Bristol*, Housing and Mental Health Group Research, Bristol: Avon Voluntary Housing Forum.

Bines, W. (1994) *The health of single homeless people*, York: Centre for Housing Policy/Joseph Rowntree Foundation.

Bristol City Council (1993) *Bristol's Housing Strategy Statement 1994–1997*.

Bristol Cyrenians (1993) *Annual Report*.

Burrows, R., Pleace, N. and Quilgars, D. (eds) (1997) *Homelessness and social policy*, London: Routledge.

Cabinet Office (1999) *Modernising local government*, London: HMSO.

Carter, M. (1995) *Extending the RSI: Will the London model work?*, London: South Bank University, CRISIS and CHAR.

Caton, C. (ed) (1990) *Homeless in America*, Oxford: Oxford University Press.

Cochrane, A. (1994) 'Restructuring the local welfare state', in R. Burrows and B. Loader (eds) *Towards a post-Fordist welfare state?*, London: Routledge, pp 117-35.

Cohen, C.I. and Thompson, K.S. (1992) 'Homeless mentally ill or mentally ill homeless', *American Journal of Psychiatry*, vol 149, no 6, pp 816-21.

Connelly, J. and Crown, J. (eds) (1994) *Homelessness and ill health*, London: Royal College of Physicians.

Drake, M., O'Brien, M. and Biebuych, T. (1982) *Single and homeless*, London: DoE/HMSO.

Goss, S. and Kent, C. (1995) *Health and housing: Working together? A review of the extent of multi-agency working*, Bristol: The Policy Press.

Ham, J. (1996) *Steps from the street: A report on direct access hostel provision*, London: CHAR.

Hambleton, R., Essex, S., Mills, L. and Razzaque, K. (1996) *The collaborative council: A study of inter-agency working in practice*, Joseph Rowntree Foundation/LGC Communications.

Hirst, J. (1998) 'Victims and villains', *Community Care*, 8-14 January.

Hudson, B. (1997) 'Caring sharing', *Inside Community Care*, 25 September.

Kemp, P. (1997) 'The characteristics of single homeless people in England', in R. Burrows, N. Pleace and D. Quilgars (eds) *Homelessness and social policy*, London: Routledge, pp 69-87.

Knight, M. (ed) (1994) *Housing, homelessness and health*, Working Group Report, London: Nuffield Provincial Hospitals Trust for the Standing Conference on Public Health.

Lee, P. (1998) 'Housing policy, citizenship and social exclusion', in A. Marsh and D. Mullins (eds) *Housing and public policy*, Buckingham: Open University Press, pp 57-78.

Malpass, P. and Murie, A. (1994) *Housing policy and practice*, 4th edn, London: Macmillan.

Marsh, A. (1998) 'Processes of change in housing and public policy', in A. Marsh and D. Mullins (eds) *Housing and public policy*, Buckingham: Open University Press, pp 1-29.

Means, R. and Smith, R. (1996) *Community care, housing and homelessness: Issues, obstacles and innovative practice*, Bristol: SAUS Publications.

Mental Health Foundation (1994) *Creating community care*, London: Mental Health Foundation.

Mullins, D. (1998) 'Rhetoric and reality in housing policy', in A. Marsh and D. Mullins (eds) *Housing and public policy*, Buckingham: Open University Press, pp 246-59.

Mullins, D. and Niner, P. (1998) 'A price of citizenship? Changing access to social housing', in A. Marsh and D. Mullins (eds) *Housing and public policy*, Buckingham: Open University Press, pp 175-98.

Oldman, C. (1997) 'Working together to help homeless people: an examination of inter-agency themes', in R. Burrows, N. Pleace and D. Quilgars (eds) *Homelessness and social policy*, London: Routledge, pp 229-42.

Parry, S. and Means, R. (1999) *Getting through the maze: An evaluation of housing advice services for older people*, Bristol: The Policy Press.

Pierson, C. (1994) 'Continuity and discontinuity in the emergence of the "post-Fordist" welfare state', in R. Burrows and B. Loader (eds) *Towards a post-Fordist welfare state?*, London: Routledge, pp 95-116.

Pleace, N. (1997) 'Rehousing single homeless people', in R. Burrows, N. Pleace and D. Quilgars (eds) *Homelessness and social policy*, London: Routledge, pp 159-71.

Randall, G. and Brown, S. (1994) *Falling out*, London: Crisis.

Randall, G. and Brown, S. (1996) *From street to home: An evaluation of Phase 2 of the Rough Sleepers Initiative*, London: HMSO.

Sanderson, I. (ed) (1992) *Management of quality in local government*, Harlow: Longman.

Social Exclusion Unit (1998) *Rough sleeping – Report by the Social Exclusion Unit*, London: Cabinet Office.

TWELVE

Models of resettlement for the homeless in the European Union

Brian Harvey

Introduction

The general purpose of this chapter is to examine models of resettlement for the homeless in the European Union. The specific purpose is to outline the particular paradigms of settlement that are to be found in the European countries; to examine their main characteristics and principal outcomes; and to comment on their implications.

The writer has drawn on material assembled by the European Observatory on Homelessness, run by the European Federation of National Organisations Working with the Homeless (FEANTSA), in Brussels; principally on papers prepared by its EUROHOME project (*Emergency and transitory housing for homeless people – needs and best practices*); and has consulted with experts on homelessness in the European countries[1].

The area of research into homelessness is especially burdened with problems of definitions. For the purposes of this chapter, the following definition of settlement will be used:

> **The movement by a homeless person (or family) from temporary into long-term sustainable accommodation, with services and support as appropriate.**

The context of poverty and social exclusion in Europe

Homeless is a small but distinct and acute part of the wider problem of poverty in modern Europe. It is estimated that 57 million Europeans now live in poverty (Eurostat, 1997). Worryingly, these figures showed an upward trend of 10% over the years 1988-93. The problem of European poverty was first recognised when in 1975 the European Communities initiated the first of three programmes against poverty (1975-80; 1985-89; 1989-94). In 1989, the Council of Ministers adopted a resolution on social exclusion. Subsequent substantial policy documents of the European Communities, later termed the European Union, stressed how social policy objectives must be developed in tandem with the completion of the internal market and European economic integration (European Commission, 1993, 1994). The current round of the structural funds (1994-99) includes a Community Initiative Programme INTEGRA designed to assist those excluded from society and the labour force. The Social Action Programme, the present governing document of European social policy, includes a chapter on measures, actions and proposals to promote a more inclusive society.

Dealing specifically with the question of homelessness, the first programme against poverty identified homeless people as a distinct element within the broader problem of poverty and groups working with the homeless were targeted for support in the second programme. In 1990, the European Communities gave support to the notion of a European Observatory which would study the nature, extent and causes of homelessness and track its changing trends. The Observatory depends on a network of national correspondents who present annual reports on homelessness in their state or region. A specific theme within homelessness is identified and studied each year. The national reports are then synthesised in order to make possible a European overview. These reports have covered services for the homeless, the characteristics of the homeless population, access to housing and youth homelessness (Daly, 1992, 1993, 1994; Avramov, 1995, 1996, 1998).

The context of homelessness in Europe

It is currently estimated that just over 1.8 million people are homeless in Europe (Table 12.1). The figures in Table 12.1 should be treated with caution, since the means of gathering information on homelessness varies from state to state, as do the definitions of homelessness used and the rigor of the information-collection agencies. Higher numbers may reflect efficient information-gathering, as much as the size of the problem itself. These are conservative estimates, for they do not include homeless people using services other than night shelters and similar providers. Even with these riders, they suggest that homeless in Europe is a significant social problem meriting a strategic response (Daly, 1993).

Table 12.1: Estimates of number of persons homeless in Europe

Country	Homeless on an average day	In the course of a year
Austria	6,100	8,400
Belgium	4,000	5,500
Germany	490,700	876,450
Denmark	2,947	4,000
Spain	8,000	11,000
Finland	4,000	5,500
France	250,000	346,000
Greece	5,500	7,700
Ireland	2,667	3,700
Italy	56,000	78,000
Luxembourg	194	200
The Netherlands	7,000	12,000
Portugal	3,000	4,000
Sweden	9,903	14,000
UK	283,000	460,000
	1,133,011	*1,836,450*

Source: Based on Avramov (1996)

Services for the homeless in Europe

The Observatory has provided basic information on the nature, profile and operating environment of services for the homeless in Europe. This is important if the role of settlement services is to be understood.

- Most services for the homeless in Europe have been developed by non-governmental organisations. Overall, over two thirds of all services are provided by voluntary or non-governmental organisations (NGOs), but in some countries the figure is over 90%. This is especially so in countries of strong philanthropic, religious traditions.
- There is much fragmentation of services. Many provide a small range of services for a defined and delineated target group. Few provide comprehensive services for a wide range of target groups.
- Services concentrate on meeting basic needs, such as food and shelter.
- Following the meeting of basic needs, information services are the most widespread.

- Reintegration services come third as the main area of work in services for the homeless. These are subdivided into training, accommodation and other support services.
- Lobbying and research activities are a low priority among services for the homeless.

These findings are discouraging. Fragmentation, the concentration on basic needs and the absence of research are conditions which militate against the emergence of settlement models as part of comprehensive and planned services. Table 12.2 provides details of the prominence of settlement services within the overall picture.

Whereas in some countries services with settlement aims are very important (for example, Belgium, Denmark, Luxembourg), they are much less important in a number of other member states (for example, Spain, both parts of Ireland, Greece). The report of the observatory commented that basic needs services were of themselves insufficient to prevent homelessness. Services of a reintegrative nature were needed and these are seriously underdeveloped in many states (Daly, 1993, p 12).

Table 12.2: Prominence of settlement aims in services for the homeless in European countries

Country or region	Settlement services as % total services
Belgium – Wallonia	66
Belgium – Flanders	99
Denmark	90
Germany	54
Greece	30
Italy	61
Luxembourg	94
Portugal	43
Republic of Ireland	30
UK – Northern Ireland	16
UK – Scotland	33
Spain	2

Source: Daly (1992, p 5)

European policy context

Homelessness generally, and services for the homeless in particular, must be seen in their proper policy context. Government policy responses to homelessness in Europe have come largely as a result of political action, media pressure and the campaigning work of NGOs. Government policies have been reactive and short-term (eg government drives to increase the number of shelter places during mid-winter). Government articulations of policy toward the homeless tend to emphasise their commitment to organisations providing shelter and immediate relief. Because of the short-term nature of such policies, settlement strategies are unlikely to be found within them.

Few governments in Europe have devised comprehensive, national, proactive attempts to address homelessness, establish a series of state responses to the problem, set targets for the reduction of homelessness, or monitor the outcomes. In its comments on policies for the homeless in Europe, the European Observatory divided them into three groups:

- The majority of member states, which had failed to develop any national policies for the homeless.
- A small number of states which had established national or regional responses. In general, such responses were more in evidence in the northern and Scandinavian states and those with the longer traditions of social welfare responsibilities.
- A group in between which recognised some, but limited, obligations to the homeless under particular conditions.

The crux of the policy context is housing. Governments throughout Europe have been generally unwilling to make homeless applicants an integral part of their housing programmes, because of a combination of factors: acute pressure on housing, restricted public funding, disbelief that homeless people can 'manage' housing, denial that accommodation is at the core of the problem of homelessness and the stronger pressures of other groups for attention.

Relationships between voluntary organisations and governments are either tenuous or hostile. The European Observatory on Homelessness commented that governments show a marked reluctance to recognise the role and value of the voluntary sector, sometimes acting contrary to its advice. As a result, coordinated national strategies are not devised and the knowledge of model approaches to homelessness (including settlement) is poorly circulated.

The evidence points to the existence of settlement *services* for the homeless in Europe. However, they operate in the context of underdeveloped, underfunded and fragmented services provided by NGOs. The evidence for settlement *strategies* is much less encouraging. Settlement *strategies* suggest a coordinated, planned national (or regional) effort to settle homeless people resident in hostels, night shelters or similar institutions, in accommodation of a transitional or permanent nature. They will be, by definition, accompanied by settlement services. However, the fragmented nature of services and the absence of government policies, whether for settlement or any other aspect of responding to homelessness, suggest that many countries may have settlement *services* without there being settlement policies or *strategies* at work. Thus, NGOs may be engaged in the settlement of homeless people in the absence of a governmental policy.

Toward a model

Despite these difficulties, it is evident from the reports of the Observatory, the EUROHOME project and a study of current practice that three approaches to resettlement are in evidence in the European Union. Apart from the work of FEANTSA, policy responses to homelessness have not been well studied or debated at a European level, which must lead one to approach categorisation hesitantly. The terms used here are those of the author and would not automatically be recognised by those working to resettle homeless households. Nevertheless these three approaches are discernible paradigms, with distinct characteristics, definable philosophies and different underlying assumptions. This is the first time that they have been defined in this manner. Table 12.3 illustrates these three models. One does not wish to over-dogmatise about these categories, for elements of each may sometimes be found in the same member state.

In order to illustrate more clearly the differences between these approaches, the operation of these strategies and models will now be examined in particular detail in three countries. Those chosen are Germany, Austria and Sweden. These countries were selected because the richest data were available in these cases; and because evaluative material is available in two of them (Germany and Austria) and critical commentaries available on a third (Sweden).

Table 12.3: Strategies for settlement in Europe

Model	Normalisation	Tiered	Staircase of transition
Working basis	Move people direct to 'normal' housing	One or more interim stages before moving to normal housing	Series of stages, with sanctions in progress toward normal housing
Countries where model is in evidence	Germany Finland Scotland	Austria UK France Italy Greece	Sweden The Netherlands

Normalisation model

The first model under examination is termed here the normalisation model. This takes as its starting point that homeless people have the same needs as other citizens for shelter, housing and support; that what homeless people desire, need and are suited for is normal, conventional, mainstream housing; that homeless people, while still needing support, should be moved directly from the night shelter or hostel into conventional accommodation as rapidly as possible. It plays down, even denies, homeless people as deviant, pathological, inadequate and with limited abilities or expectations. It even opposes the notion of transitional housing that trains a homeless person for later independent living.

The notion of settlement for homeless people in Germany may be found in the 1962 German Federal Welfare Act (amended 1974) #72, which specifies that the state must provide 'support and assistance' for people in overcoming social difficulties. The Act underlined the principle that the state should secure the economic position of homeless people and facilitate their participation in community life. The integrative concepts of the Act were, at the time, more of a challenge to voluntary organisations than the state, for the former ran quite institutional services for the homeless, some dating to the labour colonies of the 19th century. The Act forced them to revise their approaches: many started housing projects, developed housing associations, or rented flats for their former residents.

This shift in perspective was reflected in government when the German Federal Department for Spatial Planning, Construction and Urban Development ran seven pilot schemes in settlement. The pilot schemes were called EXWOST (EXPerimenteller WOhnungs und STädtbau). Conceptually, all were based on the provision of accommodation for homeless people with normal, inexpensive housing with standard tenancy arrangements in non-stigmatised surroundings. The pilot schemes covered a wide range of groups – families, single homeless, ex-offenders and people discharged from care. They were located in Bielefeld, Hannover, Berlin, Hagen, Jena, Rüdersdorf and Stuttgart. The numbers of homeless people involved were quite small, ranging from nine to 25 in each project. All involved NGOs, the transition from shelters to permanent accommodation and the provision of social worker support. They operated from 1990-94, being then evaluated over the period 1994-97 (Busch-Geertsema and Ruhstrat, 1997). From the perspective of this study, the level of evaluation has proved to be unusually detailed, especially in the cases of Hanover and Bielefeld (Busch-Geertsema and Ruhstrat, 1997).

First, in Hanover, homeless people were resettled from six different shelters into 12 flats, each 30m², in one 12-floor building. The project was run by *Soziale Wohnraumhilfe,* part of the large German protestant welfare organisation, *Diakonisches Werk.*

The evaluation covered the histories of 16 people: the original 12 who settled in the flats and four new people who replaced four original residents who left. For the first 12 residents, three left for other flats and one was evicted for failure to pay rent, related to drug addiction. Of the original 12, three managed to get work and one went to college. The evaluation followed the psychological experience of those who had been resettled. For most, there was great joy at being rehoused in a normal flat, but this was followed quickly by loneliness and a long period of time rebuilding relationships in the block and outside it. The evaluation provides quite detailed information on the type of services that were a necessary part of the settlement strategy. Support for the residents was provided by social workers, in the pattern shown in Table 12.4.

All residents required help at the very beginning with sorting out the physical aspects of their tenancy and in making financial arrangements. After this period of moving in, some residents required no further help at all. However, others required infrequent help with social relationships and attempting to find work. For some, though, intensive crisis support was occasionally necessary. The average amount of support time given was 6.5 hours per resident per month. The evaluation observed that after a period, relationships between all the tenants of the buildings were normalised and were not markedly different among the homeless category.

The evaluation provided some detailed information on the costs of

Table 12.4: Nature and intensity of social worker support require for settlement

Phase of project	Start	Mid-term	Occasional
Type of support required	Furnishing Furniture Finance	Jobs Training Social relationships Getting on with other residents	Crisis
Frequency and intensity	Frequent	Infrequent 1-3 hours a month For some, none	For those who need it, between 6 and 20 hours a month

the strategy in Hanover. The costs of settlement services were calculated as shown in Table 12.5 and then compared to the costs per month of shelter accommodation.

Evaluation of the project concluded that, purely in financial terms, the cost of resettlement is ultimately about half that of keeping people in night shelters. New housing does have a considerable start-up charge. However, night shelters have very high staffing and running costs compared to permanent accommodation.

Second, in Bielefeld, homeless people were relocated from a traditional hostel. Altogether 26 places were allocated to homeless people in flat complexes, the buildings concerned having additional places for other categories of public housing need. The project was funded by the housing

Table 12.5: Costs per month of settlement and shelter services (€)

	Settlement services	Shelter
Rent and related	292.00	1,809.00*
Social welfare	276.80	
Building (capital charge)	30.50	
Housing administration	96.50	
Social work support	224.20	
Total	920.00	1,809*

Note: * Elsewhere, the costs of providing shelter accommodation in Germany have been variously calculated at between €1,240 and €2,100 monthly. The current rate of exchange is €1 = UK£0.65.

Source: Busch-Geertsema (1998); see also Busch-Geertsema (1997, p 27)

and other public authorities of the region (North Rhine Westphalia and the City of Bielefeld). The resettled residents were elderly, many had poor health, half abused substances. The average length of homelessness was 13 years. One fifth had never managed independent accommodation before.

The new flats were built close to the old shelter, which meant that existing contacts in the neighbourhood were preserved. Shelter staff were reassigned to the settlement project, but the number of staff overall was reduced by about half. Residents received support when they requested it.

The settlement process appears to have been successful in enabling the men to reach a degree of independence, to manage their own accommodation and finances and to maintain and form social relationships. About one third continued to need ongoing social work support, mainly in crisis situations, but also for help in getting health services, filling in forms, the organisation of leisure time activities and in problems with other tenants. The overall need for support services declined over time.

Post-evaluation found that most of the settled residents engaged in more activities and had developed more skills after they moved compared to beforehand. They maintained or expanded their neighbourhood contacts. They themselves expressed the opinion that their situation had improved, that they were less stressed and felt more independent. Some received visitors in their flats, some acquired telephones, while others restored family contacts. They required more healthcare than before, but this may have been related to the fact that they were ageing. Of the first round of 18 who resettled, five quickly dispensed with the need for personal assistance. Six required on-going professional assistance and seven required help at a level that could be provided by volunteers. While the residents experienced ongoing problems with payment of rent, noise and cleanliness, these were manageable. One of the findings of the resettlement service was that it was not always a straightforward matter to predict which individual homeless person would require help, at what intensity and for how long. Some required none, others a lot, for some it was recurrent (Busch-Geertsema, 1998, p 43).

As in the Hanover pilot programme, the project was likely to result in significant financial savings in the medium and long term. The staff of the old hostel numbered 6.5, whereas the housing project required 0.5 staff to run.

The principal conclusions reached by the German experimental projects were:

- Settlement works when homeless people are provided with normal, mainstream, inexpensive housing in non-stigmatised surroundings.
- With a good flow of people into settlement, it is possible to reduce places in shelters.
- Rehousing puts an end to homelessness, but not to poverty or exclusion from the job market. Homeless people moving to independent accommodation found that their new levels of income were quite low. There was no *financial* incentive for the move to independence.
- Likewise, these new-build and conversion projects were not in themselves a solution to the housing of homeless people in Germany. Even if there were a large number of such projects by voluntary organisations, the homeless problem would still remain. They are too small in scale, compared to the size of the problem. Ultimately, better access to mainstream housing and to the existing stock must be confronted. There is a limited amount of finance for new building and new projects, so the homeless must receive greater opportunities within the existing housing stock.
- Financially, the cost of settlement services was about half the cost of shelter services.
- The staff numbers required for running housing settlement projects are much less than those required for running night shelters, about half.
- Settlement services must be as tailor-made and individualised as possible. Most homeless people, while requiring initial assistance, did not need significant help after about three months, but some needed occasional, intensive intervention.
- It is not risk-free and there will be tenancy problems, but they are manageable[2].

In addition to these experimental pilot projects, a number of other activities in accord with the normalisation model have also occurred in the 1990s. Many are the result of political initiatives in city governments, in practice where there are Social Democrat and Green coalitions.

The City of Hamburg developed a number of settlement-orientated innovative programmes for the homeless in 1994. They were partly motivated by the silting up of the city's shelter places, which then numbered 2,500. The programme comprised the reduction in the number of shelter places in the city by half, to between 1,200 and 1,400; work projects (*arbeitsladen*) for reintegration to the labour market; and an increase in the range of housing options available. The city recruited a team of specialists to find and earmark flats for homeless people, locating a thousand flats. The city then approached the landlords with a view to placing homeless people in these flats. The provision of social work support was considered an essential element in selling these proposals to landlords[3].

In 1993, the city of Berlin government took an initiative to combat the rising level of homelessness in the city, which had increased from 5,577 in 1988 to 11,603 by then (Senate of Berlin, 1995). The decision was taken to allocate 2,000 homes a year for the settlement of homeless people in what was termed a protected part of the housing market (*geschützes Marktsegment*). Two thirds were for single homeless people. The accommodation was earmarked by quotas in each of the city's 19 social housing agencies. The initiative cut homelessness in the city to 10,558 in 1994, its first full year of operation and to 9,551 by the end of the first quarter of 1995. Since then, the quota of allocations for homeless people was raised to 3,000 homes a year. However, with a change in the city government and the Christian Democrats assuming responsibility for social programmes, the strategy was pursued less vigorously.

The city of Hanover has housed homeless people, mainly families, in significant numbers since the 1980s. In 1988, the city introduced a plan to speed up the housing of homeless people, upgrade the quality of accommodation provided, allocate homes in a wider range of areas and refocus the programme around settlement. It was called 'New ideas about accommodation' (*Neukonzeption der Unterkünfte*), led by a project group and was executed by the city's housing agency, GBH (*Gesselschaft Bauen und Wohnen*). Under the programme, new flats were provided; existing city flats were modernised, improved and made more attractive; and rents were subsidised. The key objective was to maximise the ability of homeless people to stay in their new accommodation. A lavish level of social worker support was provided – medical, psychological, educational, training, addiction-prevention, work opportunities, programmes for the renewal of family contact and community participation. Participants were invited to draw up personal plans. For homeless people with a history of debt, a temporary tenancy was provided until the debt was cleared. The programme emphasised the importance of newly-homeless people being relocated as soon as possible. Over a six-year period, homelessness in Hanover was reduced from 1,853 in 1990 to 600 in 1996, down by two thirds (City of Hannover, 1996). Another consequence was that there was a reduction in the number of shelter places in the city from 2,450 (1995) to 1,200 (1997).

Tiered model

The tiered approach shares a number of features in common with the normalisation model. This approach seeks to limit the numbers of homeless people in shelters; and hopes to settle significant numbers of homeless people in normal accommodation. There is one crucial difference. This model has less optimistic expectations of the ability of homeless people to quickly manage in independent accommodation. Placed immediately in normal housing, even with support, the model argues, some homeless people will have difficulty in surviving and managing. What homeless people need and require is transitional housing, designed according to individual and group needs, to prepare homeless people for normal housing. This transitional housing can be adapted to suit different people, profiles and ability. It can therefore claim to be more realistic than the more inflexible normalisation model. It argues that for some homeless people, a residential home may be a more realistic ultimate form of accommodation than normal accommodation.

Under this model, the homeless person moves from one tier to another: from the street, to the shelter, to transitional housing, to normal accommodation, breaking the cycle of homelessness in a flexible system that is carefully adjusted to the ability of the homeless person at the appropriate stage. Thus it is termed here the tiered system, a phrase which is used and understood by groups working with the homeless, particularly in the British Isles.

The City of Vienna, Austria has developed a model for the housing of homeless people, called the 'Implementation plan for the gradual integration of the homeless' (1989). Homelessness had not been a serious problem in Vienna in modern times until the 1980s. The city authority had a long commitment to municipal housing (Vienna City Council is one of the largest landlords in Europe, with responsibility for 220,000 flats) and there was strong legal protection for tenants in both public and private sectors. Homelessness began to rise in the late 1980s with the increase in unemployment and with the pushing up of rents due to market factors.

In 1989, the city decided to make a systematic effort to confront the problem of homelessness in the city and introduced a five-point plan. The project involved the city funding voluntary organisations to manage supported housing units which took homeless people from shelters, placed them in supervised housing with an assistance programme for a period of time and then later rehoused them permanently in city flats. The supervised housing and support services were provided by eight voluntary organisations (eg Caritas, Gruft, Volkshilfe Verband, Salvation Army, ARGE Nichtseßhaftenhilfe, WOBES, Wiener Hifswerk) and by the city, all of them meeting together in a working group *Wohnplätze für Bürger in Not* ('Living places for citizens in need').

These flats were ring-fenced for homeless people: in effect, allocations to these flats side-stepped the normal waiting list procedures for people applying for housing. The supervised housing units were flats at various locations around the city, paid for by the city, where homeless people in the programme were expected to stay for periods from six to 12 months. A total of 958 supervised flats were provided during this period.

This project operated between 1989 and 1995 when a total of 2,966 people entered the programme. By 1995, a total of 1,863 people had completed the final stage and had settled in permanent accommodation, with the following outcomes shown in Table 12.6.

The figures in Table 12.6 indicate a high crude success rate, with 84% of people who entered the programme during 1989-95 in housing at the end of 1995.

The length of stay in supervised housing is illustrated in Figure 12.1. This provides data on the length of the period in transitional, supervised housing. The main finding was that whereas the average period of time in supervised housing was 398 days, a little over a year, what is also striking is the considerable number of people who stayed only a short period in supervised housing before moving on and, at the other extreme, the significant numbers who required supervision for more than two years. One must question whether the numbers in the under three month phase required a transitional stage at all; conversely, at the other extreme (over 25 months) whether another form of residential care might be appropriate. Another striking feature is that it was possible to leave

Table 12.6: Outline results of settlement programme, Vienna, Austria (%)

Outcome	%
Remaining in city accommodation	70
Proceeded to other housing	14
In hostels, jail, emergency accommodation	13
Returned to streets	3

N = 1,863.
Source: Based on EUROHOME (see note 1)

Figure 12.1:Vienna Programme: length of stay (Days)

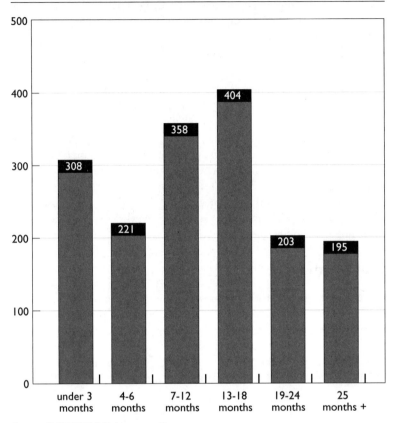

Source: EUROHOME 2 (see note 1)

supervised housing quite quickly, suggesting that efforts were made to prevent the system from silting.

The project examined the outcomes for those who entered the programme of transitional housing: 565 people succeeded in getting employment in the course of the programme. This represents over 30% of participants. This figure may seem high by international standards, but should be seen in the context of low unemployment rates in Austria (now 4.5% but then much lower).

The following were adjudged to be the lessons of the programme:

• By providing a continuing stream into supervised housing, it was possible to reduce the number of hostel places in the city.

- For 84% of programme participants, the programme was successful.
- The period of supervision required varied, significant numbers needing only a short period of supervision, while, at the other end of the scale, others required a long period.
- Settlement plans had to be closely tailored to individualised needs.

Although those who reported on the project made little mention of it, the settlement project also appears to be an unusually successful example of voluntary–statutory cooperation.

Austria is the principal country which, in the city of Vienna, has operated the tiered model in a large-scale, planned manner in recent years. There have been a number of positive outcomes from this experience. The development of tiered NGO settlement services may be seen in Italy, Britain and more recently in Greece, where a number of sophisticated and adaptable models may be found. However, in the absence of government strategies, these have limitations.

Staircase model

A third model for a settlement strategy is in evidence in Sweden. This model builds on the axiom of the tiered model that homeless people are, for the most part, not ready for the immediate transition from night shelter to independent accommodation. The process of transition is a necessary one and, in the Swedish model, is broken down into a number of stages. What marks it as different from the tiered model is that it is systematised, legally regulated and involves the use of sanctions. Like the other models, support services are provided and these are an integral element of the programme.

Sweden operates a staircase model of settlement for homeless people and those in similar categories of need (see Figure 12.2). This is widely, but not universally, in use by the local authorities in Sweden. It first started in the city of Gothenburg in the 1980s. It is estimated that about 80% of Sweden's 284 local authorities now use the staircase system. About 10,000 people are on the staircase at present, comprising, according to the area, between 0.4% and 1.2% of municipal housing. For example, Stockholm's current plan for the homeless (1997-2000) makes use of the staircase of transition. The city has about 3,000 homeless people. The numbers on the staircase are to expand from 2,098 in 1996 to 2,213 in the year 2000.

Figure 12.2: Staircase model of settlement, Sweden

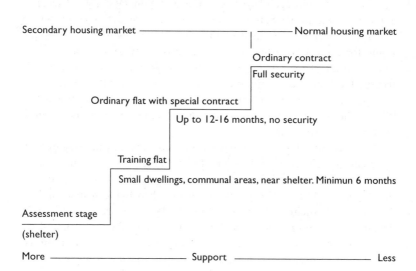

Secondary housing market ———————— ——— Normal housing market

Ordinary contract

Full security

Ordinary flat with special contract

Up to 12-16 months, no security

Training flat

Small dwellings, communal areas, near shelter. Minimun 6 months

Assessment stage

(shelter)

More ———————————— Support ———————————— Less

The principle of the staircase is that one moves from a night shelter up a series of steps to become a full tenant with the full legal rights of a tenant (including security of tenure) with what is termed an ordinary contract. On the way, there are a series of intermediary steps, such as training and transitional flats. The objective of the system is that one moves on to a normal housing system with full tenancy rights. The amount of security and the value of the contract increases as one climbs the staircase. The social worker support one receives diminishes. Movement up the system is based on social worker reports. But a tenant causing a problem or difficulty at one stage on the staircase may have to fall back to the previous level, or further and start again. The time spent on different levels is expected to vary, but it is presumed that it will take a few years to climb up the whole of the staircase[4].

The staircase of transition operates by way of a set of subleased flats spread out in residential areas. Analysts in Sweden term this the secondary housing market. Local authority social work departments rent these flats from landlords, who could be private, social housing or municipal owners, and sublease these flats to tenants who would not otherwise be acceptable to landlords.

On the way up the staircase, the tenant (homeless person or otherwise) signs a special contract. This is often an individually designed tenancy agreement (Sahlin, 1998, p 6). These state the terms of eviction (which may include eviction on the day), the right of social workers to enter the home for inspections (this may include drug testing) and may include individual mandatory work plans (Sahlin, 1998, p 23). As leasor of the flat, the local social authority presents the landlord with the details of the homeless person who is to be housed in a training or transitional flat. The landlord is in a position to approve, disapprove or lay down fresh conditions for the contract.

The staircase of transition, and the associated secondary housing market, is a recent development in Sweden. In the late 1980s, the country had a very low level of homelessness. Large-scale public housing programmes, developed by municipal housing companies, had reduced the numbers dependent on shelters, institutions and single-room-occupancy hostels. The total number of shelter beds in use was down to about 100 nationally. This situation changed with new government policies which promoted the growth of owner-occupation. Municipal housing companies were privatised or forced to compete with private landlords, thus forcing them up market. Public housing became less the norm and more the feature of residual groups. Municipal housing was faced with the problem of how to distribute those it saw as problem tenants. They were allocated housing, but only with landlord consent and on special conditions (Sahlin, 1998, p 11). The local social authorities would take over the lease, remove the tenant's legal protection, guarantee the rent, and enforce good behaviour on pain of eviction. Originally, the notion was that such tenants would obtain a full contract after a year. During this period, the local social authority would provide preparation for independent living. Assuming good behaviour and reliability, the tenant could then expect to graduate onto the normal housing market.

The staircase of transition did not emerge from a particular paradigm of the understanding of homelessness and the development of a model in response. Rather, it was a response to unique conditions in the housing market at a particular point in time. The concept of deeming people capable or incapable of independent living, which is at the root of the staircase approach, was an entirely novel one for Sweden. The policy marked an abrupt contrast to the 1982 Social Services Act, which laid down the principle that housing policy should strive toward the normal housing of all people. Now, legal notions of incapacity and conditionality were introduced.

From the point of view of housing management, the staircase has many advantages. The social work authorities pay the rents in the flats of problem tenants, take charge of repairs and day-to-day management, and respond to complaints. Landlords avoid a range of costs and procedures (for example, evictions). According to the chief analyst of the policy, Sahlin, it is based on a persuasive vision of cooperation between and within the private, public and voluntary sector. It is comparatively cheap and has an immediately appealing design.

Despite being in widespread use, the model has been criticised:

- The outcomes have been disappointing, people moving down the system as well as up.
- Tenants with special contracts are in a situation of legal and practical inferiority. Landlords have disproportionate and unwarranted power. The power relationship is qualitatively different from the ususal ones between landlord and tenant, between social worker and client.
- The system confuses social care with issues of legal responsibility.
- It is a model built on control, discipline, exclusion and supervision rather than assistance and empowerment.
- Behavioural conditions imposed on tenants at particular stages are so severe that it is virtually impossible for them to move up to the next step on the ladder.
- Although one would expect the settlement services provided to be of high quality, this is often not the case.
- Many homeless people stay stuck at the bottom of the ladder and do not move up.

Table 12.7: Comparisons of rates of homeless in cities operating the staircase of transition and those not

Prototype	Number of special contracts per 100,000 inhabitants	Numbers homeless, per 100,000 inhabitants	Number of homeless people adjudged incapable of living independently, per 100,000 inhabitants
City with staircase system	167	78	38
City without staircase system	0	12	12

Source: Sahlin (1998)

- Even when tenants move to the top of the staircase and remain on good behaviour, the landlord often refuses a permanent or ordinary contract. There are no incentives for the landlord to offer ordinary contracts, nor are there sanctions which could be invoked against landlords in these circumstances. Many people therefore remain stuck at the top of the staircase.
- The designation of tenants as 'problem tenants' creates neighbourhood resistance.
- It is ineffective in reducing homelessness. For example, although Stockholm issued a thousand special contracts in three years, the numbers of homeless people fell by only 144 in the same period.

Sahlin concluded that the landlord role of the local social authorities corrupted their function and compromised their task as a settlement service (1998, p 34). Support services in effect become a form of surveillance. Visits often take place on the day when rent payments are made in order to ensure that they are paid, thus reinforcing the controlling nature of the support.

Overall, Sahlin describes the system as a "staircase of exclusion" (1998, p 40). The way upwards and outwards from the staircase of transition is often too narrow to allow a reasonable flow through the system, she comments (p 28). New homelessness leads to an expansion of the secondary housing market, without necessarily leading to an increase in the numbers of homeless people being settled. Sahlin cited one case in a town in Sweden where night shelters had to be reintroduced after the appearance of the secondary housing market, because people were moving down the ladder of transition faster than others were moving up. Indeed, social workers claimed that they needed more night shelter places to run the staircase efficiently! In examining the operation of the staircase model across Sweden, Sahlin found that those few local authorities which did not use the staircase of transition had few or no night shelters. By contrast, those city authorities which used the staircase most were also the main users of night shelter services. She made a comparison of two prototypical cities – one which operated the staircase and one which did not (see Table 12.7).

These outcomes are significant. They indicate higher levels of homelessness in those cities operating the staircase system, linked to a judgement by the authorities that homeless people there are less capable.

Discussion

There are three main models of resettlement at work in the European Union. The tiered model is probably the most widely used. This strategy embodies the concept of movement from shelter through transitional housing and eventually into permanent accommodation. The Viennese example is the most systematic version of this model. By the standards of other countries, the staircase model is highly regulated, requiring a level of supervision that might be regarded elsewhere as intrusive. Nevertheless, the Swedish experience confronts real problems which affect housing management throughout the European Union, such as capacity for independent living, 'difficult' tenants and anti-social behaviour.

The strongest challenge to the tiered and staircase models comes from Germany, where the EXWOST pilot projects bypassed the second stage of interim accommodation and the notion of tiers. In effect, they argue that one may go directly from night shelter to a permanent residential environment, with a planned level of social worker support. The normalisation model argues that the efforts that go into organising the transition process could better be diverted into immediate but permanent accommodation. Transitional housing, they argue, institutionalises and creates its own obstacles. As EUROHOME 2 recorded, "the necessity of having so many steps in the reintegration process, during which a person is accommodated temporarily, was questioned"[5]. The emphasis should instead be on getting homeless people into permanent accommodation, with as low levels of support as possible, as soon as possible. The German examples are illuminating in providing detail on the costs of settlement and social work supports. They hold out the promise of a reduction not just in the numbers of homeless people in hostels, but in the overall cost to society of shelters, the voluntary organisations necessary to sustain them and their staffing.

The various models of settlement have limitations. First, it is evident from all these studies that settlement itself, regardless of which model one follows, will only deal with part of the problem of homelessness. Settlement strategies on their own do not solve the problem of poverty and unemployment. Other measures, critically in the areas of work and income, are required if one is to confront the broader problem of poverty among people who have been homeless for a long period. Granted that a significant number of those studied have been elderly, the labour market is not an option for all of them. In Austria, settlement was associated with a return to work, but that may be partly due to the high level of labour demand there.

Second, all models of resettlement depend on the availability of onward accommodation. Neither the normalisation, tiered nor staircase model can operate unless there is onward housing provision for people leaving shelters or transitional housing (the problem of silting). Although all settlement strategies have grasped the theoretical importance of avoiding silting, only the examples of Vienna appear to have overcome the problem. All settlement strategies depend on a critical, sometimes high flow of people into independent accommodation. This requires the allocation of sufficient resources by the responsible housing authorities and mechanisms which ensure such a flow. The experiences of Vienna showed that not only was there a commitment to the making available of public housing, but homeless people were prioritised within these allocations. As well as financial resources, significant planning efforts were also applied. In the cities of Germany and Austria, settlement strategies received high-level attention within their respective city administrations, demanding significant financial, planning, administrative and personnel commitment. As noted by the editors, the fiscal crisis of the state in late 20th century industrialised nations mean that this has been an unpropitious time to seek funds for the scale of resources necessary to sustain settlement strategies.

Third, these European lessons demonstrate the importance of scale of undertaking and governmental leadership. Conversely, they emphasise the danger that without sufficient resources, settlement strategies degenerate into settlement services without strategy, with resulting frustrations. Not only must sufficient resources be made available on a wide scale, but they must be applied over a long time-period. In Berlin, the 'protected market' approach designed by the one administration was pursued less enthusiastically by its politically different successor.

These models set a challenge to the way in which responses to homelessness are funded. Regrettably, cost-benefit analysis is available only in the case of the German settlement experience, but it is unequivocal in showing that there are high, up-front costs in settlement strategies, certainly within the normalisation model. However, there is a substantial trade-off, for successful settlement has led to a reduction in the costs of providing shelter and related services. The overall costs of providing services for the homeless fell by half. It is possible to speculate that the costs of shelter services also declined in Austria as the numbers of homeless people staying there fell. These experiences suggest that a key element in successful settlement strategies is the switching of resources from shelters to housing and support instead. This must have serious implications for the work and role of voluntary organisations.

The three models are a challenge to the way in which we think about homelessness and its roots in individual causes or structural circumstances. The models differ in their underlying assumptions as to the preparedness of homeless people for independent accommodation. The normalisation model minimises (but does not dismiss) the difficulties homeless people will experience in living independently; the tiered model acknowledges these difficulties and adjusts its tiers to those anticipated levels of difficulty; whilst the staircase model institutionalises them.

A central problem highlighted by these studies is the capacity of homeless people for independent living and who makes that assessment. Champions of the normalisation model argue that negative assessments of the capabilities of homeless people lead to their being allocated poor quality housing which they have difficulty in keeping, thus establishing a self-fulfilling circle in which housing solutions are perceived to be inappropriate for their problems. One's judgement of the capacity and desire of homeless people for housing tends to determine the model and strategy followed. A positive assessment leads one in the direction of the normalisation model; a negative one toward tiered or transitional models. This core issue of the assessment of the nature of homelessness and its root causes is at the heart of the issue.

As noted earlier, governmental responses to homelessness have been more in evidence in the northern and Scandinavian states of the European Union than in the southern or Mediterranean states. Yet national responses to homelessness have often defied such attempts at classification, the best example being the existence, side-by-side, of radically different approaches to homelessness in the neighbouring states of Sweden and Finland. Finally, there are lessons concerning the voluntary–statutory relationship. Although most settlement services in Europe are provided by voluntary organisations, the settlement strategies outlined in this chapter have been the initiative of national or regional governments. These governments have taken the lead, engaged in large-scale planning and allocated resources accordingly. Some strategies, especially in Germany, have found strong political champions at city and regional level. Hitherto, the burden of meeting the needs of the homeless in Europe had been thrust unreasonably and disproportionately on voluntary organisations. Successful settlement strategies outlined in this report have been careful not to do this. Instead (Vienna is the best example), there have been positive examples of voluntary statutory partnerships. Voluntary organisations have played a secondary, limited, but carefully designed, important and specific role.

Although these models of resettlement and the outcomes thereof have important policy implications for the way in which services and policies for the homeless in the European Union should be organised, the prospects of their doing so are poor. Resettlement is a small subset of the debate on homelessness within a limited circle of NGOs and academics at European level. Most national governments in the European Union take the view that homelessness is a national (or even regional) responsibility and reject the principle of cooperation on the issue at European level. They guard this principle jealously and, as a result, the prospects of a policy debate as to how to address homelessness effectively and share models of good practice are limited. This issue is discussed further by the current author elsewhere (Harvey, 1999). Poor information exchange is, most probably, one of the reasons why homelessness remains such an intractable problem across Europe.

Notes

[1] These are: *Selected papers,* Workshop held in Vienna, 11-13 July 1996 (henceforth EUROHOME 1); *Report on emergency and transitory housing for homeless people – needs and best practices,* Report on seminar held in Athens on 4-5 October 1996 (EUROHOME 2); Papers from seminar held in Milan, 23-4 May, 1997 (EUROHOME 3); Papers from seminar held in Copenhagen, 1997 (EURHOME 4). I am grateful to Mary Higgins, Director of the Homeless Initiative in Dublin, Ireland, for her permission to have published here research undertaken for the initiative. I wish to also record my thanks to the following for their information and advice: Dr Dragana Avramov, Director, European Observatory on Homelessness, Brussels, Belgium; Dr Volker Busch-Geertsema, Gesselschaft für innovative Sozialforschung und Sozialplanung, Bremen, Germany; Dr Thomas Specht-Kittler, Bundesarbeitsgemeinschaft Wohnungs-losinitiativen, Bielefeld, Germany; Dr Helmut Hartman, City of Hamburg; Dr Inger Koch Nielsen, Danish National Institute for Social Research, Copenhagen; Dr Ingrid Sahlin, Lund University, Sweden; Anne de Gouy and Isabelle Sery, FNARS, Paris, France.

[2] EUROHOME 2, 12, see note 1.

[3] EUROHOME 3, 6, see note 1.

[4] Sahlin (1998, p 13). For a further discussion of this model see Sahlin (1995, 1996).

[5] EUROHOME 2, 20, see note 1

References

Avramov, D. (1995) *Homelessness in the European Union – Social and legal context of housing exclusion in the 1990s*, Brussels: FEANTSA.

Avramov, D. (1996) *The invisible hand of the housing market*, Brussels: FEANTSA.

Avramov, D. (1998) *Youth homelessness in the European Union*, Brussels: FEANTSA.

Busch-Geertsema, V. (1997) *Normal Wohnen ist nicht nur besser, es ist auch billiger*, Bremen: Gesselschaft für innovative Sozialforschung und Sozialplaning.

Busch-Geertsema, V. (1998) *Rehousing projects for single homeless persons – Innovative approaches in Germany*, Bremen: Gesselschaft für innovative Sozialforschung und Sozialplaning.

Busch-Geertsema, V. and Ruhstrat, E.-U. (1997) *Wohnungsbau für Wohnungslose*, Bielefeld: VSH Verlag Soziale Hilfe GmbH.

City of Hannover (1996) *Lebensraum mit Ausblick*, Hanover: City of Hannover.

Daly, M. (1992) *European homelessness – The rising tide*, Brussels: FEANTSA.

Daly, M. (1993) *Abandoned: A profile of Europe's homeless people*, Brussels: FEANTSA.

Daly, M. (1994) *The right to a home, the right to a future*, Brussels: FEANTSA.

European Commission (1993) *Growth, competitiveness and employment – The challenges and ways forward into the 21st century*, White Paper, Luxembourg: European Commission.

European Commission (1994) *European social policy – A way forward for the Union*, White Paper, Com 94/333, Luxembourg: European Commission.

Eurostat (1997) *Statistics in focus – population and social conditions, 1996/7*, Luxembourg: Eurostat.

Harvey, B. (1999) 'The problem of homelessness: a European perspective', in S. Hutson and D. Clapham (eds) *Homelessness: Public policies and private troubles*, London: Cassell, pp 58-73.

Sahlin, I. (1995) 'Strategies for exclusion from housing', *Housing Studies*, vol 10, no 3, pp 381-401.

Sahlin, I. (1996) 'From deficient planning to "incapable tenants" – changing discourse on housing problems in Sweden', *Scandinavian Housing and Planning Research*, vol 13, no 3, pp 167-81.

Sahlin, I. (1998) *The staircase of transition*, Mimeo, Lund.

Senate of Berlin (1995) *Geschützes Marktsegment – ein Berliner Modell zur Wohnungsversorgung für Bürgerinnen und Bürger die von Obdaschlosigkeit bedroht oder betroffen sind*, Berlin: Senate of Berlin.

Index